AF449426

TOYNBEE HALL

AND SOCIAL REFORM

1880–1914

THE SEARCH

FOR COMMUNITY

STANDISH MEACHAM

YALE UNIVERSITY PRESS

NEW HAVEN AND LONDON

Designed by Sally Harris
and set in Caslon type by
Graphic Composition, Inc.
Printed in the United States of America by
Thomson-Shore, Inc., Dexter, Michigan.

Library of Congress Cataloging-in-Publication Data

Meacham, Standish.
Toynbee Hall and social reform, 1880–1914.
Includes index.
1. Toynbee Hall (London, England)—History.
2. Social settlements—England—London—History.
3. Community—History. I. Title.
HV4236.L66M43 1987   362.5′574′0942   86–28269
ISBN 0–300–03821–6

2   4   6   8   10   9   7   5   3   1

CONTENTS

Following page 110:
Figure 1. Samuel A. Barnett and Henrietta O. Barnett.
Figure 2. Toynbee Hall.
Figure 3. Toynbee Hall.
Figure 4. Toynbee Hall.
Figure 5. An evening concert, Toynbee Hall.
Figure 6. *Toynbee Record* calendar, November 1893.
Figure 7. Toynbee Hall committees, clubs, and associations,
October 1896.
Figure 8. Advertisement for Lectures on Labour Questions by
W. H. Beveridge and R. H. Tawney.

Figures 1, 2, 5, 6, 7, and 8 are reproduced with the kind permission of
Toynbee Hall; figures 3 and 4 with the kind permission of the Tower
Hamlets Library.

Toynbee Hall, founded in the slums of London's East End in 1884 by the Reverend Samuel Barnett, was the first settlement house established in England or America and probably remains the best known. Chicago's Hull House, its closest rival in terms of fame, was patterned on its assumptions and its programs. For over one hundred years the men and women who have worked at Toynbee Hall have attempted in a variety of ways, and with a mixed measure of success, to improve the lives of their Whitechapel neighbors and of other English men, women, and children forced to live less than decent lives.

This book is neither a history of the hall nor a biography of its founder. Its subject is an ethos, fostered by Oxford and Cambridge in the late nineteenth century, particularly by Balliol College, Oxford, and embodied in the activities of the hall during the first twenty-five years or so of its life. This particular brand of social reform was one of several propounded in the 1880s as a means of addressing the increasingly complex social problems generated by advanced capitalism. International competition, industrial obsolesence and technological change, chronic underemployment, and urban decay were forcing social critics and reformers to rethink older attitudes and propose new solutions. Growing numbers of politicians were prepared to countenance state intervention beyond the limits delineated by earlier generations. Schemes such as those enunciated as part of Randolph Churchill's Tory Democracy, Joseph Chamberlain's Unauthorized Programme, and the tracts of the recently founded Fabian Society were a response to the realization that public health and sanitation, factory regulation, slum clearance, and the like were the particular and constant business of government.

Toynbee Hall was founded as an expression of the belief that before such issues could be effectively tackled, a more fundamental question of social organization had to be addressed and answered. The hall's existence proclaimed its supporters' conviction that community was of transcendent importance. They believed that industrialism had subjected English men and women to centrifugal pressures which, in league with the precepts of philosophical individualism, economic laissez-faire, and class consciousness, had accelerated a dangerous, nationwide drift toward social disintegration. Their goal was social reintegration. Its accomplishment would result from the imposition of enlightened authority and hierarchy to achieve community, a community in which they saw themselves both as teachers and—at least for the foreseeable future—as governors. The lessons they would teach, the virtues of self-reliance, industriousness, and an appreciation of "higher" things, would help working-class men and women realize their "best selves" (a favorite phrase), thereby benefiting not only them and their community but the community of the nation as well.

The book traces the history of this ethos, first acknowledging the contribution of late Victorian thinkers such as Matthew Arnold and the Balliolites T. H. Green and Arnold Toynbee to the enrichment of an older, public school–bred tradition of high-minded service. The middle chapters then focus on Toynbee Hall. Designed to bring recent university graduates together into community with working-class Londoners, the hall was perceived by its founder and supporters as a device that would bridge the gulf separating class from class and allow men and women to connect "one by one" with each other as human beings. Connection was to be effected by means of a multitude of educational programs, most of which were consciously designed to impose a hierarchy of values upon the pupils for whom they were designed.

Although the hall appeared to flourish during the first ten or fifteen years of its existence, by about 1900 Barnett was compelled to admit that it had not brought East London into much closer communion with its "leaders." Meanwhile, the philosophical assumptions of the Toynbee ethos were challenged in a direct way by those socialists and centralizers who argued that the solution to England's difficulties lay not in the promotion of local connection but in a sharply increased measure of state intervention. The ethos was challenged too by the militant proclamations of a revived Christian Socialist movement and by the rational assumptions of scientifically minded sociologists. Responding to the implied assertion that the hall was little more than an anachronism and an irrelevance, Barnett, while never abandoning his earlier beliefs, acquiesced in a refocusing of its activities away from education and in the direction of social investigation. The result was the training of a new kind of elite, no longer to serve as disinterested mentors at the head of a local community but to assume instead positions of disinterested leadership within the expanding national bureaucracy.

The book's final chapters examine the early careers of William Beveridge and R. H. Tawney, two men who were educated at Balliol and served an apprenticeship at Toynbee Hall in the early 1900s. Beveridge and Tawney both grew beyond the Toynbee ethos they had absorbed as young men. Yet they lived their lives with its mark upon them. Beveridge, though he could not sympathize with Barnett's attempts to recreate community in "small doses," allowed the notion of disinterestedness to encourage his belief in himself as an enlightened bureaucrat par excellence. Tawney, while he emphatically rejected the antidemocratic implications of hierarchical social organization, nevertheless remained convinced of the need for individual connectors—"pontifices" he called them—who could bring together men and women of different classes and encourage them to derive a common purpose together. Tawney's later service as just such a pontifex, like Beveridge's as a bureaucrat, was rooted in the ideas and experiences of the social-reform tradition that is examined here.

These two important careers suggest that analysis of the Toynbee ethos can contribute to a more general understanding of twentieth-century British history. Grounded in the attitudes described and analyzed in the pages that follow are the very hallmarks of the modern British welfare state: confidence in the decisions of a supposedly disinterested elite on behalf of everyone else, and concern about the well-being of a community that is more than the sum of its individual members.

I am pleased to acknowledge assistance from the following friends: Richard Cockett, Eileen Gallagher, Laura Mayhall, and Claudia Siegel, for help in preparing the manuscript; T. W. Heyck, who was kind enough to read an early draft of the manuscript and to make valuable suggestions for its improvement; and R. K. Webb, whose thoughtful, telling criticisms made me understand what I was trying to say and how to say it. At the Yale Press, I have enjoyed the continuing support of Charles Grench and have profited from the careful editing of Otto Bohlmann.

Research was conducted with assistance from the American Council of Learned Societies and the University Research Institute, University of Texas at Austin.

For permission to quote from manuscript sources, I gratefully acknowledge the Warden of Toynbee Hall, Donald Chesworth (Toynbee Hall Papers); the Greater London Record Office (Barnett Papers); His Grace the Archbishop of Canterbury and the Trustees of Lambeth Palace Library (Tawney Letters); University of Oxford, Department for External Studies (Tutorial Classes Committee Papers); The Workers Education Association (Early Tutorial Classes Correspondence); Michael Vyvyan (Tawney Papers); and J. S. M. Booth (Booth Papers).

ABBREVIATIONS

BP	Barnett Papers, Greater London Council
BevP	Beveridge Papers, Library of Political and Social Science, London School of Economics
CCHF	Children's Country Holiday Fund
COS	Charity Organisation Society
CSL	Church Socialist League
CSU	Christian Social Union
CUB	Central London (Unemployed) Body
LPSS	Library of Political and Social Science, London School of Economics
OUED	Oxford University Extension Delegacy
RH	Rewley House, Oxford
TH	Temple House, London
THP	Toynbee Hall Papers, Greater London Council
TP	Tawney Papers, Library of Political and Social Science, London School of Economics
WEA	Workers' Educational Association

1

THE QUEST FOR NEW COMMUNITY

England in the years after 1850 found itself governed by a new ruling class. Though still drawn to a degree from landed society, the membership of this elite came increasingly from the ranks of upper-middle-class professional families, whose sons had had the ideal of selfless public service preached to them at the schools where they had been sent by earnest and ambitious parents to be educated as Christian gentlemen. These are the young men whom G. M. Young labeled "Arnoldians," men "disposed to bring everything in the State of England to the test of Isaiah and Thucydides."[1] The label acknowledges the degree to which the new governors were the intellectual heirs of Dr. Thomas Arnold, headmaster of Rugby in the 1830s, and of other equally reform minded though less highly publicized heads—G. H. Moberly at Winchester and Christopher Wordsworth at Harrow. The late Victorian founders of the East London settlement house, Toynbee Hall—the men who are the subject of this study—were the spiritual legatees of this breed, a second generation as determined as the first to put England to the test, to find the source of its defects, and to work change upon the land and its people.

Though Darwin had shaken their religious faith, they remained dedicated to the high-minded moral absolutism of Isaiah and Thucydides, determined like their forebears to take their nation's measurement, to judge according to a demanding standard, to distinguish true from false, sham from genuine. As David Newsome has remarked in his study of Thomas Arnold's legacy, these Victorians, though prepared to acknowledge that "it was beyond anyone's powers to force people to be good," believed nonetheless in the need to teach "that it was the duty of man to strive towards the good, and that his true happiness lay in making the attempt."[2]

The hallmark was high-mindedness; the consequence, a compulsion to lead. The secret of the reforming headmasters' influence lay in their ability to capitalize on this compulsion, to understand that old habits of authority were waning, and to give them life by providing them with renewed religious and historic justification.[3] Into the consciousness of the schoolboy sons of the gentry and of the growing professional upper-middle class they implanted the belief that effective leadership should be defined as "disinterestedness." The task of leadership would be to reconcile the conflicting interests of class for the good of the community as a whole. Education, grounded in the universality of Christianity and the classics, would, by placing the new leadership above class, teach the disinterestedness so absolutely necessary to the art of authoritative leadership. The reward would be power, the ultimate goal of any ruling class; in this case, power to redirect society to the noblest possible ends, as defined by those who took upon themselves the task of redirection.

Historians have variously identified and analyzed these Victorians. Harold Perkin would include them in what he has labeled a "fourth class," distinct from the landed aristocracy, the entrepreneurial middle class, and the industrial working class, and possessed of an ideal of its own. Noel Annan, in his often-cited essay "The Intellectual Aristocracy", has shown how several generations of like-minded Victorians shared not only ideals but also many of the same grandparents and great-aunts and -uncles.[4] They came, if not from the same homes, then from homes bound together by kinship. They attended the same schools, formed friendships with one another, and together developed a system of values and a set of common resolves. It was from this class, this aristocracy, that the social reformers of Toynbee Hall emerged in the years after 1880.

Their primary concern—how to reestablish community within a society increasingly polarized by class divisions—was by no means peculiar to them or to the ethos they inherited. The "condition of England question" that so fretted social critics of all political and philosophical stripes from the 1820s on was essentially a question about the best way to restore community to a disintegrating commonwealth. Robert Owen's socialism responded to this concern, so did Jeremy Bentham's artificial harmony of interests, Samuel Taylor Coleridge's proposals to reintegrate the Church into the social order, and Thomas Carlyle's insistence upon the need for enlightened "captains of industry." So did the Chartists' demand for equal participation by all adult males in the affairs of state.

When Arnoldians addressed the issue of community, however, they did so in the firm conviction that the term implied not equality but hierarchy. Community for them was a set of vertical relationships, bound together, it is true, by obligations and responsibilities that were mutual yet governed by an authority that emanated from the top down. It is tempting to label this a kind of latter-day paternalism. Indeed, Toynbee Hall residents sometimes characterized themselves as urban squires. "Paternalism," though, is a slippery term, as David Roberts's recent study suggests,[5] one not easily transplanted from the preindustrial society in which it is rooted. Traditional paternalism, as practiced in small rural communities, was grounded in a set of direct economic relationships between landlord, tenant, and laborer that contradicted the Toynbeeites' insistence upon their own disinterestedness. If they thought of themselves as modern Allworthys, it was because they were anxious to impose upon a localized population an authority they believed to be benevolently altruistic, so as to draw that population together. Yet an eighteenth-century squire's task was above all self-interested, actuated by his need to extract economic profit in order to guarantee himself a continued position as the head of a community to which he was permanently bound by ownership of his estate.

Desire to impose authority and hierarchy was characteristic of many Victorians keen to reintroduce order into a society pulled apart into classes by industrialization. Benthamites were enthusiasts for authority, and often authoritarian. Evangelicals, too, welcomed opportunities to tell others what to do and how to do it. Though the conscientious among them judged most harshly of themselves, far more hastened to sit in judgment upon those less fortunate. When doubt denied middle- and upper-middle-class Victorians the certainty of orthodox Christianity, they nevertheless continued to preach moral improvement as a means to the end of revitalized community and to assume an authority that licensed their preaching.

Community, authority, and hierarchy: a reforming spirit based on that quintessentially Victorian trinity became the hallmark of the ethos espoused by the men of Toynbee Hall. These Toynbeeites were motivated as well by the equally Victorian conviction that by participating in the recreation of community they were assuaging collective guilt for the damage their material success had done to those at whose expense it had been achieved. Beatrice Webb wrote in her autobiography, *My Apprenticeship*, of a growing "class consciousness of sin"[6] as a primary motivating force within herself and those who shared her compulsion to improve the lot of the poor. The process of social service consequently appeared to demand a direct relationship between giver and receiver, those who ministered and those ministered to. "There was," as Margaret Simey has written of charitable effort in Liverpool, "a yearning to do good to the poor in person. . . . Guilt sought relief in contact with the injured."[7]

The purpose of reform was thus not only to reestablish social order but also to reconnect individuals of high and low estate to a set of commonly shared goals. Both would experience the true meaning of reform and thus derive a clearer sense of life's high purposes for themselves and for the community to which they belonged. This was the gospel preached by the mid-Victorian reformer Edward Denison, who went to live among the poor of Stepney at a time during the 1860s when economic distress and a consequent flood of well-meant but indiscriminate charity drew public attention to the chronic problems of London's East End. Denison argued that the doling out of food, clothing, and shelter by public officials to any who bothered to ask for them demoralized a parish by turning its residents into irresponsible beggars. Though well-intentioned, such ill-conceived effort failed to benefit either giver or receiver; regeneration by means of personal connection was impossible when charity was bestowed in mass doses and from afar. When "the lever has to be applied from a distance," Denison wrote, "the sympathy is not strong enough to bear the strain." He argued instead that reformers go and live among the poor, not only to administer assistance personally but also to recreate genuine community—defined as a collection of men and women of high and low estate dedicated to a common purpose. "There are no rich people in the district," he lamented. "It is this unbroken level of poverty . . . which is *the* blight of East London."[8]

Denison was conscious that his particular remedy had to be coupled to at least a measure of state activity to siphon off the excess number of unemployed and casually employed laborers that blighted East London. Yet he was convinced that there was much that individual reformers could accomplish from their position as disinterested authority. They could certainly see to it that charity was not provided with so lavish and indiscriminate a hand as to damage community by encouraging the wrong sort of dependence. Denison wanted the poor residents of Stepney to depend upon him for moral leadership, but not for their own economic well-being. For that, they must be encouraged to look to themselves. "Build school-houses, pay teachers, give prizes, frame workmen's clubs, help them to help themselves; lend them your brains." But do not give them money. What he called "bread and meat doles," instituted by rich West End Londoners either out of a sense of guilt for the condition of the poor or out of fear of the unrest that condition might engender, accomplished nothing but the further degeneration of a population whose environment was already conspiring to rid it of any sense of purpose.[9]

Denison's ill health resulted in his premature death at the age of thirty in 1870. A volume of his letters and addresses, published in 1872, became a kind of sacred text for later reformers attracted by his particular brand of high-minded authoritarianism. Another whose work served equally as a model was Octavia Hill, who began to preach and to practice a similar ethic at about the same time. Granddaughter of the early Victorian crusader Southwood Smith, whose investigations of East London squalor had fueled the public-health movement in the 1840s, Hill was born into that aristocracy of talent that bred so much high-minded reform.

Friendship with John Ruskin encouraged her to seek his financial support for her first scheme, the reconstruction of a dreary set of buildings in Marylebone into an urban village. Her plan, like Denison's, reflected the notion that her business was not simply the remodeling of a particular environment but of the character of its inhabitants as well. Her ultimate hope lay, she wrote at the outset of the experiment, not in the improvement of "outward arrangements, . . . but in these as a means of *knowing and training the people to work and to trust. It is with me entirely a question of education.*"[10] Reiterating Denison's determination to produce economically independent men and women, she insisted that the attention she and her fellow workers were bestowing would succeed only if it made genuine individuals of the working-class poor in their care.

Octavia Hill's endeavors were not confined for long to a few courts in Marylebone. Using an increasingly large corps of trained rent collectors, whose role was in fact that of general organizer, remodeler, sympathizer, and disciplinarian to those in their charge, she extended her domain to other parts of London. Landlords, impressed by her ability to manage property in such a way as to improve its physical condition and the character of its inhabitants while returning a 5 percent profit on investment, entrusted further buildings to her management. The early 1880s saw her charged with the general administration of 378 families—approximately two thousand men, women, and children.

The success of the enterprise depended upon the hard work of rent collectors who, although they generally did not live within the precinct over which they ruled, in all other respects acted the role of a benevolent female authority. Of their duties, Hill wrote in 1874: "They must take the position of *queens* as well as *friends,* each in her own domain, . . . I should like them to take complete control as they would of their own house, garden or field; to take them as bits of God's earth, which He has entrusted to them to make of them the best possible; to take the people in the same way under their wings and carefully respecting their independent right as tenants, to make them the best possible."[11] The assignment was a great deal more demanding than the superficially similar one of district visitor for the Poor Law Board of Guardians. In the latter case, Hill reminded a worker, "if anyone did not welcome you, you could just stay away." But because these families were her tenants she insisted she had a duty to make their welfare her concern, no matter how difficult that task, no matter how unwelcoming their initial response. Respect for their "independent rights"—which Hill never defines—could be no excuse for the avoidance of disinterested intervention on their behalf. "From the greatest to the least the problems have implied some duty on your part. Nor have you chosen for whom the duties shall be undertaken: the family are tenants; that fact implies your relation to them. You know they are yours; they know it, and as the years go on this sense of attachment will deepen and grow."[12]

Social regeneration along the lines advocated by Denison and Hill had been preached and practiced previously by various reformers in other cities. The Scottish divine Thomas Chalmers had reorganized a wretched Glasgow parish in the early nineteenth century, placing a deacon as overseer of no more than fifty families, each deacon possessed of the personal authority to intervene in the lives of his charges, tutoring them in the ways of economic independence, and discouraging their reliance on parish charity. In 1850 Mary Carpenter, later famous for her work on behalf of ragged schools and the reform of juveniles, had purchased a court in the slums of Bristol to improve its accommodations for working-class families, much as Hill was later to do. The American Unitarian Joseph Tuckerman, himself inspired by Chalmers' work, in turn influenced many well-placed and philanthropic Unitarians, among them the Liverpool minister John Hamilton Thom, who encouraged "domestic missions" among the poor, preaching the importance of "heart acting on heart, conscience on conscience, soul on soul, man on man."[13]

These ideas and experiments, undertaken earlier and away from London, suggest the degree to which elements of the particular reforming ethos we are tracing penetrated the conscience and consciousness of Victorian reformers throughout England. What remains noteworthy is the degree to which the founders and early resident reformers of Toynbee Hall drew their inspiration almost exclusively from metropolitan experiments such as those of Denison and Hill. In the 1880s "outcast London," whose "bitter cry" the Congregational minister Andrew Mearns sensationalized in his 1883 pamphlet, had replaced the giant industrial cities of the north as the focus of national concern and apprehension.[14] Beyond that fact, young men who had received their education in public schools and at the ancient universities naturally directed their attention toward more familiar London, rather than the culturally distant north. The metropolis, whose industrial geography of small workshops and specialty trades gave to its economy a peculiarly preindustrial character in the second half of the nineteenth century,[15] would seem a more congenial focus for their concern and endeavor than northern cities, where uniformity and scale might appear insurmountable obstacles to any sort of satisfactory connection. One might, however, hope somehow to reestablish community in the idiosyncratic neighborhoods of working-class East London, whose venerable names—Bethnal Green, Whitechapel, St. George's—bespoke a history congenial to minds taught to revere the past.

Oxford did more than contribute a metropolitan bias to the reforming ethos that produced Toynbee Hall. A handful of its graduates, dons, and masters transformed the public-school notions of authoritarian high-mindedness and disinterested service to the state into a philosophical statement of intention that instilled intellectual rigor into the work of a generation of reformers. Once the university had begun to acknowledge after 1850 that its primary responsibilities were not to the private fiefdoms of its colleges but to the nation, it then started to argue about the definition of that responsibility. During the 1860s and 1870s Oxford debated the question, some contending that the finest service the universities could render lay in the cultivation of pure scholarship, whether philosophical or scientific, others urging their colleagues to understand their commitment as the training of a generation of able and authoritative politicians and administrators. In time, the two camps came to be identified with their leading protagonists: Mark Pattison, rector of Lincoln, and Benjamin Jowett, master of Balliol.

Jowett and Pattison had been reformers together in the 1850s. But though the two agreed in insisting that Oxford assume its rightful and necessary position as a national institution, Jowett's view of that position and the means necessary to achieve it contrasted markedly with Pattison's. Jowett believed that Oxford should begin to do what Pattison continued to insist that it should not: educate men to take their place as national leaders. Pattison defined Oxford's mission in terms of pure intellect; Jowett defined it in terms of disinterested duty. Both valued it as something apart from the world. But, unlike Pattison, Jowett hoped that once men had experienced it they would carry it with them out into society, where it had to be carried if it was to serve its purpose most fully.

Jowett differed from Pattison as well in insisting that, although the university ought to possess a sense of itself as a single institution, its colleges and their tutors should be allowed to remain the heart of its life and teaching. Pattison warned that to rely principally upon college tutors, rather than university professors, would be to run the risk of subverting Oxford into little more than a kind of greater public school. His fears stemmed from the fact that after mid-century, and in response to the dissemination of Arnoldian ideals, the post of college tutor was perceived more and more as that of moral preceptor. If education meant understanding one's duty, then education was not simply erudition and scholarship. This was the philosophy Arnold had preached at Rugby, which when it spread to Oxford and Cambridge produced what Sheldon Rothblatt has called "the revolution of the dons."[16] A profession that had till then usually involved little more than the often degrading and seldom rewarding task of coaching students for examinations took on a new and nobler purpose. By translating the example of the schools to the university, "tutors found that in forming the character of students, by which they meant restoring the influence of the teacher, they regained their self-respect."[17]

Tutors in colleges such as Balliol thus came to resemble a less formal but no less formidable equivalent of the public-school master. They understood themselves as standing in loco parentis, undertaking to educate their students as to character and goals by presenting themselves as worthy examples. Friendships between dons and undergraduates flourished in college essay societies and on vacation reading parties. College communities, bound together by the common experience of schooling and earnest intellectual endeavor, were the breeding ground of the godliness and good learning Newsome analyzes, of what Rothblatt calls a "mode" which the university could then translate, through the life and work of its graduates in the world at large, as its singular contribution to the nation's well-being.

Because of the increasingly intimate relationship between the public schools, the colleges, and the men who passed between them as students, dons, and masters, the mode would in time grow to reflect the values esteemed within the circle of those connections. In some cases, this would perhaps mean little more than devotion to the sort of spirit exemplified by group emotion and attention to the prowess of college teams, expressed in later life as simple-minded, conformist loyalty. But in others the mode amounted to far more, an essential link, in the case of Balliol, between older traditions and developing attitudes toward the methods and purposes of social reform.

Balliol, like all colleges, had natural connections with the gentry, with the Anglican clergy, and hence with the practices and precepts of authority and hierarchy. And like most colleges, it was experiencing through many of its most talented undergraduates an infusion of that seriousness of purpose which was at large in upper-middle-class Victorian England. The Balliol community built its particular mode upon that bedrock. While never turning its back upon learning, as the Pattison caricature would have it, it continued to insist on the sterility of learning for its own sake—thus in turn, perhaps, caricaturing the Pattisonians. Balliol's mode was an insistence that learning was a part of education, that education meant understanding the role men should play in the world, and that learning could help men to the certainty that the role was one of disinterested service to their fellow human beings.

The mode was of course by no means confined to Balliol, though the activity of Balliol's most talented and conspicuous graduates in time came to epitomize its expression. The fact of its more general prevalence was due in some measure to the writings of Matthew Arnold, the son of Thomas, whose preaching of the need for civilizing reform from the late 1860s on corresponded to the message that would emanate from Balliol. Matthew Arnold defined disinterested service to accord with his own hope of transforming England into a nation of "sweetness and light," a nation possessed of a valuable and commonly valued culture. He decried the extent to which class consciousness had prevented the connection so vital to such a culture and hence to the community of the nation. "The humanising, the bringing into one harmonious and truly humane life, of the whole body of English society—that is what interests me," he declared in an address to the Ipswich Working Men's College in 1879.[18] Late nineteenth-century social reformers were to share with Arnold this desire to be able to move throughout society without ever feeling oneself in an alien world. They understood it as their particular mission to destroy the walls that class had erected and then to bring to all within the nation a culture from which they might equally profit.

These sentiments formed a basis for the crusade Arnold hoped reformers would undertake on England's behalf. The isolation and consequent degradation of each class was to be overcome through the preaching of a common culture. Yet it was to be culture as defined by Arnold. A hierarchy of values was imperative, accompanied by an authority anxious to encourage and capable of imposing those values most essential to the perfectionism that was Arnold's goal. The authority once exercised by the aristocracy, Arnold argued, should now be entrusted to the state. He asked his readers in *Culture and Anarchy,* "What if we tried to rise above the idea of class to the idea of the whole community, *the State,* and to find one centre of light and authority there?" The obvious danger would be that in doing so the English might make use of the power of the state in order to press the claims, not of the unified nation as a whole, but of one particular class. Suppose, though, that a few citizens could rise above class, could exercise power in accordance with the reason that Arnold insisted resided within our "best selves"? Such persons do exist, Arnold maintained. Within each class "there are a certain number of aliens, . . . persons who are mainly led, not by their class spirit, but by a general humane spirit, by the love of human perfection." These individuals, privileged in the sense that they are already possessed of a knowledge of their "best selves," could be entrusted with the authority of the state in order to induce (or if necessary to coerce) the rest of the nation to subscribe to culture as they had defined it. "We want an authority, and we find nothing but jealous classes, checks, and a deadlock; culture suggests the idea of *the State*. We find no basis for a firm State power in our ordinary selves; culture suggests one to us in our *best self*." An authority, disinterested in the sense that it has risen above the interests of class, would employ the engine of the state to impose perfectionism, knowledge of "the best which has been thought and said in the world," [19] upon the rest of society.

That goal would appeal to the men of Balliol, as would Arnold's definition of cultural reform as active commitment and participation. Arnold was himself a school inspector, whose experiences as he traveled in that capacity across England had helped to shape his point of view. He defined learning's purpose as Jowett did: "The great men of culture are those who had a passion for diffusing, for making prevail, for carrying from one end of society to the other, the best knowledge, the best ideas of the time." [20] Though Arnold criticized Victorian middle-class society for its unwillingness to put aside its business long enough to seek out and appreciate what was truly best, he was at one with the "philistines" he belabored in his insistence that great men must be men active within the world. Arnold's compulsion to be up and doing betrayed the extent to which he and those who attended to his message were together the heirs of the moral activism his father and other headmasters had preached, and were still preaching, at Rugby and elsewhere.

The philosopher T. H. Green was another believer in the importance of doing. As Melvin Richter has pointed out, there was a close resemblance also between the religious beliefs of Thomas Arnold and of Green, who, although he entered Rugby eight years after Arnold's death, nevertheless experienced what Richter has described as that "singular atmosphere, characterized by incessant activity and corporate morality" which had survived the headmaster. [21]

Green argued, as had Thomas Arnold, for the infusion of Christian principles into national life. By the time he had begun to teach and to write in the early 1870s, however, serious-minded young men anxious to strengthen the community of the nation through the introduction of Christian principles found themselves compelled first to decide if they could any longer subscribe to the theological beliefs upon which the Church insisted the principles were founded. Green came to their rescue. He had himself abandoned Christian orthodoxy in the 1860s. He knew that for many other young men the loss could be almost unbearably difficult. As tutor, he took it upon himself to ease the hardship of the struggle by insisting to undergraduates that to lose one's faith need not—indeed, must not—mean the abandonment of the vital principles that lay at the heart of the Christian message.

In an introduction to two lay sermons which Green preached at Balliol and which were published after his death in 1882, his colleague Arnold Toynbee explained that Green recognized a responsibility to redefine for his listeners, as he had redefined for himself, "the practical character of Christian life," not only what one could believe but what one must do.[22] First-generation Church of England Evangelicals at the beginning of the century had insisted that religion must be "practical," that it must teach men and women how to live their lives in this world so as to prepare for life in the world to come. Green, though compelled to abandon all certainty as to the existence of an afterlife, preached duty as devoutly as had the practical Christians of an earlier generation, and he defined that duty as the constant cultivation of one's higher self. Duty meant self-subordination, in the sense that subordination of self to the needs of one's fellow human beings should take the place of subordination to the will of God. In the struggle to recognize their higher nature, men and women were strengthened by a God immanent within them. Though Green abandoned belief in a transcendent God, he insisted he did not therefore abandon what was of value in that belief. "An immanent God, a God present *in* the believing love of him and the brethren, a Christ within us, a continual resurrection": this sense of communication with the eternal and absolute would remind human beings of their insignificance and yet of their potential greatness. God was "the possible self."[23]

Green's affinity with the thought of the German idealists is reflected in his doctrine of an immanent God. It proclaimed the fact that men could trust to something more than self-generated instinct in their search for certainty. Evangelicalism's injunction to look for authority within oneself had too often either encouraged a sloppy, personal emotionalism or resulted in an honest doubter's thinking himself out of religion altogether. Philosophy, using reason and the perceptions accorded rational man by modern thought, would provide tools necessary to establish a new understanding of the relationship between God and man.

The doctrine of God's immanence allowed doubting undergraduates to understand how they might realize a higher self. It supplied renewed self-confidence to thoughtful young men at a time when the challenges and implications of scientific inquiry and higher criticism might otherwise have left them with a sense of ultimate human inadequacy. Green's injunction was simple and straightforward: to know that God is within you, act always in harmony with your higher self; to realize that harmony, act always to promote the common good.

Man was part of society, never an individual disconnected from the community in which he lived and which he had a duty to serve. Freedom meant something very different from doing what one wanted, even if that doing caused no actual harm to others. Freedom meant the opposite of willfulness; it often meant sacrifice. Speaking of the community of early Christian believers, Green declared that the Christian love manifested there was testimony to the fact that men and women could realize their best selves only in community—"the higher life," not just of each individual but, in this case, "of the Christian society."[24]

Green's persistent focus on community led him to teach that citizens' rights were defined by society. Individuals, Green declared in his *Lectures on the Principles of Political Obligation*, possess attributes and rights only insofar as they recognize the common interests and objects of the society in which they live, interests and objects defined, as with the individual, in terms of a higher, and in this case a communal, "self."[25] Yet despite that insistence, Green retained an ambivalent attitude toward state power and state intervention. His interest lay in the development of community, defined as an association among human beings equally free. To the extent that the state could assist in that development, he was prepared to see it act. He believed that state action was justifiable when it worked to promote a freedom that would, in turn, encourage individual citizens to cultivate their higher selves. Until men were perfect and therefore able to understand where true freedom lay, the state must "take the best security it can for the young citizens growing up in such health and with so much knowledge as is necessary for their real freedom." Injury to the health of individuals was a public injury, "an impediment to the general freedom," a diminution of "our power, as members of society, to make the best of ourselves."[26] Green argued that the Education Act of 1870 should have made primary education compulsory. Education was more than a parent's moral duty: its purpose was to prevent the hindrance of a child's right to freedom. Hence the state's authority to intervene.[27]

Laws of contract and of property, Green believed, restricted the freedom of too many for the benefit of too few. The freedom of a worker to negotiate wage levels over which, in fact, he had no control was no freedom at all, but instead "an evil incident . . . of that historical process by which the development of the rights of property has been brought about, but in which the agents have for the most part had no moral objects in view at all."[28] The statement reflects Green's conviction that ultimate responsibility rests with the individuals who comprise community. Without a moral object in view, their interference will serve the community ill. Voluntary action is therefore to be preferred wherever possible to state intervention, because voluntary action, resting as it does upon personal morality, is far more likely to promote a moral response on the part of both giver and receiver. To the extent that the state was forced to compel action, it was discouraging the development of morality, since morality depended on individual will operating apart from the compulsory machinery of the state. As Melvin Richter has rightly pointed out, Green distrusted machinery, looking instead to direct contact with the poor as the means of community integration.[29] Good citizenship more often meant individual rather than collective commitment to the well-being of one's fellow man: commitment to community, but by means of personal connection.

Green provided philosophical substance to the set of beliefs that would soon sustain the work of early Toynbee Hall reformers. Not only did he emphasize the importance of community and individual connection; he argued as well against the intrusiveness of class. He looked forward to its elimination, and welcomed the Reform Act of 1867 as a promise of that eventual goal. "The whole nation wins by a measure which makes us for the first time one people."[30]

Though Green spoke out against class division, he continued to preach communal unity in terms of the same sort of cultural hierarchy that appealed to Matthew Arnold. He welcomed the establishment of the Oxford High School in 1881 as a milestone on the road to a future when the phrase "the education of a gentleman" would have lost its meaning, since "the sort of education which alone makes the gentleman in any true sense will be within the reach of all."[31] That "sort of education," however, was to be defined by those whose duty and privilege it was to bring culture to the Oxford High School students. If education meant the discovery of freedom it meant a discovery in harmony with a middle-class world view.

Green, like Arnold, trusted that a cadre of dedicated and disinterested leaders would come forward to teach workers how they might become part of the larger community by shedding their class consciousness and realizing their higher selves. He himself undertook the role of teacher in this sense and was thus at one with the Balliol mission "to put Oxford in communication with the rest of the nation."[32] He campaigned for secondary education as a founder of the Oxford High School and as a member of the Taunton Commission, appointed in 1864 to investigate endowed secondary schools. He served on the Oxford Town Council and promoted the admission of women to the university. In the *Lectures on the Principles of Political Obligation*, he spoke of the nation's pressing need for "intelligent patriots," men with "a passion for serving the state."[33] Green hoped that his philosophy and his personal example might encourage those young men who heard him to undertake that service.

There seems to be little doubt that though Green's influence on undergraduates could be profound, on most students it was no more than general. Henry Scott Holland, who was perhaps as close to Green as any of his students, acknowledged that his lectures were not easy to follow: "His message was tough and tangled; the Hegelian jargon was teeth-breaking and head-splitting; and the way of speculation was hard and grim to tread." It was his obvious, passionate concern that convinced the serious minded that they must come and listen, no matter how much or how little they might understand. "Green's very figure, the tone of his voice, the piercing glance of his deep-set eyes, all meant that the apparently dominant forces of modern thought were running against the plain acceptance of Christian faith. he had won a foothold at a cost greater than any young man could measure."[34] For those students who came to know him well, his influence was extraordinarily powerful. "You have taught me everything of importance that I have learnt at Oxford," Holland wrote following notification of his first class in Final Schools, "and, for the Schools, you gave me a standpoint, by the fact of which I felt at once in a better position towards the papers than outsiders could be. And if I am grateful for the teaching, I am far more grateful for the great kindness you have shown me the last three years."[35]

What was the standpoint Green inspired undergraduates to occupy, as they came to hear him lecture or read and talked with him during term time or on holiday? First, to understand that loss of orthodox faith need not mean an end to life's purpose, that philosophy might restore the certainty, self-confidence and optimism that doubt had all but destroyed.

Second, that purpose must be defined in terms of self-denial and service to a community ideal. Third, that community implied personal connection between those who were to serve and those who were to be served. And finally, that their own lives could not be better spent than in that service.

Green, who had been teaching at Balliol in various capacities since 1860, was at the height of his influence as tutor and fellow when Arnold Toynbee matriculated in 1875. Though Toynbee's academic work was as an economic historian and not as a philosopher, the assumptions that shaped it reflected the powerful influence of Green's idealist thinking. Like Green, Toynbee wished to see religion "stripped of all accidents." Like Green, he was an immanentist. And like Green he insisted that the immanentist's ideal of an individually realized holiness could be achieved only through a life of duty—duty to "the perfect purity of inner life or *being*, and the duty of living for others, that they too may be perfectly pure in thought and action."[36] Freedom for Toynbee, as for Green, came to mean a self-restraining "perfect service" to one's fellow man and thus to God.

Toynbee's life was spent in pursuit of that service. "For the sake of religion," his friend Alfred Milner wrote, "he had become a social reformer; for the sake of social reform he became an economist." Toynbee acknowledged his own share of that "class-consciousness of sin" which Beatrice Webb believed inspired so many late nineteenth-century reformers. As he confessed to an audience of London workers in 1883: "We have neglected you; instead of justice we have offered you charity, and instead of sympathy we have offered you hard and unreal advice."[37] Toynbee used his profession as an economic historian to atone for the sins of his class, teaching his students to reject the "iron laws" that had been proclaimed as the theoretical basis of laissez-faire. He insisted instead that historical circumstance mandated flexibility when men attempted, as they must, to mitigate economic reality with human compassion. Toynbee lectured on the industrial revolution not as a set of propositions but as history. Enclosure, the factory system, the Poor Law, were the consequences of human activity at a particular time. If his students could be made to understand this, if they could realize the extent to which human factors and institutions—custom, public opinion, trade unions, law—shaped human events, they could be convinced of the possibility of change in the direction of the ideal.[38]

Change, for Toynbee as for Green, implied a larger role for the state, as arbiter of the community as a whole. The state's responsibility was to promote community by encouraging "the highest form of life"; in other words, "to secure freedom by compulsion."[39] But Toynbee pressed the case for state intervention further than Green did. "Where people are unable to provide a thing for themselves, and that thing is of *primary social importance*, . . . the State should interfere and provide it for them."[40] In a lecture entitled "Are Radicals Socialists?" which Toynbee delivered to audiences of northern working men and employers, he argued specifically on behalf of state-subsidized housing for the poor. The nation would not achieve genuine community "until all citizens have the chance of living decent lives; the poorest class need to be raised in the interest of all classes." By providing housing and education to the poor, the state would establish them upon a footing secure enough to enable them to understand their responsibilities as citizens and thereby "enter upon a purer and higher life."[41] Proposing a series of popular courses in political, industrial, and sanitary education to cooperative societies, he reiterated this insistence upon education beyond class and on behalf of community. "The whole scheme, Toynbee declared, "is framed not with reference to the education of the individual man, but of the citizen with a view of showing what are his duties to his fellow-man, and in what way union with them is possible."[42]

Toynbee argued that this union would produce a kind of fraternal government, in contrast to the paternalism of Randolph Churchill's Tory socialism. Yet Toynbee, like Green, advocated the leadership of a disinterested elite. He told workers that in return for the willingness of upper-middle-class men and women "to give up the life with books and those we love" to help the poor, the poor must be prepared to pledge themselves to "lead a better life" according to the ideals established for them by their mentors. And he was prepared to press the claims of the university men as just such disinterested teachers. Speaking to working-class audiences on the subject of "Industry and Democracy," Toynbee rested his right to address them "on the fact that I am a student" and argued that, as such, "I have . . . certain qualifications not possessed in an equal degree by the politician and man of business." With an assurance that would prove characteristic of the generation of social reformers he did much to inspire, Toynbee declared that the student would not "be suspected of class prejudice or political prejudice," and that, additionally, his training and temper had equipped him well "to take those wide, connected views of things which are often to the politician and the practical man impossible."[43] Hence his particular suitability not only as lecturer on a subject such as "Industry and Democracy" but, by implication, as mentor—connector—to the nation as it struggled to put behind it the conflicts of class in its search for communal citizenship.

Toynbee's life outside Balliol accorded with that declared belief. In Oxford he served on the Board of Guardians. He lived for a time in East London, lecturing in Whitechapel and Tower Hamlets. He spoke frequently to working-class audiences and campaigned for adult education and a more responsive Church establishment. The effect of his teaching and example, while probably not as profound as that of Green, was nonetheless impressive. Milner, a far from inconsequential personage even when an undergraduate, declared that "no man has ever had for me the same fascination, or made me realize as he did the secret of prophetic power—the kind of influence exercised in all ages by the men of religion and moral inspiration."[44] Perhaps because of his early death, Toynbee became a mythical figure and as such a portent of the effect the Balliol mode was to have upon the imagination of young social reformers. "That eager, impetuous scholar of Balliol," Albert Mansbridge, founder of the Workers' Educational Association, described him. He "flung himself into the haunts of workmen, lived with them, talked their best talk, . . . spending the last efforts of his all-too-brief life in the endeavour to secure unity between scholars and working people."[45]

Though Green died in 1882 and Toynbee in the following year, the young men they had taught and the examples they had set kept both their reputations and their ideas alive for more than a decade. While Jowett remained master of Balliol until his death in 1893, the college continued to give public expression to the ethos he had fostered. Power over self was the goal. It was Jowett's expectation that once his students were armed with that power they would move into the world as leaders, confident of a mission they believed to be the opposite of self-serving and assured by the assumption of tradition and training that there would be those who would as willingly follow them as their ancestors had followed the governing class of old.

Nor did the tradition die with Jowett. The philosopher Edward Caird, who succeeded him as master, possessed none of Jowett's public persona: "Frank as a landscape," his biographers remark, "and just as willing to be over-looked."[46] Caird was a Scot who had come to Balliol from St. Andrews in 1860, recently liberated from Protestant orthodoxies by Carlyle and of a mind and disposition to be further liberated by Green. He returned to Glasgow in 1866, where he remained to lecture and write until his election as master of Balliol more than a quarter of a century later. The distance did nothing to detach him, however, from ideas that mark his thought as reflective of the Balliol mode. Again, as with Green and Toynbee, conflict between individual and society was resolved by insistence that freedom and association could be defined only in relationship with each other, not as abstractions but as a union reflecting society's organic nature. And that assistance which society gives individuals "cannot be real aid unless it be such as to call out and stimulate their individual energy."[47]

Caird defined the responsibilities of the rich toward the poor very much as other Victorian reformers had defined them: as a means of improving the character of both rich and poor and, therefore, of society. "The only real charity, according to the ancient meaning of the word, 'which blesseth him that gives and him that takes,' is that which we pay not merely with our purses, but with our persons as well." Caird's conviction that a general wish for such work was growing among the young encouraged his optimism for the future. More than once he spoke, much as Beatrice Webb had written, of the "generous shame" that he believed must motivate the reformer working to bring men and women of different classes into communion with each other: "generous shame for the advantages that have fallen to his lot"; "generous shame that the heritage of humanity was, so much, the possession of the few."[48] Generous shame on the part of the giver and generous gratitude on the part of the receiver would insure the maintenance of the connections that fostered community.

Caird called upon Balliol students to take up their responsibility outside the college and within the world. In a lay sermon preached in the college hall, he defined what he called "the double ideal": "Unity, brotherhood, passionate enthusiasm of humanity and readiness to give up everything for the weal of the community"; "manly independence, free acceptance of responsibility, and willingness to undertake all the cares and difficulties of an individual life."[49] Community on one hand, the individuals within it on the other. Between them the intrusive presence of special interest and class, to be overcome only when individuals connected, as individuals, with each other, through the agency of a benevolent, disinterested elite.

The injunction to serve was by no means confined to the moralizing of the masters and tutors of Balliol. But the inspiration imparted by Green and Toynbee combined with the authority first of Jowett and then of Caird in a way that placed Balliol at the center of an invigoration of that collection of reforming impulses we have been tracing. The influence of those particular teachers was of a breadth that transcended the particular ethos they were refining. In 1889 a group of young High Church clergymen, the best known of whom were Charles Gore and Scott Holland, published the collection of essays entitled *Lux Mundi*, which, despite their avowal of orthodoxies which Green had abandoned, still bore the imprint of his immanentist teachings. Gore, Holland, and others among the essayists had been students and friends of Green's. Although they and the other *Lux Mundi* authors emphasized dogma, sacrament, and the Church, they were at one with Green in their willingness to define religion in terms of a consciousness of God at work constantly within the world. That definition led them, in turn, to echo Green's insistence that such consciousness was manifested by dedicated participation in the activities of a state whose own actions must reflect the values of an immanentist religion, and whose purpose was the fulfillment of Christian promise in programs of social justice and welfare.

Gore and Holland, as we shall see, pressed beyond Green to the borders of socialism, applying their religion to the problems of modern industrial society. Another of Green's ablest students, Sidney Ball, crossed the borders and organized the Oxford branch of the Fabian Society in 1895. Yet Ball's socialism amounted to little more than Green's idealist liberalism on the march to a logical conclusion. "Collectivism," he wrote, "implies the consciousness by society of a social ideal, of a better form of itself, and its distinction lies in its clearer consciousness of the end to be attained and its conception of the means of attaining it."[50]

Though logic might have encouraged a move toward socialism beyond the mild interventionism Green and Toynbee preached, the traditional appeal of hierarchy and authority acted as a powerful brake upon any such impulse. Thoughtful Oxford and Cambridge students, freighted with that tradition, amalgamated what their mentors taught them in a way that accorded with what they had already been encouraged to believe: that their background and education qualified them for their future role as disinterested leaders, and that their leadership would assist in the recreation of community far more genuine and enduring—because more personal—than that which socialism promised.

Further confirmation of that belief came to them with the publication in 1888 of Mary Ward's extraordinarily influential novel *Robert Elsmere.* The author was the niece of Matthew Arnold and a disciple of T. H. Green. Her hero's Oxford mentor (Green thinly disguised as Henry Grey) preaches Green's doctrine to his pupil Elsmere, but with the initial result that Elsmere takes orders. In poor health, Elsmere retires to recuperate in the hills of Westmorland. There he meets and wins his future wife, Catherine, the daughter of a strict Evangelical, dedicated to the preservation of her father's precepts and practices. Together they begin married life in the Surrey parish of Murewell, where they wage an ultimately successful battle against the absent squire's agent and on behalf of his tenants, who live in unhealthy squalor. Elsmere shows himself a conscientious modern reformer, "armed," as Ward describes him, "not only with charity but with science."[51] He is a campaigner for drains, for classrooms, for an institute, and is beloved within the community for those campaigns.

Yet while Elsmere is winning battles against ignorance and diptheria, he loses the battle for his faith. The squire, Roger Wendover, said to have been modeled to a degree upon Mark Pattison, returns home from scholarly researches in Germany. In the course of long conversations with Elsmere, Wendover's cynical, anticlerical arguments eat at Elsmere's beliefs, until he must declare to himself, and to Catherine, that he has no choice but to resign his living. A last-minute visit to Grey is of no avail, in the sense that Grey does nothing to dissuade him from resignation. But Grey preaches him a sermon that provides him with the hope upon which he is eventually able to build. Elsmere's present despair, Grey tells him, "is the education of God. Do not imagine it will put you farther from him! . . . Learn the lesson of your own pain—learn to seek God, not in any single event of past history, *but in your own soul,*—in the constant verifications of experience, in the life of Christian love."[52]

Elsmere determines to seek God in the slums of East London, first as a teacher in a Unitarian Sunday school, ultimately as the founder of a new religion based upon Grey's teachings and calling itself the New Brotherhood of Christ. The task of the New Brotherhood is "to reconceive the Christ," to proclaim him risen, not in legend or miracle, but in "wiser reverence," in "a more reasonable love," and in "new forms of social help inspired by his memory."[53] Before he is able to do much more than enunciate his goals, Elsmere dies of consumption—though we are to believe that his message and his personality have impressed themselves sufficiently upon the community to enable his work to go forward without him.

Throughout the novel Ward emphasizes the singular impact of Elsmere's manner and bearing. He is clearly a leader; and it is that fact, as much as what he has to say, that results in the ultimate power of his cause. Elsmere declares when first arriving in East London that he is there "to learn, not to lead." Even if he does listen and learn from working men, however, Elsmere continues to be a leader because it is in the nature of one bred and trained as he has been. He stands at the head of a community whose territory is men's spirits rather than their land. And he must prove, by his own conduct and his manner of inspiring others, that he is worthy of their confidence and trust. This of course he does, connecting with other individuals until he has created his new brotherhood.

Robert Elsmere's beliefs and work epitomize the ethos that inspired the reformers of Toynbee Hall. A young man, university educated, loses his faith. yet the lessons he learned from his tutor and his friend sustain him and provide the basis for a life of more perfect service. He moves into a depressed and fragmented wasteland and, by the force of his personality and his ability to lead others—as a consequence of his commitment to authority and hierarchy—creates a community in its midst, one in which he, the giver, is restored along with those poor men and women to whom he is giving. As Melvin Richter has remarked, Green himself looked forward to the foundation of communities not unlike the one Elsmere established. In a letter to Scott Holland in 1869, Green predicted the eventual existence of new forms of religious society or "simple religious citizenship," and declared his faith "that the new Christianity, because not claiming to be special or exceptional or miraculous, will do more for mankind than in its 'Catholic' form hampered by false antagonisms it has ever been able to do."[54]

The optimism that rings in that declaration was characteristic of the reformers' ethos. In a conversation with Mary Ward, W. E. Gladstone (who considered *Robert Elsmere* disturbing enough to review it in *Nineteenth Century*) took her to task for having forgotten sin. Mrs. Ward replied with the same confidence that Balliol bred into its high-minded under-graduates: "Though I did not wish for a moment to deny the existence of moral evil, the more one thought of it the more plain became its connection with physical and social and therefore *removable conditions*."[55] The task was to remove those conditions, yet to realize that their removal was but the means to a far nobler end: the regeneration of individuals within a restored and revitalized community.

2

TOYNBEE HALL: CONNECTION AND
THE EDUCATION OF BEST SELVES

The man most responsible for putting the precepts of Balliol and the latter-day Arnoldians into practice was Samuel Barnett, founder and, for a generation, guiding spirit of Toynbee Hall. Balliol men made their mark because of their willingness to undertake the task of curing what seemed to them a sick society. Barnett offered continuing education to them and to others so disposed, teaching them about the nature of the sickness and encouraging them to come and work a cure with him.

Born in 1844 the son of a Bristol manufacturer of iron bedsteads and grandson of merchants on both sides of the family, Barnett grew up on the fringes of Annan's "intellectual aristocracy." The Barnetts moved out from Bristol when Samuel was eight to suburban Clifton, where they became neighbors of the family of Dr. John Addington Symonds, father of the future critic and of the future Mrs. T. H. Green. Barnett and his brother were raised within a large, wealthy family of fond grandparents, aunts, and uncles, Forsytean in their affection for each other and in their attention to each other's business. A cousin of Barnett's, writing after the death of their maternal grandfather, remarked of his household that life was lived there against "a background of indulgent aunts," fruit picking, and birthday treats—"a happy and serene existence."[1] According to Barnett's wife, Henrietta, life in his own house was serene only because Barnett's mother catered to the every whim of his self-centered father, who, though "pure-minded," "punctilious," and "just to his work people," pampered himself without regard to his wife's feelings and patronized his sons throughout their lives by treating their opinions as a joke.[2]

24

Henrietta Barnett believed her husband had himself been spoiled as a child, though her evidence for this—his parents' willingness to provide the boys with "nice food and fruit"—says more of her, perhaps, than of them. Certainly they were not particularly concerned about their sons' education. Samuel was kept from school until he was sixteen, largely on grounds of poor health. He then went as a weekly boarder to a crammer, where, not surprisingly, he found himself intensely unhappy, and from there to a clergyman who provided academic stimulation sufficient to win him admission to Wadham College, Oxford, in September 1862. Wadham was at the time a backwater, its warden a Tory reactionary and an evangelical, its dry-as-dust precincts sheltered from the exhilarating breezes blowing across Oxford from Balliol. Barnett studied hard but without much enthusiasm. "I was," he later confessed, "what we in those days called a smug."[3] He rowed a bit, attached himself to a circle of friends none of whom distinguished themselves in later life, and graduated with a second-class Honours degree in law and history.

He had already determined to take orders but postponed his career long enough to serve two years as a master at Winchester, so as to earn money for a tour of America. His wife remarks in her biography of him that his experience at the school impressed upon him "the strength of opinion in the boyish world, which strangled some characters and sustained others."[4] Barnett thus encountered Winchester's moderated variations upon Arnoldian themes after he had ceased to be a schoolboy and at a time when he would naturally evaluate the ethos with a degree of objectivity. Nothing suggests that his Winchester experience had much effect upon his thinking or his determination to begin his clerical career in London.

It was his trip to America, apparently, that set the direction of his mind and his intentions. "Born and nurtured in an atmosphere of Toryism," he later remarked, "what I saw and heard there knocked all the Toryism out of me."[5] His observation of recently freed blacks convinced him of the degree to which proper education opened up a promise of adult life as a thoughtful citizen rather than as something little better than an animal. "The real future of the nigger," he wrote in his journal, "depends on the effect education has on him; the boy nigger seems bright enough and has a most intelligent look, but he is not father of the man; the chin and forehead of the man nigger recede, the nose flattens out, and the lips protrude and nothing of intelligence is left." Yet he was encouraged by the progress toward civilization of black children he saw in a Baltimore school. "As far as I can judge, the children . . . looked as intelligent as any white children; they answered questions in geography, and did decimal fractions most correctly."[6] Barnett drew no direct parallel in his journal between the black children of Baltimore and the slum children of industrial England. But one implication seems clear: capture the mind at an early enough age, and the child stands a chance; leave him to his own devices, and he deteriorates into a threat both to himself and to the society that has so willfully ignored him. "Toryism", to Barnett, appears to have meant leaving things as they were. And that he was not prepared to do.

Upon his return from America, Barnett confided his desire for a place in a metropolitan parish to a sympathetic Bristol clergyman, who sent him as a kind of clerical apprentice to W. H. Fremantle, rector of St. Mary's, Bryanston Square. Fremantle was one of a growing number of incumbent Churchmen and Nonconformists who believed that Christians had a particular mission to preach not only the gospel but also civilization to the poor. For at least a generation Anglicans of that conviction had been laboring to make headway against religious and educational indifference, working either in concert with men and women of other denominations, as in the case of the London City Mission, or on their own in urban parishes. Those like Fremantle who attempted the latter, did so longing to believe that they might reproduce in an urban parish setting the sort of Church-centered community that they liked to suppose had characterized preindustrial England. James Fraser, bishop of Manchester, took a different view, however, as is reflected in his charge of 1872:

> The parochial system, as ordinarily conceived, admirably efficient in rural parishes and among limited populations, where the pastor knows and is known by every one committed to his charge, breaks down in the face of that huge mass of ignorance, poverty and wretchedness by which it is so often confronted in the thickly peopled areas of our manufacturing towns.[7]

The parish of St. Mary's, situated to the north of Marble Arch, was not burdened with ignorance, poverty, and wretchedness to the degree that many in Manchester—and in East London—were. Yet there was enough to strain resources and administration. Barnett's diligence appealed to the hard-pressed Fremantle, who appointed him curate following his ordination as deacon in December 1867. At that time, Fremantle later recalled, his neophyte assistant's ideas and intentions were "at most in an inchoate condition." Gradually, during the five years he spent at St. Mary's, Barnett grew more certain of what he hoped to accomplish and on what grounds. A fellow curate remembered him as more inclined to sociology than theology and as a devoted disciple of Carlyle. With a third clergyman, they read philosophy together, "on the broad common basis of liberal thought and earnest inquiry into the truth of things." Fremantle put him to work teaching school and managing a club for workingmen, practical means of instilling in his curate his own conviction that "the Church of England meant the whole nation uniting in all its parts as a Christian body, and that the attempts to narrow it must be combatted."[8]

Meanwhile, Barnett had met the two women who gave his mind the direction it needed. Octavia Hill had commenced her philanthropic experiments in Fremantle's parish. Through him she met Barnett, whom she immediately pressed into service as an adjutant. And through her Barnett met his future wife, another of Hill's apprentices, a rich and strong-willed rent collector, Henrietta Rowland. "The profound influence which Miss Octavia Hill had on Mr. Barnett it is impossible to describe," Henrietta Barnett wrote in her biography of her husband. "She came to him as a new revelation of womanly potentialities," she added with apparent satisfaction, "for which his dear mother and the women he had known at Bristol had given him no indication."[9]

Hill had assumed the role of Fremantle's unofficial almoner, administering parish relief in accordance with that determination to encourage self-reliance which she, Edward Denison, and others were attempting to instill throughout London and beyond. With Barnett she discussed applicants for assistance, relying on him for an appraisal in each case: whether or not the men and women who came to her possessed the personal history of independence and willingness to work that would stamp them as "deserving" poor. "She was very good to him," Barnett's wife wrote, and "took trouble to introduce him to interesting people. . . . His feeling for her was deep, strong, and very beautiful, founded on admiration which reached veneration, and in those days it included unquestioning obedience, uncritical agreement and fervent chivalry. They respectively worked each other hard and without pity, while counselling moderation and rest to others."[10] Of Barnett, Hill remarked to a friend in 1870: "I should not wonder if he becomes a great man; now he is simply a good man, a remarkable man, but not yet a great one."[11]

A good enough man, at any rate, to receive her blessing at the time of his marriage in 1873 to Henrietta Rowland. Barnett's suit had at first been rejected. Though only eighteen when she went to work for Hill, Henrietta believed herself ready to dedicate her life to social and charitable work as a spinster, much as her mentor was doing. Besides, Barnett was eight years older than she, and looked a good deal more than that: "I had accepted his interest as that of a kindly elderly gentleman, with small sensitive hands, a bald head, and a shaggy beard." [12] He won her round in about six months, largely because of growing mutual affection and because Barnett agreed to her insistence that they live and work among the poor in East London. Octavia Hill approved. When Barnett had written her to ask if she thought Henrietta's none-too-robust constitution could stand life in such a place, she replied with characteristic certitude: "I do not think that the East End is at all necessarily unhealthy. I do not think that there is any parish so small, or any life so narrow but that, with her nature and heart, she might easily spend, yes even readily exhaust, all the strength she has. Her safeguard will be by no means in seeking remote places—passion and pain enough are found everywhere; it will lie in noble self-control." [13]

Armed with that high-minded injunction and with their own determination, the Barnetts sought Hill's assistance in finding them a parish of their own. Through a friend of hers, Edmund Hollond, who had followed Denison's example and gone to live in Stepney, she approached John Jackson, bishop of London, who bestowed upon Barnett the parish of St. Jude's, Whitechapel, though only after warning him that it was "the worst parish in my diocese, inhabited mainly by a criminal population." [14]

The Barnetts began their work at St. Jude's in 1873, facing bleak prospects—as Henrietta recalled:

> When Mr. Barnett and I went to see our proposed home it was one of those warm winter days when drizzle seems to magnify the noise and make sunshine a distant memory. . . . The people were dirty and bedraggled, the children neglected, the streets littered and ill-kept, the beer-shops full, the schools shut up. I can recall the realisation of the immensity of our task, the fear of failure to reach or help those crowds of people, with vice and woe and lawlessness written across their faces. . . . [15]

Whitechapel was one of the worst of London's slums. Sixteen years after the Barnetts' arrival there Charles Booth found 40 percent of the district's population living below the poverty line. The majority who worked earned a precarious living, some as sweated clothing, boot, and furniture makers, others as street peddlers or casually employed dock laborers.

The district had a reputation for viciousness as well as poverty. Common lodging houses sheltered prostitutes and thieves. An extensive urban-renewal scheme, carried out in consequence of the Artisans' and Labourers' Dwelling Act of 1875, and actively supported by Barnett, eventually rid the area of some of its worst rookeries. Yet in 1885 he could still detail daily incidents of criminal violence:

> *October 6th.*—Disturbance in Fashion Street. Three women had been knocked about by a drunken man, who had a nasty gash on his left eye and was bleeding profusely. . . .
>
> *October 9th.*—Woman's head badly cut by a man. Charge brought next day . . . but not being supported by woman was dismissed. . . .
>
> *October 29th.*—Saw a woman dead drunk dragged along the length of the street.[16]

It was in the Whitechapel district that Jack the Ripper murdered five prostitutes in the fall of 1888. To the demoralization of poverty and crime was added the social tension consequent upon the continuing immigration of East European Jews, a flow that increased after the pogroms that followed the assassination of Czar Alexander II in 1881. St. Jude's, located on Commercial St. and nearby Whitechapel Rd., lay at the center of the largest concentration of working-class Jews in East London.[17] Not surprisingly, the Church's influence within these precincts had been almost nil. The work of an occasional zealous incumbent or of a lay missionary such as Denison might make some slight temporary impact. But in 1895 the rector of neighboring Bethnal Green estimated that not more than 1 percent of the workingmen of East London attended church or chapel.[18]

Despite these daunting circumstances, Barnett's intention was to undertake to do at St. Jude's what other clergymen were attempting elsewhere: to use the institutional machinery provided by a parish church to create a regenerated community.[19] In a circular issued soon after taking charge he bombarded his parishioners with proposals: day schools, Sunday schools, church repair, free seats, a mixed choir ("because I think worship should be as social as possible"), and a church council, to which he proposed to grant "most of the power which the law at present allows to the Vicar." He declared himself the clergyman not just of his congregation but of the whole parish. Everyone was to have a claim upon his "counsel in difficulty and his help to enable them to live the life and do the duty God has designed for them."[20]

By the end of their first decade, and with the assistance of a crew of benevolent and hardworking upper-middle-class laymen and women, the Barnetts had accomplished a good deal. Various organizations awakened the parish to the church's existence, with the result that attendance at morning and evening services increased. There were adult classes and a night school for girls; a literary society and annual art exhibitions; mothers' meetings and a maternity society. A penny bank and a pension scheme were established to encourage thrift; a revised system of charitable relief under the supervision of lady visitors was designed to promote self-help. Yet after ten years, despite what he had accomplished, Barnett continued to wonder if the parish was an effective solution to the multitudinous problems endemic to East London.

The petty business of parish life confined clergymen to details—often exasperating and sordid. They could so seldom raise their eyes from account books or their minds from the squabbling and importuning of their parishioners. Hugh McLeod, in his study of religion in late nineteenth-century London, cites the diary of a Bethnal Green curate of the 1880s as evidence of the enervating and endless tedium. "It is a pathetic document. Woodriffe [the curate] was plagued by beggars, tramps, cranks and parishioners in trouble, and he seems to have spent most of the day in trying to determine whether applicants for hospital letters were deserving cases, and whether seekers of advice or spiritual consolation were merely after his money." The result was demoralization, such as that reported by another East London clergyman in his visitation return of 1883. When asked what was impeding his ministry, he replied: "The deadness of the Church in so many parishes round, owing in a great measure to the incumbents being broken down."[21]

Barnett was by no means broken down. On the contrary, during the late 1870s he began to conceive and to articulate a philosophy of action derived from a growing association with Balliol and its mode. Fremantle had introduced Barnett to Jowett at a London breakfast. Barnett and his wife had paid their first visit together to Oxford at the invitation of one of Henrietta's friends, Toynbee's sister Gertrude. By 1879 Barnett was corresponding with Toynbee about the limitations of the Church as an engine for the regeneration of community. As he began to mount a national campaign on behalf of what he called "Pan-religion," Toynbee wondered in a letter to Barnett whether the Church had the vision to promote a unity of the secular and spiritual that he believed necessary for the achievement of reinvigorated national community. "The spiritualization of life in all its aspects": this was the principle upon which reform had to be grounded.[22] The immanentism implicit in this declaration found favor with Barnett, who had by this time begun to preach that same message. To be without God in the world was the great human calamity. And only within the world, in the midst of mankind, could men and women hope to find God. Octavia Hill reported of one of Barnett's sermons:

> He spoke of the mistake of those who left men with the idea of entering into nearer communion with God, that only as we lived among them could we learn the true beauties of their various natures, and that slowly, year by year, as we gathered these fragments of glory, the old notion of corrupt humanity would vanish, and we should see gradually that these fragments made up the mighty humanity which was Christ himself.

There was a good deal of Green in this; indeed, as Beatrice Webb remarked, Barnett was from this time best described as "an idealistic Christian without dogma."[23]

Several months after Toynbee's first letter to Barnett, he wrote again to report that he had founded a club at Oxford to further the cause of spiritual and secular unification. Its membership of seven included four young Balliol men, Alfred Milner among them. At its first meeting, Toynbee had read a paper on "The Organisation of Consumption," in which he indicated "the individual reforms which must accompany any great Religious and Political movement." To succeed, they would have to give practical expression to the principles of combination, "in religion, politics, and the industrial sphere."[24]

The vision was one that transcended parish boundaries, and that therefore encouraged Barnett to chafe against the constrictions imposed by parochial concerns. He found himself opposing the subdivision of large parishes, a reform that for some time had been perceived as a means of breaking down the vastness and anonymity of urban life. Now, as his wife recorded, Barnett began to argue that the parish did not provide scope enough "for men with power of organization and force of personality. 'There are no adequate places for the best men unless they consent to become Bishops', he used to say, 'and then they are apt to be strangled by their own gaiters!'"[25]

Distrust of parochial machinery was responsible in large measure for Barnett's search for another means to achieve some sort of genuine community in London's East End. The distrust was shared by others concerned with the same set of problems. Recalling the mood of the mid-1880s, Walter Besant later wrote:

> Men at the universities, especially those who directly or indirectly felt the influence of T. H. Green, were asking for some other way than that of institutions by which to reach their neighbors. . . . They felt that they were bound to be themselves true to the call which had summoned them to the business and enjoyment of life, and they distrusted machinery. . . . Philanthropy appeared to many to be a sort of mechanical figure beautifully framed by men to do their duty to their brother men.[26]

The Barnetts moved with increasing frequency and intimacy in the years following their marriage among university men of the sort Besant described. Their visits to Oxford combined the opportunity to become acquainted with Green, Toynbee and Jowett, Caird and Ball, with the chance to persuade undergraduates to spend vacation time working at St. Jude's. "From Oxford the men came to us, and we put them to such work as was possible," Henrietta Barnett recalled. "Arnold Toynbee stayed with us rather oftener than the other men, but his health was too fragile to bear the pain and strain of residence in East London, and the experiment soon ended."[27]

It was on the occasion of a visit by Barnett to Oxford in November 1883 that he proposed the idea of a university settlement. He had received a request from a group of students at St. John's, Cambridge, for suggestions as to ways they might accomplish some sort of effective work among the poor. The petition provided the catalyst, and at a meeting in Sidney Ball's rooms, Barnett read a paper on "University Settlements in East London." In it he contrasted existing college missions, staffed by resident Church of England clergymen, with the possibility of a new and far more effective way of achieving what Barnett assumed to be their goal—what had, in fact, become his own goal: "The grand idea . . .

which, like a new creative spirit is brooding over the face of Society, and is making men conscious of their brotherhood," the reconnection of men and women into community.

Barnett was critical of "ordinary parochial mechanism," ill equipped as it was to "carry to the homes of the poor a share of the best gifts now enjoyed in the University." Left to deal by himself with the protean complexities that poverty imposed upon his parish, the clergyman soon grew discouraged, he and those interested in his work convinced "that there is no way by which the best can be given to the poor."

A determination to offer the best to the poor was as essential to Barnett's scheme for the creation of community as it was to Green's and to Matthew Arnold's. To give the determination effect, Barnett proposed a settlement headed by a "chief" who was "qualified to teach" and was "endowed with the enthusiasm of humanity." This man would be joined by others fresh from the universities. The settlement house, located in some poor quarter, would become "a common ground for all classes." Lectures, conversations, and receptions would afford "all sorts and conditions of men" the chance to come to know each other. Bound by their resolve "to do something to improve the condition of the people," the settlers would insure an interchange between the universities and the world. "The condition of the English people will come to be a fact more familiar than that of the Grecian or Roman, and the history of the College Settlement will be better known than that of the boat or eleven. On the other side, thoughts and feelings which are now often spent in vain talks at debating societies will go up to town to refresh those who are spent by labour, or to find an outlet in action." Settlers, binding themselves "by sympathy and service to the lives of the people," would "bring the light and strength of intelligence to bear on their government, and . . . give a voice both to their needs and wrongs."

Barnett insisted upon distinguishing between a settlement—the institution he was proposing—and a mission. The latter were founded to proselytize for a particular sect or dogma and had existed in London since mid-century. The Church of England had established the Clergy Mission College in 1863, charged with the responsibility for drafting mission clergy into service in the parishes of the poor. By the 1880s, over fifteen public schools and university colleges sponsored similar endeavors in London and in a few other large cities. Nonconformists had cooperated toward the same end with evangelical Churchmen in founding the Conference of Christian Workers. Following the publication of *The Bitter Cry of Outcast London* in 1883, the London Congregational Union, sponsor of the pamphlet, renewed its campaign for increased missionary endeavor and was joined, in varying degrees of enthusiasm and commitment, by other Nonconformist denominations. "If any place under heaven should be made Christian, London is the place," declared the committee of the Wesleyan Metropolitan Chapel Building Fund in 1884. And within a year, the Wesleyans had established a London Mission "to carry the Gospel to such regions of London . . . as are most spiritually destitute and degraded."[28] Barnett argued that the spirit exemplified in the "best selves" of recent university graduates transcended denominational bounds. The settlement worker's nondenominational, though godly, task was to undertake the restoration of community through the example he would set and the leadership he would provide.

His ten years in Whitechapel had taught Barnett the dangers of easy optimism. "It is impossible to prophesy," he warned, "that a University Settlement will make the poor rich or give them the necessaries of true life." Yet the promise of community made the scheme's implementation imperative. "There is . . . for the settler an ideal worthy of his sacrifice. . . . He looks to a community where the best is most common, where there is no more ignorance and sin—a community in which the poor have all that gives value to wealth, in which beauty, knowledge, and righteousness are nationalized."[29]

Here was the Balliol mode expressed as an exciting but apparently practical plan. Barnett pressed his advantage, speaking the following month at the Oxford Union, where he proposed the motion, which carried unanimously, that "the condition of the poor in our large towns is a national disgrace." By early 1884 a committee that included several Balliol tutors, along with Sidney Ball and the Liberal member of Parliament James Bryce, had determined to establish a Universities' Settlement Association, which in July was registered as a joint-stock undertaking. Its objects were broadly stated: provision of "education and the means of recreation and enjoyment for the people in the poorer districts of London and other great cities"; "inquiry into the condition of the poor"; and consideration and advancement of plans to promote their welfare.[30] As means to those ends, a first property was to be purchased and appropriate buildings erected to house the settlers and to accommodate their work; a settlement director was to be named; and a trust was to be established to receive and disburse funds donated for the purposes of the association.

Henrietta Barnett took credit for the proposed settlement's name, claiming the inspiration had come to her while hearing a sermon preached by her husband in Balliol chapel at Jowett's invitation in the spring of 1884 on the anniversary of Toynbee's death. "As I sat on that Sunday afternoon in the chapel, one of the few women among the crowd of strong-brained, clean-living men, the thought flashed to me: 'Let us call the Settlement Toynbee Hall.'"[31] The association appears to have lost little time in selecting Barnett as the director—warden—of the enterprise. Tired of the parish grind that his life had become, he accepted, although he did not in fact resign the living of St. Jude's for another ten years. He immediately suggested a site adjacent to St. Jude's—that of a disused boys' industrial school—as appropriate for the hall. It was purchased for £6,250, and by Christmas Eve 1884 the first settlers were in residence.

Barnett was forty years old and, despite his sense of frustration with parish work, still "endowed with the enthusiasm of humanity." One of the young men who was to come to work for him at the hall remembered after Barnett's death the degree to which he could inspire that enthusiasm in others: "I felt myself that the whole world ought to be conquered, and could be conquered . . . it was the enthusiasm that really mattered."[32] Beyond the enthusiasm, his decade of experience in East London both as a parish priest and as community leader appeared to fit him for the job. Regardless of those assets, however, Barnett remained in many respects a less than promising candidate for the challenging position of warden as he had outlined it in his Oxford address. Time had not given him a countenance and figure any more striking than those he possessed when, in 1875, a friend of his wife's had described him in a letter as "plain and insignificant. . . . In fact, what in my old hunting days I should have classified as a 'poor thing.'"[33] Nor was he a particularly effective public speaker. Beatrice Webb, who came to know the Barnetts well as a result of her own work in East London, perceived, with characteristic sharpness, that

> he had no personal magnetism as a preacher, no fluency as a lecturer; he had no special talent in the choice and use of words. Meticulous lawyers found him muddle-headed when explaining schemes of reform; fanatics discovered indispensable links absent in the consistent working out of a creed; hard-sensed and literal-minded men and women felt that he was Jesuitical in the way he

jumped from standpoint to standpoint in search of common ground upon which might be based united action in the direction he desired.[34]

Yet despite his shortcomings, and his own consciousness of them, he proved himself capable, for a time at any rate, of engendering just such action. He succeeded because he was a man determined to discover and encourage a best self in others. By persevering, he generated devotion and loyalty in those men whom he was awakening to their potential as disinterested leaders of a revived effort on behalf of community. "In our dealings with individuals," he wrote, "we should remember more consciously their ideal selves. . . . Few realize that in the individual there is a buried life, a life which can think and love, and that the only end worth achieving is the release of this life from beneath its load of selfish, mean cares." This conviction had encouraged Barnett to press ahead with his campaign to reach out to the men and women of Whitechapel. It also informed his equally determined attempts to uncover the very best that lay beneath the surface of young university gentlemen. "My husband," Henrietta Barnett wrote, "had, by the force of his longing for the fulfilment of the best in everybody, not only the power of probing, but a stimulating and controlling influence. This was so strong that often, when people were with [him], they really were what he wanted them to be, and which he therefore believed them to be."[35]

That they often fell short of her husband's expectations, once removed from his compelling influence, was a fact his wife felt herself bound to acknowledge. Henrietta was not one to suffer fools. Beatrice Webb called her "the more masculine-minded of the two." Mrs. Barnett believed that people too often took advantage of her husband, because of his unwillingness to think of them as anything less than what he wanted them to be. Octavia Hill once warned him to beware of his "intense desire not to separate yourself by criticising, or dwelling on, differences between yourself and any single human soul you come in contact with." To all three of these strong-minded, opinionated women, there was clearly something almost childish about Barnett's faith in the potential for human goodness. Yet they understood it as the source of his strength. A doer, immersed in the business of living men and women, he nevertheless journeyed through life, as Beatrice Webb observed, "'as if' he was in continuous communion with an external spirit of love; and 'as if' man's purpose on earth was to make this spirit of love supreme in society."[36] That was indeed Barnett's mission, and one that he radiated with such intensity that men were attracted to his call and persuaded to respond to his charge upon their best selves.

Barnett talked university men into joining him by convincing them that connection with the slum dwellers of East London through the institution of Toynbee Hall offered them the best chance to discharge the duties and to assuage the guilt that their privileged position imposed. He shared with other Victorian reformers the compulsion to atone for the sins of class irresponsibility. He prayed for consciousness of public and national sin as well as private: "In our *public* life we have sinned against Thee, we have shrunk from our responsibility, from our duty to our brother man. We have preferred our own ease to doing justice. . . . We have sinned against Thee in our *national* life. As a nation we are in trouble, poverty, want. It is because we have not trusted in Thee that we are in trouble."[37] Trust in God would compel activity that would reunite men in the fellowship of community.

Barnett lamented the social gulf that had resulted when individual connection had given way to impersonal assistance, whether philanthropic or state supported. Massive, sporadic intervention in response to brief, sensational appeals harmed both giver and receiver, and was the sort of charity Toynbee Hall was designed to thwart. "To make a market of human misery, to raise money by cheap sensation, to expose suffering friends to fashionable curiosity, is alien to the very idea of the Hall," an informational bulletin proclaimed in 1887. There, in contrast, "those who really care for the poor can acquire knowledge and offer sympathy in a simple and inoffensive way; those who are ready to give a part of their leisure to the service of others, can find openings for substantial work."[38] Through intimate connection of the kind the hall offered, both giver and receiver would benefit. "Blessings not shared tend to degrade their owners," Barnett preached, and self-subordination in the activities of Toynbee Hall provided an effective means for combating such degradation. In these observations, Barnett was reiterating earlier expressions of the necessity for connection between one individual and another. "The thousands of East London labourers will never be taught by missions; they must be reached one by one; and any one educated man or woman may be the one to show to eyes wearied with gloom something of God's infinite beauty. . . . One by one is the phrase which best expresses our method, and the 'raising of the buried life' is that which best expresses our end."[39]

The vital importance of "one by one" was grounded in Barnett's belief that genuine reform was impossible without reformation of character. (We shall see, however, that this conviction did not stand in the way of his increasing support for state intervention.) As José Harris has observed, Barnett remained convinced that "'character' was the clue to social distress and the key to social reform."[40] That being so, lasting change for the better would come only when two "characters" could come together to interact upon each other. Barnett recognized that the impatient would find his methods slow and uncertain, that they would be in too great a hurry to do *for* people what should be done *with* them. "There is an absence of patience—the passionate patience—which is content to examine, to serve, to wait, and even to fail. . . ."[41] But the eventual reward would be worth the delay. "If rich and poor could see one another as God sees each, if they could get rid of the ignorance which hides from each the real goodness of the other, there would be on earth peace and goodwill among men."[42]

Toynbee Hall afforded shelter for the cultivation of "passionate patience." Barnett tried to be as explicit as he could about the methods by which the residents there were to go about the delicate, intuitive business of connection. "They take in knowledge which they do not tabulate; they absorb thought as air, they consciously become sympathetic, and lose the narrow views which kept them as a class apart."[43] The key to change was habit; to change a community, one must change the habits of its individual members. And that could only be accomplished "one by one." "The habits and tastes, therefore, which lie at the root of Poverty, Ignorance, and Sin, may best be met by the formation of other habits, which come through the example of persons, by the contact of man with man." Hence the need for Toynbee Hall. A company of righteous men "who would live simply and share their luxury, whose gain would not mean another's loss," living together and working with passionate patience to redirect the habits and tastes of the poor, might make a real and lasting difference.[44]

A difference to whom, though? To society generally—if enough righteous men in time answered the call. And a difference, certainly, to the university men, who would come to understand themselves, their fellow men and women, and the problems of poverty by their work in East

London. Above all, Barnett hoped, a difference to the poor. Barnett fought hard against a tendency to patronize the workingmen and -women of East London. He contested the notion that the poor were somehow qualitatively different from the rest of society and therefore fair game for a kind of condescending benevolence. On the contrary, Barnett argued, it was because the poor were as capable as the rich of appreciating the very best in life that the attempt to reconstitute them as part of the community was worth making. Nevertheless, Barnett believed with Matthew Arnold in a hierarchy of cultural values and in the necessity for a disinterested elite to instill that hierarchy into the minds of working-class men and women by instilling it into their habits. To do so, this elite had to inspire a trust that implied its position as leaders. "The one thing necessary," Barnett explained in an early Toynbee Hall *Annual Report*, "is that the attempt be made by those . . . who having learnt through feeling what are the needs of their neighbours, are able to put into language unuttered thoughts, and who, having shown through sharing what are their own ways of living, are trusted even when they are not understood."[45]

The new communities were thus to be established on the basis of hierarchy. The first Toynbee Hall *Annual Report* declared the "main difficulty" of poor city neighborhoods to be that their residents "have few friends and helpers who can study and relive their difficulties . . . , few educated public-spirited residents."[46] P. Lyttleton Gell, one of the hall's first residents, came closer than Barnett to stating the purpose of the institution in terms of a kind of enlightened urban paternalism. In a pamphlet entitled *The Municipal Responsibilities of the "Well-to-Do,"* Gell wrote:

The whole English system is based upon the assumption of a resident leisured class. . . . But if the well-to-do fly each evening from the cities where their wealth is created, and if the working classes are left behind when the day's work is done, too fatigued and too uninstructed to care for anything but to refresh their wearied bodies against tomorrow's toil, the social system . . . breaks down. . . . The departure of the well-to-do from out of the heart of our cities robs each community of the citizens whose duty it is to maintain the standard of administration and refinement, and leaves them to become more hopeless and more dingy still. . . . There is only one real solution. The wealthy middle-class deserters from the commonwealth must take up again their civic responsibilities. They have the leisure and the ability, which the poor have not. It is their duty to labour personally at the improvement—material, moral, spiritual—of the masses, by whose labours alone their leisured life is rendered possible.[47]

Consider the progression: from a definition of community based upon a recognition of mutual worth, we move to one that insists upon the establishment of a hierarchy of values, and from there to yet another which argues the necessity of a benevolent ruling class. Barnett and his coworkers wanted community to mean one thing: what Arnold Toynbee had referred to as fraternalism. Their own habits, despite their insistence on their disinterestedness, frequently led them to give the word a different and very distinctly authoritarian meaning, and the actions that were the words' expression a different and equally authoritarian purpose.

An instinctive fear lay behind the inability of Barnett and his coworkers to abandon authority and hierarchy in their search for community: fear of a town-bred proletariat; fear of the antagonisms of class consciousness. The dull mindlessness and mental impoverishment that seemed to so many middle-class observers to characterize the lives and outlook of the urban poor implied a threat to the social order. Pointless pleasure seeking might easily turn to gratuitous violence. Barnett was by no means immune to the theory, current particularly in the 1880s, that the city itself was the cause of the general deterioration that alarmed so many. It was easy for reformers to lay the blame on biological and ecological, rather than economic, forces. Investigators declared that "the savage and brutalized condition of the casual poor was the result of long exposure to the degenerating conditions of city life."[48]

Although Barnett was prepared to acknowledge the contribution of economic circumstances to the problem, his antiurban perceptions and point of view induced in him a degree of fatalism about the chances for regeneration within an urban environment. In this he echoed the sentiments of his fellow upper-middle-class reformers. Edward Denison despaired of the city. Green had insisted upon man's need for the countryside, the meeting point of humanity with nature.[49] The myth of the countryside was part of the mystique of still-rural Oxford and Cambridge, of Wordsworth (Green's favorite English poet), and, more generally, of the Victorian upper-middle-class mentality. The countryside was a tonic against the diseases of city living. Writing once to his brother of a walk on Hampstead Heath, where the Barnetts maintained a retreat for themselves from the oppressiveness of East London, Barnett declared that he had "felt more than ever the power of the country. Vain is it for us to try to teach men new life if we keep them in the city; it is the country and only the country which can teach so as to be obeyed."[50] The facts of East London life limited the reformer's opportunities. Whitechapel would not vanish, and while it stood as it was, it blighted the lives of those who lived within it. If Barnett hated much of what the city represented, it was because of what the city was in that area where he had chosen to work.

Fear of what city life might breed mingled in Barnett's mind with fear of what class consciousness might engender. In company with other Victorian reformers, Barnett deplored the division of society into classes. Unwilling to acknowledge the extent to which the disinterested men whom he was assembling at Toynbee Hall were themselves representative of a class, or the degree to which the culture he hoped to broadcast was the culture of a particular elite, he urged the example of his work upon the nation as a solution to the class divisions that he believed represented an alarming national threat. "When part of society is content with a low life," Barnett wrote in 1888, while social tension was running high,

and another part is indifferent to that content, class warfare is not far distant. There are tens of thousands with the thoughts and feelings of men, living the lives of beasts, greedy for what they can get, careless of the means of getting, rejoicing in low pleasures, moved by a blind sense of injustice ready to take shape in foolish demands and wild acts; there are, on the other side, thousands with the knowledge that such lives are lived by their neighbours, who go on making themselves comfortable and happy, and their hardness of heart takes shape in commissions, in lucid expositions over dinner tables that "the statistics of pauperism show no increase," and in admirable reasons, founded on political economy, that "nothing can be done."[51]

Barnett believed in the existence of that elusive species of humankind, the man or woman of good will. And he was confident that when those men and women of good will met each other as individuals, one to one, and not as the representatives of class, their differences would resolve themselves. "Conscious of being human, with human wants and hopes, labourer and employer resent being treated as if interests were supreme; the labourer resents the attempt to buy him with a gift, while he is denied a voice in the parish council, and the employer knows the agitator does him wrong when he says that the only way of making him feel is through his pocket."[52]

Toynbee Hall set itself the task of dissolving "interest," as Barnett defined it, so that the human wants and hopes of capital and labor might meet. Barnett was concerned that without such a meeting, each class would entrench itself behind what, in another article, he referred to as its "ideal": "Different ideals are more disintegrating of society than incendiary fires," he wrote, for differing ideals breed different ethical standards. "Workmen, it may be said, are better able to feel deeply than to think clearly, while the richer classes think clearly rather than feel deeply. . . . Class pulls against class. Each has its eye on an ideal in which its own members are dominant, not one in which all citizens get equal benefit."[53] Barnett did not want to see class abolished. What he did hope for was agreement upon an ideal—one consistent with his own perceptions of the "best"—an ideal that would allow classes to live in harmony, together dedicated to the achievement of a noble and common end.

Barnett's perceptions of class were circumscribed by the fact that he had experienced little of England except Oxford and London. Although he was the son of a Bristol manufacturer of iron bedsteads, he knew almost nothing about factory life or the consciousness it might produce. His only recorded impression of the evidences of industrialization in the north, in a letter to his wife in 1883, was cast in a romantic vein. The Sunderland foundry he had visited put him in mind of "a temple erected for the worship of fire. With the memory of [York] Minster on me, so it seemed. . . . A different worship from that of the Minster, suggesting a different relation to a different side of life. The life of 'progressive' England with its ships, its railways. . . ." The workers—"the priests"—did not appear happy, however. They looked "stern and weary," even though in some instances they were paid as much as £2 per week. "I can imagine that their only relaxation would be in the riot of a public-house or of the Salvation Army."[54]

Barnett's inclination was to lump workers together into a mass, label them, not "labour" or "the working class," but "the poor" and assign to them all the characteristics and habits of mind that he had discovered among the Whitechapel "residuum." On frequent occasions, it is true, he spoke and wrote of the distinction between what contemporary social reformers were calling the "true working classes" (those men and women who could command steady, decent wages) and the casually employed or unemployed remainder. But economic conditions in Whitechapel meant that much of his work lay among the latter, so that he came to assume they represented all those in one of the "two great classes" whom he hoped to see reunited. Taking his evidence primarily from London, he could remark that "the classes in our great cities are many, but the terms 'rich' and 'poor,' if not exact definitions, represent clearly enough the two great classes of society."[55] That definition made it easier for him to argue for the abolition of class differences. When class amounted to little more than poverty and greed, who could in good conscience oppose its abolition? The horizontal aspirations of working-class consciousness—what Barnett meant by the working-class "ideal"—could be dismissed as the selfishness of "have nots," just as the inclinations and perceptions of the middle and upper classes could be described as the indifferent greed of the possessors.

Class, which to Barnett meant the ignorant prejudice of the poor and the wooden-headed indifference of the rich and which threatened social order with division, was an institution to be overcome by a revived sense of community. "How may the human flickering instincts of respect and sympathy be cherished," Barnett asked, "so that they may fuse into one body the men and women divided by their interests as employed and employer?" He believed that Toynbee Hall provided a setting that would teach men and women to give the same answers he gave to that question: by coming to a fuller understanding of the character of God, as "formed out of contemporary experience"; by encouraging rich and poor to live in closer proximity; and by promoting "higher thinking" for the poor and "simpler living" for the rich.[56]

Barnett's apologia for Toynbee Hall and its work contained nothing that was new. His thoughts, as Beatrice Webb remarked, were no more than "the tools whereby his feeling expresses itself."[57] He had felt the lessons preached by Green and Toynbee, just as he had felt the examples set by Denison and Hill. His contribution was the amalgamation of lessons and examples into an apparently practical scheme, whereby community might be reestablished at the hands of a disinterested and benevolently intentioned authority.

Throughout his years as warden of Toynbee Hall, Barnett held himself personally responsible for the recruitment of residents. Not surprisingly, he looked primarily to Oxford to supply them. During the early 1880s, Oxford—not merely Balliol but the university community at large—invited, heard, and heeded speakers of various political points of view, all of whom preached the dangers of neglecting the problems of the cities. Cambridge, awakened in much the same way, responded by throwing major support behind the campaign for university extension, though Cambridge men—among them J. R. Seeley, the historian—assisted in the foundation of the Universities' Settlement Association. Toynbee Hall was the expression of Oxford's mood and mode, however, and contributed the majority of Barnett's recruits. Jowett gave the enterprise his blessing, entertaining the Barnetts on their frequent trips and making two visits to the hall, although Henrietta Barnett recalled that he did not much enjoy them. "Whitechapel was rough and noisy, the number of interests confusing, the freedom of equality too apparent, and everybody perhaps over-anxious to please him. . . . The Master referred more than once to all we had seen during his visits to the East End, but he evidently preferred to see us amid the dignity of Balliol."[58]

A year-and-a-half after the founding of the hall, Barnett could report of a meeting at the college that he had "once more fiddled on the Settlement string and found the men ready to dance. In fact the men altogether are as responsive as ever and put us in good heart." A year later he reported enthusiastically once more, remarking that "the Balliol boys are the best." By 1893, the tone is less optimistic: "We have seen men after men and ground out the old tune. I hope we may have got one or two."[59] Yet for the first ten years or so, Barnett had reason to be generally satisfied with the success of his call to the young undergraduates of Oxford and Cambridge. From 1884 until 1900, one hundred and two residents lived at Toynbee Hall. Of the eighty-seven of these that have been traced, fifty-two came from Oxford (twelve from Balliol, the highest number from any college) and twenty-seven from Cambridge.[60] All were required to remain in residence for at least three months; the average stay, according to the *Annual Report* of 1892, was between one-and-a-half and two years.[61]

There was no religious test for residency, a reflection of Barnett's determination to distinguish between the settlement worker and the Church or chapel missionary. The criterion was Barnett's personal reading of a candidate's willingness to subscribe to the purposes of the hall. The list of Barnett's choices includes a number about whom nothing more than their residency is known. Among those for whom more information exists, there was a considerable diversity, despite the similarities of background and commitment that drew the residents to settlement life. Numerous early residents were already clergymen or civil servants, disinterested types with which the residents of Whitechapel would perhaps have been warily familiar. Many others went to work outside Whitechapel by day; one of Barnett's expectations was that men who led "normal" middle-class lives and were not professional social workers would mix more easily with the East London poor and contribute more variety to their lives. "You were encouraged to go on with your profession, if you had one," a resident later recalled, "and to give what time you could to the work of the Settlement. It was somehow made impossible for you to think that you were doing anything out of the common, or conferring any obligation by living in the East End."[62]

A remarkable number of residents from the early years later achieved reputations as social reformers: Bolton King and Cyril Jackson, as educational administrators; T. Hancock Nunn, a member of the 1909 Royal Commission on the Poor Law; Ernest Aves, collaborator with Charles Booth on the latter's survey of London life and labor; E. J. Urwick, first director of the London School of Sociology, forerunner of the London School of Economics; Hubert Llewellyn Smith, first head of the Labour Department at the Board of Trade. But there were other less predictable men among the mix: the young journalist J. A. Spender; the soldier–war correspondent Henry Nevinson; the writer and arts-and-crafts enthusiast C. R. Ashbee; the aristocratic commander of the Toynbee Hall cadet company, Francis Fletcher Vane. Residents were admitted as paying visitors for a three-month, probationary period, and then elected to residency by those already enjoying that status.

To enrich the life of the hall further, the Barnetts persuaded a number of well-established scholars and public figures to give their time and talent on a part-time basis as associates. They cultivated acquaintanceships with the great and near great at dinner parties in the St. Jude's vicarage. Henrietta Barnett was proud of their "daring" experiments in "blending East and West," boasting of having brought together Jowett, Walter Besant, Herbert Spencer, and the duke of Devonshire with the likes of William Morris and the radical trade unionists Ben Tillett, Tom Mann, and John Burns.[63] As a consequence of proselytizing on occasions of this sort, these and others such as Leslie Stephen, Alfred Milner, Graham Wallas, Augustine Birrell, Mary Ward, Walter Crane, and Thomas Hughes were among the interdenominational and eclectic host of notables who taught or lectured as part of the various educational programs sponsored by the hall. Meanwhile, the Universities' Settlement Association, with an elaborate committee structure distributed throughout the Oxford and Cambridge colleges, worked to generate enthusiasm and raise money.

When Barnett preached "simpler living" for the rich, he undoubtedly had the residential accommodation at Toynbee Hall in mind as a pertinent example. If young university graduates were to make effective connection with East London working-class men and women, Barnett reasoned, they would need to do so from an unostentatious center. The result was a set of buildings representing a rather severe blend of country house and Oxford quadrangle.

An illustrated article in the *Cambridge Review*, written shortly after the opening of the hall, provides evidence of the manner in which Barnett and his architect, Elijah Hoole, translated simplicity into bricks and mortar. The accommodations included rooms for sixteen male residents, a classroom for three hundred, a large dining room, a conversation room, a drawing room, and appropriate "offices." The style of the fittings, the *Cambridge* author reported approvingly, was "rather that of a comfortable country house than of a London Club." (Barnett himself, in discussing the design of the hall in a letter to his brother, referred to it as "a manorial residence in Whitechapel.") "The dining hall," the *Review* continued, "—a veritable 'combination room'—is also used as the library of the establishment and is . . . much frequented by the residents and their friends." The room was decorated by Ashbee and a class under his direction with sunflowers and the crests of Oxford and Cambridge colleges. A resident's suite (sitting room and bedroom or bedsitter) differed "in no essential aspect from an ordinary college room," with the exception that Henrietta Barnett supervised the decoration, seeing to it that lively colors banished any sense of institutional drabness. The design as a whole, the author concluded, was "admirably suited to its purpose, which is the maintenance amid East End surroundings of the usual civilised existence, without undue luxury or display. It is not second Sybaris, nor is it, on the other hand, a hermitage for anchorites."[64]

The pattern of daily life within the hall was regulated by a committee composed of warden and residents. Charges for bedroom, board and service were thirty shillings a week. "To our surprise," Barnett reported to his brother, "we find it costs 6/6 a week to give a man a room, fire, light and only necessary service. How can people live?"[65] Luncheon and dinner were taken communally at a long table at specified hours. Rules regulated such matters as the time for lights out and prohibited dancing and Sunday tennis, "a curious decision," Henrietta Barnett observed, "by a body of men who. . . included Churchmen, Roman Catholics, Nonconformists, Jews, Quakers, and Agnostics."[66]

A resident's sense that he had not left Oxford or Cambridge far behind was reinforced by the general absence of women. Although Barnett was a convinced feminist and supporter of women's suffrage, he believed, according to his wife, that the introduction of female residents would encourage the impression that the settlement had been "captured" by women and thereby frighten the ablest university men away. Although advised by well-wishers to hire only male servants, on the model of Oxford scouts, the committee engaged young maids, and without untoward incident, although "occasionally, in the early days," Henrietta Barnett primly recalled, residents had to be warned "that offers to carry the heavy trays or fetch the coals were liable to generate mistaken notions"—an injunction suggesting that "connection's" writ ran up to but not beyond the green baise door separating servants from masters. "To old-public-school and University men," a resident recalled, "Toynbee Hall with its collegiate atmosphere, had a familiar feeling. There was the society of contemporaries, there was the kindly guidance and supervision of an elder man, there were the meals in common and the community life." The sole potentially jarring element was the presence of Henrietta Barnett, but she was perceived by most as a kind of sexless partner in her husband's work.[67]

When the decision was made in the late 1880s to add two further residential units—Balliol House and Wadham House—to the existing buildings, Oxford and Cambridge were again the model. The new residences were designed to encourage and facilitate the study of university subjects by men living in the East End. "Schoolmasters, clerks, and artisans," while attending Toynbee Hall or university extension lectures or while preparing for qualifying exams in fields such as architecture and medicine, would be afforded a chance to enjoy the benefits of collegiate life. "It would seem," an article in the hall's recently founded monthly magazine, the *Toynbee Record*, declared, "that there is something in college life of substantial worth; that the discipline, the manly *savoir faire*, the refuge from sentimentalism which it gives, have more than counterbalanced the false ideals and the false standards that have sometimes clustered in Oxford and Cambridge Colleges; and that where there is a fair field for more real and strenuous life the college may be of saving worth in solving many a social problem." Barnett hoped that Balliol House and Wadham House might be the forerunners of a "great democratic university" in the East End, "as popular and far-reaching as the medieval universities were, when the 'poor students' crowded in thousands round the feet of the great scholastic teachers."[68] Meanwhile, along with the rest of the hall, they would benefit the East End populace as exemplars of England's collective cultural best self.

Two important observations emerge from consideration of Toynbee Hall's architectural and institutional setting, both directly related to its ultimate goal of community and both reminders of the continuing strength of hierarchical assumptions and habit. First, by insisting that the buildings and the pattern of life they embodied should represent "the best" as he and his like-minded associates defined that term, Barnett helped to confound the connection he was so anxious to promote. Toynbee Hall was a physical expression of the hierarchy of values so important to Matthew Arnold, T. H. Green, and Barnett himself. In its dining hall and its drawing room, men and women from East London were to meet "one by one" with young university graduates, so that both groups might better understand each other. Yet the building stated, at the outset, that the understanding was to be on terms established by the residents.

The hall was a conscious part of the design to inspire and uplift. When it came to decorating the drawing room, Henrietta Barnett reported that "we finally decided to make it exactly like a West-End drawing room, erring, if at all, on the side of gorgeousness." G. F. Watts lent paintings, of which Barnett wrote that "they warm hearts by their colour, and suggest thoughts which cannot be put into words. . . . Men and women who turn away from preachers and from books stop before pictures which tell of Life and Death, or of 'the joy in widest commonalty spread.'"[69] Paintings, rooms, buildings were weapons in the cultural battle that had become part of Barnett's definition of connection. "At Oxford," Arnold Toynbee had written a friend in 1875, "one's ideal of a happy life is nearer being realized than anywhere else: I mean the ideal of gentle, equable, intellectual intercourse, with something of a prophetic glow about it, glancing brightly into the future, yet always embalming itself in the memory as a resting-place for the soul in a future that may be dark and troubled after all. . . ."[70] An Oxford life bred the disinterested temper that, if left to exercise its power within society, would shed light and dispel trouble. Life within the precincts of Toynbee Hall might be but a shadow of the Oxford ideal, but it was a shadow very much worth projecting.

The second point to make about the surroundings and atmosphere of the hall is that they encouraged a kind of theater that could, once again, only serve to impede connection. Toynbee Hall was, literally, the setting for the transformation Barnett hoped to see enacted in the East End. In the sense that the buildings and the style of life lived in them were alien to the environs of Whitechapel, they were inevitably artificial, in a way designed to discourage a sense of natural fellowship between residents and their working-class neighbors. The sensations experienced by a young Oxford-educated social reformer in East London were in all likelihood similar to those described by Leonard Woolf, as he recalled his setting sail for Ceylon as a young civil servant before the First World War. "In Cambridge or London we were undergraduates or dons or barristers or bankers; and we *were* what we were, we were not acting, not playing the part of a don or a barrister. But in Ceylon we were always, subconsciously or consciously, playing a part, acting upon a stage."[71] Transplanted to the alien slums of East London, as Woolf found himself transplanted to the alien purlieus of Jaffna, the determined Toynbee Hall resident would find himself perforce acting a part. And his artificial, manorial environment would encourage him in his role, to the detriment of his prescribed mission.

A. P. Laurie, a resident who eventually moved from the hall into his own East London flat, complained of "an atmosphere about Toynbee Hall which irritated us. . . . We were supposed to be noble young men engaged in trying to do good to the poor," Laurie wrote. Of course that was just what Barnett hoped they would not suppose. To the extent that Barnett's goal was to impose the culture of one class upon another, however, and to the extent that the buildings and the atmosphere of Toynbee

Hall were an expression of that goal, the responsibility for Laurie's malaise was Barnett's. Another resident, the Quaker Stephen Hobhouse, reported a similar uneasiness. "I established myself [at Toynbee Hall], but soon realized that it was much too comfortable, . . . an 'oasis' of Oxford and Cambridge academic life, whose doors shut one off from the drab poverty of most of the humble homes around." He took himself off to live alone in Hoxton, as Laurie had departed for Stepney. "We did not feel noble," Laurie wrote, "and we had no desire to do good to anybody. . . . We wished a closer contact with the people and lives of East London." [72]

Barnett was conscious of this sort of criticism. He countered by suggesting that those who felt compelled to leave did so because of a willfulness unsuited to the demanding, self-denying work of reconnection. "A place like Toynbee Hall may offer what seems to be more comfort than is possible in East End lodgings, but it requires what is often a greater sacrifice—the surrender of self-will and will-worship. In fact true individuality survives, I think, better in a settlement than in lodgings, where eccentricities are often cherished, and where useful conventions succumb to the influences of East London." [73] What were to Barnett the "useful conventions" of a superior culture were to men like Laurie and Hobhouse habits of mind and action whose theatrical artificiality inhibited true connection.

B arnett disparaged the machinery of charitable and philanthropic enterprise on the grounds of its impersonality. He nevertheless believed that one of the hall's most important functions was to provide a variety of specific opportunities designed to help residents get to know their East End neighbors and to enable them to enrich the life of their adopted neighborhood. The result was a vast educational network of classes, clubs, organizations, and projects: the machinery of connection. The pages from the *Toynbee Record* of November 1893 and October 1896 reproduced here as plates 6 and 7 are evidence of the range of educational organizations that flourished at the hall during its heyday and of the degree to which, despite Barnett's disavowal, machinery was an integral part of the business of connection. Membership in the Toynbee Travellers' Club or the Dalgleish Street Boys' Club, attendance at the Toynbee Literary Association's lecture on Jowett or at the Economic Club's discussion of the employment of school children: it was all activity designed to promote that "higher thinking" for the poor which, along with "simpler living" for the rich, comprised Barnett's formula for the breaking down of class barriers and the consequent strengthening of the bonds of community.

From the time the Barnetts came to St. Jude's in 1873, both Samuel and Henrietta had worked to improve the quality of education offered in the East End. Barnett had attempted to enliven the instruction in the Voluntary (Church-supported) schools attached to St. Jude's, opposing as he did the system of payment by results and the consequently monotonous and unimaginative teaching that was too often geared to nothing beyond the passing of standard examinations. He encouraged the introduction of special subjects—physiology, geography, Shakespeare, clay modeling, and carpentry—and persuaded volunteers to teach them. The Barnetts looked beyond St. Jude's for means to achieve their goal of more imaginative teaching. They served as local board school managers; they raised money to support pupil-teacher training centers; they campaigned to improve the standard of teaching in Poor Law schools. The same year that Toynbee Hall was founded, Barnett took the lead in establishing an Educational Reform League whose general object was "to infuse more life into the dry bones of State-aided Elementary Education" by further teacher training, more creative use of school buildings, and an improved system of inspection.[74] Barnett pushed Toynbee Hall into the forefront of these battles, lending its facilities and its growing prestige to campaigns on behalf of an increase in evening classes and of scholarships to encourage secondary education among the children of the poor.

Barnett had not established the hall as an agency to lobby the interests of the poor, however. If it was to serve its purpose, it had to do so by bringing rich and poor into close personal touch with each other. Hence the heavy emphasis on lectures and classes taught by residents and associates to groups small enough to allow for some sort of exchange between teacher and pupil. These were the real stuff of Toynbee Hall educational programs. The subject matter of most courses, particularly in the early years, was clearly intended to induce "higher thinking": "The First Four Tudor Reigns," with S. R. Gardiner as lecturer; "Physical Properties of Air and Water"; "Eighteenth Century Music: The Works of Handel, Bach, and Scarlatti"; "Voltaic Electricity and Electromagnetism"; "The Morality of Common Sense." Interspersed among courses of this sort was utilitarian instruction in dressmaking, lifesaving, and the like, and, after

1893, in bookkeeping and accounting. In addition, the hall was used as a center for the teaching of university extension courses, in connection with which such luminaries as James Bryce, Henry Morley, and J. R. Seeley spoke and tutored.

For those fortunate enough to be able to afford it—mostly minor civil servants and elementary school teachers—there were the Toynbee Travellers' Club which organized excursions abroad and, after 1902, the Workmen's Travelling Club, whose itineraries were designed to accord with a more limited budget. The young were provided with youth clubs, sports clubs, a cadet corps, and a series of evening continuation classes, the best known being those conducted by the Old Northeyites Club, founded in 1887 to encourage further education for boys from the Northey Street Board School. In the summer, children were sent from East London into the country under the auspices of the Children's Country Holiday Fund, an organization separate from the hall but founded by the Barnetts and staffed by Toynbee residents.

These myriad endeavors represented no more in one sense than a continuation of the philanthropic campaign to educate the poor that had flourished throughout much of the nineteenth century. The YMCA and YWCA, workingmen's clubs, Boys' Brigade, Church Lads' Brigade, Working Men's College, adult school movement, university extension—all these and others had been established to promote not only education but also social harmony. The Working Men's College, founded in 1854, declared as its aim the establishment of a society "of which teachers and learners are equally members, . . . a society in which [men] meet not as belonging to a class or caste, but as having a common life which God has given them and which He will cultivate in them." One of its founders, Frederick Denison Maurice, a man whom Barnett acknowledged as an influence on his own thinking, declared that he had made it his mission to "persuade men to recognize Christ as the centre of their fellowship with each other, so that they might be united in their families, their countries, and as men, not in schools and factions."[75] Though the purposes of other institutions might not have been as broadly inspired as those of the college, they together professed a sense of responsibility for the poor and a recognition of the power of education to bind society to a set of common ends.

Barnett would claim, however, that Toynbee Hall was attempting something different from such organizations, worthy and important though their goals were. At the hall, educational programs were no more than a means to the end of one-by-one connection. What lay at the center of hall life, Barnett would insist, was individual personal acquaintance-ship and subsequent friendship between the residents and those men and women they had come to East London to meet. Hence, if residents found themselves unable to make connection by means of a particular club or society, they were encouraged to abandon it and to look about them for some other way to befriend people and thereby create community.

In an interview for Charles Booth's survey of London religious life, Ernest Aves argued that this approach was unique to Toynbee Hall, contrasting it with that of Church missions "where the men work under authority; are told off to do this or that. At Toynbee the method has been rather to find out what a man is good for, and let him do it in his own way."[76] An 1884 brochure advertising the work and purposes of the hall provided a long list of possible activities by means of which residents might achieve the purpose of their settlement: "attendance in working men's and boys' clubs; joining in conversation and discussion; helping in entertainments and excursions; teaching on behalf of the University Extension Scheme; conducting men and boys over museums and picture galleries on Saturday afternoons; promoting good music and art."[77] One of the early residents illustrated this flexibility in his description of a typical week's work:

My mornings were devoted to reading and private coaching, but my afternoons till Friday were spent visiting in Limehouse. Monday evening was first set down for a class at the "Whittington" [the boys' cadet corps]. This was at 9 o'clock, but I generally spent some time beforehand in chat with the boys. Afterwards came Mrs. Barnett's weekly "At Home," at which we have had many enjoyable discussions. When the Whittington classes were reconstituted I relinquished my elementary class for a share in a dramatic class on Wednesday. Tuesday was normally my free evening, but actually was spent usually in assisting at the entertainments, conversaziones, at Toynbee Hall, whenever my service either at the piano or otherwise might be required. On Wednesday I have a literature class for pupil teachers and my Thursday evening is pleasantly spent in assisting at the Boys' Club.[78]

The popularity of many of the hall's educational programs thwarted the goal of one by one. When crowds of as many as five hundred attended an evening conversazione there was little chance for a coming together "to know each other's characters, thoughts, and beliefs."[79] Residents were therefore encouraged to give small parties, asking just a few men and women whom they might have encountered in the classroom or on a local committee to join them and other friends for refreshments and conversation. Barnett described the process in an article entitled "Hospitalities":

> The resident carefully chooses friends to meet the guests who will get and give enjoyment. He has the tables daintily spread and decorated with flowers, and he provides that food shall be simple and abundant. Again he himself, in the drawing room, receives each guest as he arrives, and, about half an hour after the time, conducts them all to the dining room. At first the appearance of the room will cause a sort of awe to fall on the party, not an unpleasant one, but one which yields to the influence of good food and good company. As supper ends there will be two or three short speeches, and then the whole party will adjourn to the drawing room to smoke, to sing songs, to tell tales until they part at twelve o'clock conscious that the world is larger than it seemed and full of good fellows.[80]

The degree to which "theater" intruded upon evenings such as these must have depended almost entirely upon the personality and sensitivity of the host. Here one does sense the hesitancies and tensions that were a constant accompaniment to life at Toynbee Hall and to its experiments in connection.

Barnett was never more than tentatively confident of the success of his educational programs. One of his favorite projects was a series of annual art exhibitions, to which West End artists and collectors were requested to contribute and from which—as from conversation with residents—the men and women of Whitechapel might be expected to experience some sense of "higher things." After a particularly popular exhibition attended by more than fifty-five thousand, however, Barnett confessed his own uncertainties in a letter to his brother: "What does it mean? An increase in respectability—a greater desire on the part of all to be uniform and do what others do—a wider love of decency, or does it mean that more are conscious of their divine relation and more anxious to cultivate it?"—a direct echo of Green.[81]

What, indeed, did it mean? Not just this particular exhibition, but the whole network of educational programs, formal and informal, institutional and personal, that occupied so much of the thought and effort of the Barnetts, the residents, and the associates. The beginning of an answer lies in Barnett's declaration in an 1893 article for the *Toynbee Record* that "the social problem is at root an educational problem." Barnett proceeded with this argument in two directions. If one defines "the social problem" in terms of poverty and its consequent potential for civil discontent, then education must somehow be designed to alleviate both. "The object [of education] must be that there may not be so many wretched, homeless people on Commercial Street doorsteps, so many unemployed half-fed in their single-roomed homes." Those who possess education possess a passport to a better material life. But education will not only help rid East London of poverty. It can, if it is education of the right sort, help guarantee a more tranquil society as well. Its object is therefore "that the problem of capital and labour may not be settled by bullets." Those who "accept" education of this kind will "feel in honour bound to become servants of the community of the nation. . . . The acceptance of the teaching will be to them as the acceptance of the Queen's shilling by which the receivers are pledged to be loyal fighters on her side."

Education thus represented an important and useful way of solving the social problem by promoting social harmony. But because Barnett understood the social problem as something more than poverty and social desperation, he saw education as serving a further end. If, Barnett argued, one defines the social problem as an inability to distinguish good from evil or to recognize that "no happiness is satisfactory except that which comes from 'the inward eye,'" then education must correct that inability by providing "schemes of study which are set forth as trustworthy guides for those who want their minds fitted to be always learning."[82] Education, then, was a means to the ends of social harmony and the liberation of the human spirit.

The programs of Toynbee Hall expressed the attempt of Barnett and his fellow workers to address these two aspects of the social problem as an educational problem. Much of the teaching, particularly in the boys' clubs, reflected the desire to instill social harmony by means of a respect for tradition, order and authority. In East London schools, the *Record* reported in 1889, "there is a total want of tradition—of obligation on all who belong to the school to be worthy of those who went before them, such as·forms the very lifeblood of our public schools, and this want of tradition entails also a want of unity of the feeling that all . . . are working together for the success, not merely of a class or a department, but of their school."[83] The Old Northeyites Club, whose name echoed public school habits of mind, had as one of its primary purposes the establishment of "a school esprit de corps." Francis Fletcher Vane, commandant of the Whittington Cadet Corps, reported his belief that "self-restraint, order, and respect for authority are taught better on the parade ground than anywhere else."[84]

Sentiments such as these must, of course, be matched against Barnett's own less strident arguments on behalf of social order as well as his hopes for a more liberal and humane elementary-school curriculum. Yet Barnett himself, despite his concern for the human spirit, believed that respect for authority was among the most important lessons education had to teach. One of the dangers of a district like Whitechapel, he wrote, was that its inhabitants, "hopeless for want of large ideas, became antagonistic to authority."[85] He believed that "large ideas," by encouraging in men and women the desire to stretch beyond themselves, must make them understand the necessity of an authority that circumscribed their own interests on behalf of community: a subtle and not particularly palatable lesson even when preached to social equals by an Oxford don; far less palatable, in all likelihood, when delivered to East London workingmen by young Toynbee Hall residents, few of whom had the ability to reason with the gentle tone Barnett himself apparently possessed.

In practice, education at Toynbee Hall often came to mean following the example set by one's betters. Barnett appears to have taken some comfort from his perception of the poor as children—and therefore as pupils particularly open to instruction. "The working classes may possess special virtues and purer insights," he wrote, "but the virtues are the virtues of children and the insights the insights of children." Or, after watching a crowd at a cornerstone laying ceremony: "The sight was depressing in many ways . . . the faces were empty—weary—or self-indulgent. These poor are children, and the danger is lest they become men in feeling before they become men in reason."[86]

With the very poor, education thus meant teaching those things one might teach a child: punctuality, the practice of framing rules, or dressing with care. It meant bringing men and women into the houses of the rich, not so much that both rich and poor might come to know each other, but that the poor might learn good habits and make worthy resolves. "Very pregnant of influence are these introductions into a house scrupulously clean and tastily furnished," Henrietta Barnett wrote, "a house kept as the dwelling of every human being should be kept."[87]

Toynbee Hall teachers apparently did not concern themselves unduly with the contradictions inherent in an educational policy that, like most, professed both the habit of authority and the spirit of liberation. The ability to survive the contradiction may well have been in part the result of Barnett's readiness to encourage residents to work with students in whatever way seemed most natural and effective to them. Thus, while Francis Fletcher Vane drilled his cadets, another resident led a working-men's discussion of Henry George. "Some of the men showed great enthusiasm for these meetings," he reported, "reading George by themselves during the week and entering with spirit into my plan that they should give me their practical experiences as workers on matters of which a student fresh from Oxford must necessarily be ignorant."[88] If this left hand did not know what Vane was up to on the right, Barnett presumably did and saw no inherent conflict between what the two were about. Education, he wrote in the 1890 *Annual Report*, "must come as an aid in life," bringing a sense of power, derived from the discipline that comes with the exercise of "truer judgment." The best education would encourage men and women to think for themselves, but in such a way as to "see through the froth of propaganda to the deep waters of social life."[89]

This was the educational goal closest to Barnett's heart, as it was closest to the ideals of Balliol and the Arnoldians; it was the one he was fondest of preaching and the one he believed an institution such as Toynbee Hall could most effectively foster, by helping men and women to recognize and then to encourage the growth and development of their best selves. He talked frequently of the challenge of leisure, of the need to encourage workingmen and -women to use what little free time they had in worthwhile ways. He recognized, unlike a great many of his reforming contemporaries, that few people could be expected to enjoy the work they were forced to do. He understood as well how workers might resent the fact that, while more and more members of the middle class had the time and opportunity to enjoy the world in a number of new ways, such enjoyment was to a great extent closed to them. "Workmen live in the new world of the nineteenth century, they hear of sights which their fellowmen rejoice to see, they read in books of possible joys to be found in travel. . . . They see possibilities, and they resent the bondage of work which holds them back."[90]

Yet Barnett despaired of the shallow aimlessness that seemed to him to characterize so much of the leisure-time activity of the working class. Writing to his brother of the bank holiday scene on Hampstead Heath, he reported that "the majority were content with rather aimless walking and exhibition of clothes. . . . What one feels is the emptiness of the people. Their unconsciousness of that in which they live and move and have their being. Their effort to feed souls on husks."[91] Residents stood ready to teach that true enjoyment was an active art, an enterprise to which the participant must make a conscious contribution if it was to be of any lasting benefit.

The hall's crowded monthly calendar of events is convincing evidence that it was an educational enterprise of sizable proportion. Figures on library use, published proudly each year by the *Record*, bear out the same impression. During the library's first five years, when readers' tickets were required, the attendance total was between eight thousand and ten thousand annually. In the first year after tickets were abolished, attendance jumped to over thirteen thousand, where it apparently remained.[92] Regular visitors, readers, and students came from beyond the East End as the hall's reputation grew. Ernest Aves estimated that in the late 1890s the educational programs, although they attracted a clientele from across London, drew about 70 percent of their participants from the east, northeast, and southeast sections of the city.

Aves went on to remark that while "none, of course, are the poorest class, . . . nearly all have been educated in a public elementary school, and a large portion would be described as of the working rather than the lower middle class."[93] His report accords with evidence in the hall's annual reports and elsewhere which establishes the not surprising fact that the large majority of the students in attendance at Toynbee Hall lectures and classes were either from the upper-working or lower-middle classes. A resident reported, for example, of his political economy class that it "consists of almost a dozen of the best sort of workingmen, . . . steady, thrifty, interested in the improvement of their order." And another reported of his Latin and Greek students: "The majority were of the lower middle class, but there was a pupil teacher and one [was] a foreman at the docks." University-extension pupils were even more likely to be teachers, clerks, shop assistants, or foremen; Balliol House and Wadham

House were, by their very purpose, limited to an upwardly mobile, lower- middle-class clientele. Many of the clubs also drew their membership from men and women of a similar background. The Toynbee Travellers, whose excursions could cost as much as £30, were in the main minor civil servants and board-school teachers. When, in response to requests for a club with a comparable but less expensive program, the Workmen's Travelling Club was formed in 1902, its membership was recruited exclusively from trade unions, friendly societies, and cooperative organizations.[94]

The fact that it was so often "the best sort" that explored the opportunities Toynbee Hall offered for connection did not unduly disturb Barnett. To him, foremen, clerks, board-school teachers were as much in need of improvement as were the very poor. Membership in the lower-middle class could induce a kind of poisonous smugness as disheartening to Barnett as it had been to Matthew Arnold. Describing his guests at a gathering for elementary-school teachers, he wrote despairingly to his brother: "They are a set which need culture. We had thirty concertedly ignorant, comfortably ugly men and women to whom is entrusted the power once held by students and priests. We brought them face to face with Mr. Holman Hunt and other real creatures." Two years later, the same lament: "Dear me, the teachers do want to be sent on the quest of the Holy Grail. They are so cocky and so ignorant." It was from the ranks of these men and women that the leadership of the working class would come. It was these teachers whose daily contact with poor children made them logical potential "connectors." All the more important, then, that they move beyond the notion which, according to Barnett, was the distinguishing characteristic of so many—"that the main chance ends in their stomach"—that instead they learn to stretch their minds toward the culture and values that reflected a best that was permanent, ideal, and ennobling.[95]

It is impossible to generalize with much accuracy about the hall's educational influence upon the vast numbers who attended at homes, conversaziones, and art exhibitions. One can guess that some came away impressed, entertained, enlightened, instructed and that under the guidance of a sympathetic tutor or visitor they may well have pursued interests first awakened during visits to Toynbee. One can suppose as well that in a few cases, individual one-by-one connections resulted in genuine friendship and exchange between rich and poor. But no general shift in cultural values occurred, whether by individual or institutional means. One reason for Toynbee Hall's relatively modest impact in this regard was its location in Whitechapel, whose divided population of under-employed and therefore transient unskilled workers was the least likely to respond to the hall's educational message. Remarks in the *Record* and elsewhere suggest that the residents soon lost heart with the very poorest: "No doubt good work can be and has been done by direct contact with the classes holding the lowest moral standards," Barnett himself wrote as early as 1885, "but there is disregard of economy of labour in such dealings, and vitality seems to pass out of the worker so quickly without a corresponding gain."[96]

The temptation in that case was to forsake one-by-one connection and to attempt instead an authoritarian attack against the institutions of working-class culture, which, the Barnetts believed, kept the poor from a discovery of their best selves. Residents who possessed little or no first-hand experience of industrial communities also possessed little familiarity with the complex web of social institutions which existed beyond individual and family relationships to help bind working-class communities together. They tended to treat class consciousness, neighborhood networks, and the like as hindrances to their goals. Elaborate funerals, which to a working-class neighborhood were an important way to define hierarchy and celebrate solidarity, in the eyes of Henrietta Barnett merely obstructed an individual's perceptions of proper duty. "It is the common practice to make much fuss," she wrote, "and to spend large sums of money on funerals, and in buying ugly black clothes. . . . Does not a little thought teach us that this exaggerated mourning and ostentation is both unlovely and untrue to what the highest and best have taught us about life and death?"[97]

The authoritarian habits of hierarchy often all but obliterated the advertised goal of connection. Barnett failed to perceive that although the men and women of Whitechapel were poor, they were not without a culture of their own. To him, Whitechapel represented a cultural void, into which his own culture had to be poured. Yet, as Helen Meller has remarked in her study of Bristol, by the 1880s, "all levels of society were subject to a far wider range of influences, above all, those generated by their own experiences and own response to change." Meller describes T. W. Harvey, a Bristol clergyman and warden of the Church of England Clifton College Mission, as sensitive to this fact, and therefore as anxious to serve as "midwife to an independent culture," to provide "some of the conditions in which it might flourish." But she is wrong to suggest that in this Harvey's intentions echoed Barnett's. Barnett instead resembled the Congregationalist clergyman H. R. Thomas, with whom Mellers compares Harvey. Like Thomas, Barnett saw himself as a "conveyor of culture" and Toynbee Hall as the means of conveyance.[98]

Because Barnett believed that the minds of the poor could "take in the same joys" as those of the rich, he was all the more insistent that the culture of his community be the worthy culture which residents were there to impart as any true friend would wish to impart a precious gift. All the more frustrating, then, when the poor, despite their ability to appreciate what was being offered, turned their backs upon it, preferring instead their clearly "inferior" pursuits and way of life.

3

TOYNBEE HALL: DEMOCRACY, POLITICS, AND THE STATE

Samuel Barnett's compulsion to improve the minds of the poor reflected his fear of the potential political power of the masses and his dread of the direction in which unimproved minds might in future decide to lead the nation. Asked once if he had "unbounded faith in the people," he replied: "I have, so long as we keep educating them."[1] In fact, he was not usually inclined to so sanguine a view: the task of education, as he had learned from experience, was so everlastingly frustrating, the pupils so generally uninspired. The middle- and lower-middle-class shopkeepers who had gained political power over the past half-century had done little with it, in his opinion, to inspire confidence. There was not much evidence, Barnett declared, that they could be trusted to promote "the welfare of any end so wide as 'humanity' or so high as 'truth.'" What real hope, then, that working men would prove themselves any worthier of the nation's trust, unless by means of some massive program of training in the responsibilities of democracy? "Selfish working men will not be much more desirable as governors than selfish tradesmen and the advancement of those who will use their advancement to make for themselves comfort and happiness does not seem to be worth any very great sacrifice. There is something rotten in our state of progress."[2]

There was, however, something inevitable about it as well. Barnett, like a great many late Victorians, resigned himself to mass democracy as a fact of Britain's political future. All he could hope was that disinterested leadership might succeed in connecting with the proletarian demos to promote the idea of government on behalf of community rather than class interest.

62

The working men have not the knowledge which is gained in years of study. They have not learned to take wide views. They are not in the modern sense scientific. Theirs is the power, but unless they take into their confidence the talented young men and women who are thinking about the future and are "Pilgrims of the Invisible," unless they bind their spirits with the generous, cleareyed spirits of cultural people, . . . the vision which will inspire their . . . movement will be one which will lead the world in a weary circle in which rights clash with rights rather than onwards to a unity of classes made happy and strong by that which each member supplies.[3]

Visits to India and to the United States with his wife in 1890 and 1891 did little to encourage Barnett's hopes for this future. In India he saw the results of an administration that claimed disinterestedness while succumbing in matters large and small to the self-interest of maintaining power. He wrote in his journal of the opportunities for service afforded the English in India. "A Collector's work is certainly one of the fullest open to a man. Nowhere in the world could he exercise such power and in so many directions." Yet how infrequently did he do so. Of an acquaintance in Bombay, Barnett wrote: "Typically English—superior, well-disposed and tyrannical. He does not respect the nation whom he lives to serve." The tragedy was all the greater given the incapacity of the Indians, who could not begin to govern themselves, "who cannot be left even to issue papers without supervision," and who therefore so desperately needed the sort of instruction that a truly dedicated and disinterested administration might provide.[4]

To Barnett, India illustrated the hollowness of paternalist government when it ignored the ideals which justified its authority. The United States exemplified the social chaos that resulted when a society in its haste to abolish hierarchy turned its back on community as well, abandoning itself to narrow-minded and vulgarising individualism. Henrietta Barnett, an even more tepid democrat than her husband, reported in the journal with some satisfaction that "the Vicar's belief in democracy and in the virtue of the ignorant classes has been more shaken by this three weeks in California than has ever happened to us. The whole tone of the conversation with everyone one meets is the same—ignorant and brutal greed. . . ." They were shocked at the tyranny of the California monopolies and at the absence of a public-spirited resentment that might have curbed them. Above all, there was the rudeness, "the loud laughing, the free and easy relations of men and women and their resentment of control." On their way to visit a glacier in Yosemite, "the owner of the horses with the ungracious bluntness which marks American manners refused to assist anyone to walk." Henrietta Barnett was appalled: "Was there ever such an argument for the Church and Aristocracy as the condition of this country? . . . In no place in England would both the squire and the parson have allowed such actions as this!!"[5] Connection in the democratic United States presented problems and embarrassments less easily managed than in the controlled precincts of Toynbee Hall.

Little wonder, given this lack of enthusiasm for democracy, that Barnett displayed an equal disinclination toward politics. He labored to portray Toynbee Hall and its residents as above the political fray. Hoping to avoid the appearance of partisanship, he continued to insist that the hall no more spoke for a particular political persuasion than it did for a single religious point of view. "There is no such thing as a 'Toynbee Hall policy,'" Barnett declared, "and it is never true to say that 'Toynbee Hall' favoured one candidate in an election." Candidates were enjoined not to use the Toynbee Hall address on their literature; nor could residents write to the newspapers from that address without first checking with Barnett.[6] Residents or former residents stood for election with the endorsement of both sides—Progressive or Moderate—in local elections, the most notable case occurring in the 1890s when G. L. Bruce and Cyril Jackson both won seats on the London School Board, the former as a Progressive, the latter as a Moderate.

The claim of impartiality was disingenuous, however, as critics did not hesitate to assert, and as Barnett eventually all but admitted. Although he continued to argue the apolitical nature of Toynbee Hall itself, as opposed to its individual members, he conceded that the public might mistake its dedication to reform as partisanship. "It is, of course, easy to explain the mistake," he wrote in the *Record* in 1900.

> So far as Conservatism is based on the principle of "leaving well alone," so far there must be a tendency to label as Radicals or Progressives all who are intent on reforming what is bad. And in every Settlement the Residents, whatever their "politics" may be, are certain to be united in their desire to reform many things, and so far may be said to have a progressive bias. But it is just because we believe this desire for improvement is, or ought to be, shared by

all—whatever their party—in all matters with which local government has to do, that we object strongly to the party labels in the
election of the·Borough Councillors.[7]

In a genuine community "politics" was a matter for quotation marks,
since unity of purpose meant basic political agreement. Parties were
therefore divisive agents, like classes, keeping men of good will apart
under false pretences when they should be working together.

The political activities of Toynbee Hall residents expressed their determination to do no less than that "required of every citizen—a citizen's
duty in his own neighborhood."[8] Barnett believed that the only way to
teach the difficult lesson of democracy was by disinterested example at
the local level. He acknowledged that borough government was too often
characterized by selfish squabbling, too prone to settle for the short-
sighted and the inconsistent. Yet "the advantage of local government is
that it . . . brings home to every member of the community the fact that
he is himself a governor of the country and a responsible member of the
community."[9]

Barnett thus considered participation in the affairs of local government, under the guidance of disinterested instructors, as another form of
education. Local politics without the benefit of such disinterested leadership, however, either brought the kind of squalid chaos one found in
the boss-ruled cities of America or produced the sort of unimaginative
pettiness that soured so much of the activity of Poor Law boards and
school boards in England. Workers could not yet be trusted with much
more than a very junior partnership in the management of their own
political affairs. Meanwhile, residents would set them a worthy example.
In addition to running for a variety of local offices, they busied themselves in a successful campaign for a free library and an increase in the
Whitechapel water supply. Members of Toynbee Hall played an active
role in the administration of the Poor Law and the distribution of charity
in East London. Both Samuel and Henrietta Barnett sat on the Whitechapel Board of Guardians. By 1888, two residents were almoners for the
Society for the Relief of Distress and one had joined the Barnetts as a
guardian.[10]

What exactly was the lesson that the East End neighbors of Toynbee
residents were expected to learn from these examples? Was it that they
should begin to organize their own battles under leadership of their own

choosing? Or, rather, that they should remain content to serve as field soldiers under the generalship of their disinterested political leaders? Toynbee Hall answered ambiguously. Barnett was prepared to see the "better" sort of citizen afforded a chance to participate actively in local government. He advocated a lowering of the rating qualifications for election to Poor Law boards, for example, so that poor people "of humanity and intelligence" could stand for office.[11] For the rest there seemed no answer beyond the very general one of thoughtful connection and careful education, only then to be followed by participation. At Toynbee Hall politics was of two sorts, and a direct reflection of Barnett's own tentativeness: there was politics *with* the better sort, that privileged minority accorded a very limited partnership, and there was politics *on behalf of* the rest.

Trade unionism for a time appeared to offer an escape from the confusion of policies that conceded the inevitability of democracy, while continuing to practice the habits of hierarchical authority. The new union movement during the last years of the century saw radical members of skilled-craft unions assuming the lead in the organization of the unskilled. The resulting agitation was exciting, and also a potential threat to the status quo. Both exhilarated and worried by its implications, residents of Toynbee Hall tried hard to reach out to its leaders. They believed in the need to educate them to responsible politics, hoping that through them they might discover a way to connect with the "residuum" as well.

Characteristically, Toynbee Hall's avenue into the affairs of trade unionism was by way of the Co-operative movement. Co-operation's methods of production and distribution, which aimed to benefit workingmen and -women both as producers and consumers by eliminating profit-taking entrepeneurs and middlemen, corresponded with the hall's commitment to enterprise on behalf of community. One of Barnett's early Balliol supporters, A. H. D. Acland, the former college bursar and a Liberal M. P., was instrumental in arranging classes for London Co-operators at the hall. In 1888, Barnett lent his support to the establishment of a Co-operative Aid Association, organized to provide loans to East London producing co-operatives. More and more frequently, the hall played host to groups of Co-operative mantle makers, boat makers, cigar makers, and the like; in this way its residents grew increasingly familiar with the difficulties facing workers determined to organize and bargain collectively in their own interests.

From the late 1880s, Toynbee Hall encouraged trade unionists to use its meeting rooms. In February 1888, it sponsored a conference on the utility of strikes at which representatives from unions and management were asked to air their opinions and points of view. Lord Herschell, the chairman, struck a moderately radical note in his summation of the discussions by declaring that "under many circumstances [strikes] were justifiable, and also that under conceivable circumstances, even the altruistic form of labour contest, called the 'strike on principle,' would become necessary."[12] Over the course of the next several years it was on the basis of that broad principle that residents of the hall, and Barnett too, lent their sympathy and support to the strikes of new unionists such as the Bryant and May matchmakers and the London dockers.

Strikes, as expressions of class consciousness, were socially divisive and destructive of community. But on these occasions, men and women hitherto excluded from the community of the nation because of the menial and insecure nature of their work were using the strike as a responsible means to petition for membership; hence the strikers' appeal to the community-conscious reformers of Toynbee Hall. At the time of the 1889 dock strike, whose modest goals were the reorganization of hiring practices and a minimum wage of sixpence per hour, residents and former residents lent their active support to the cause—Hubert Llewellyn Smith and Vaughan Nash on the picket lines, Ernest Aves as the first president of the Trafalgar branch of the Dock, Wharf, Riverside and General Labourers' Union, Barnett as presiding officer of the first Trafalgar branch meeting at Toynbee Hall, and a number of others as distributors of relief to dockers' families. The central strike committee celebrated its victory with a supper at the hall, attended by the heroes of the occasion, Tom Mann, Ben Tillett, and John Burns—all three of whom continued to appear over the next several years as speakers at Toynbee Hall lectures and conferences.

Despite these manifestations of support, Toynbee Hall committed itself to new unionism only to the degree that it saw the movement as a means to the greater end of better general community understanding. Barnett was convinced that the rich must be shocked into consciousness of their social derelictions. The dockers' strike had, in his opinion, delivered a proper and much-needed jolt. Sympathy for the men—"the scramble round the dock gates, the sight of the wretched creatures"— was at last bringing home a sense of duty to those who should have felt it before. Sympathy by itself was not what he wished to see engendered, for community could not be constructed from sympathy alone. "I should like to smash up the sympathy which does nothing," he wrote to his brother during the Hull dockers' strike of 1893, "the sympathy which keeps knowledge and beauty to itself."[13] Duty, on the other hand, pledged one to what he once called "the high character of service" that was necessary to achieve community. If the strike had awakened both masters and men to a sense of that duty and that service, then it had been worth supporting.

Barnett remained uneasy about the ability of the new unions' officers to carry the burden of their leadership. He wrote his brother that while he could understand Tillett's resort to inflammatory techniques, his "habit of meeting extravagance with extravagance has been tried in vain." He worried that the new members would not remain committed, that they "don't know what union demands," and that their ignorance and lack of determination might lead to a long series of bitter strikes and even more bitter defeats.[14] His concerns provided justification for Toynbee Hall's continued role in trade-union affairs. If union leaders needed further instruction in the proper habits of authority, what better classroom than the hall, what better teachers than its sympathetic yet sensible residents and associates?

Through its support of responsible new unionism, the hall was able to claim connection with the "residuum." Trade unions, if properly directed, taught lessons of self-restraint and fellowship. By guaranteeing dockers the chance of settled employment, they promoted steadiness, regularity, and thrift. These were the lessons and habits of community, a contribution to be passed from Toynbee Hall to union leaders and on to the rank and file. In a talk on wages and work, Barnett declared that trade unions were, in fact, the "effect of Christ's call. . . . Men feel bound to raise themselves, they unite, and by union have done great things." These unions, because they partook of the divine, would be no threat to community; instead, they would teach social obligation. "Christ tells the workman to do good work. He reminds him of his calling as a Man. He forbids him to scamp, to dawdle, to make work. He forbids him to bully or to threaten others, to do anything unworthy of his nature, of his comradeship or anything hurtful to others' nature."[15]

Lessons of this sort were not soon learned. Barnett, though, as always, preached the dangers of haste—"the haste which, shrinking from examination, takes cries, agitations, and noise for evidence." Those who worked alongside the trade-union leaders had to bring passion to their work. But passion informed of the facts and awake to the dangers of apparently simple solutions: what Barnett was so fond of calling "the passion of patience." Above all, it needed to be passion that was pure, disinterested. "If men do not feel that as reformers they are doing the will of the righteous God—if, that is, they have no reverence—and if, when they agitate for their neighbour's good, they have not charity—are not, that is, empty of self—it is not hard to foretell that the indignation and pity which now move them to action will be short-lived."[16] The passion of patience and the reverence and charity of an ideally inspired disinterestedness were the hallmarks Barnett hoped would distinguish Toynbee Hall's politicians and the campaigns they pursued or sponsored on behalf of the goals of connection and community.

While Barnett continued to believe in the virtues of localism as a means of political education, he grew increasingly to believe that the problems of poverty and unemployment were not local problems, but ones demanding the attention and intervention of the state. This despite the fact that he began his work in Whitechapel a confirmed advocate of the dogma of self-help, as proclaimed by the most prominent organization for charitable reform of the day, the Charity Organisation Society (COS). Founded in 1869, the society wore the armor of self-confidence as a public declaration of its certainty that it could solve the problems of urban poverty and social degeneration. Its apologists lamented the rapid spread of the disease of pauperism, believing the primary cause of the disease to be an aversion to work on the part of the great body of unskilled laborers. Given the chance, men and women would accept a dole—whether administered by private donors or through the agencies of the state—rather than seek or remain at unpleasant work at low wages for long hours. The more money well-meaning charities or generous Poor Law guardians placed in the hands of these weak-minded individuals, the more they were contributing to the contagion rather than to the cure of the disease.

The COS campaigned in favor of these constantly reiterated principles. Wherever the society established branches, it preached the same set of doctrines: that the poor, before they could be treated for the disease of pauperism, had to be divided into two classes, those who might be encouraged to help themselves and those clearly unwilling to do so; that this division and any subsequent assistance had to be the result of carefully and scientifically conducted investigation; and that those in the latter category could be afforded no relief whatsoever, other than that provided by the Poor Law, strictly enforced by means of the workhouse test.

Barnett initially endorsed these precepts with enthusiasm. In the severe winter of 1880–81, the Whitechapel guardians were prepared to offer families from twelve to fifteen shillings per week, but only on the understanding that unemployed husbands and fathers would agree to come into the workhouse. Barnett wrote approvingly of the scheme. It provided relief sufficient (in Barnett's opinion, at any rate) to keep the families from debt. By imposing the workhouse test, it insured against exploitation by the ne'er-do-well. And "it brought home to the men rather than to the women the hard results of inadequate wages, of laziness, or waste"—the assumption being, apparently, that somehow inadequate wages were as much a workman's fault as his laziness or wastefulness.[17]

Such authoritarian prescriptions, whatever their effectiveness in reducing pauperism, generated understandable resentment and consequently made the task of connection just that much more difficult. George Lansbury, the East London socialist who made it his life's work to battle for more generous and humane provision for the poor, declared in his autobiography that his determination had been fueled by memories of the unnecessary hardships inflicted by the guardians, Barnett among them, upon his neighbors. Lansbury's mother was rebuked by the clerk of the Whitechapel Board for the dinners and nursing she was providing to various indigent families. "I wrote Canon Barnett about these cases," Lansbury recalled, "and was told by him that 'the workhouse was the best place for such people.' This message and my later inquiries made me a most bitter enemy of the Charity Organisation Society and all its works."[18]

Lansbury's recollection confirms by inference what we have already perceived about the nature of connection as defined by Barnett: that its purpose was instructional, and that the instruction, if it was to be effective, needed to be left to the disinterested. Why was Mrs. Lansbury not as capable of connecting with her poor friends as some Toynbee Hall resident? Because presumably *her* friendship was not of the disinterested sort that could distinguish between temporary and permanent benefit. Barnett insisted that settlement workers befriend their poor neighbors. But the nature of that friendship had to rest upon an understanding of the ultimate good, rather than the immediate pleasure, it might bring with it. "Relief if it is to be helpful," Barnett preached to an Oxford audience in 1884, "must follow and not prevent friendship, it must strengthen and not weaken character, it must have for its object the *good* and not the *comfort* of individuals." As with education and politics, so with relief and charitable assistance: the end was the improvement of character. "Gifts must aim at developing the high in the low, at bringing out the manlike qualities in those who live as animals. It is not by treating a man as well as a pet dog that he will become manlike, it is by recognizing his brotherhood with the best."[19] For Barnett, teaching a worker and his family to recognize their brotherhood with the best was a worthier and more important goal than was Mrs. Lansbury's of sharing with them as members together in the brotherhood of fallible humanity.

Although Barnett never forsook the principles which shaped his policies as a guardian and which identified him in the eyes of opponents like Lansbury as a doctrinaire apologist for the COS, experience and observation did eventually lead him into serious disagreements with the society. They arose primarily because of Barnett's increasing willingness to ascribe at least a portion of the misery in East London to environment rather than to individual moral failing alone, and because of his consequent advocacy of state intervention. Octavia Hill, Henrietta Barnett noted, "expected the degraded people to live in disreputable conditions *until* they proved themselves worthy of better ones." Toynbee Hall, however, began to argue "that for most folk, decent environment is essential to the promotion of decent life."[20]

The implications of that gradually dawning environmentalist perception were spelled out in a series of articles and talks by both Samuel and Henrietta Barnett published or delivered in the 1880s and issued as a collection under the title *Practicable Socialism* in 1888. A second edition, which included more recent writings, appeared in 1894; another collection, *Toward Social Reform*, in 1909; and a new series, using the original title, *Practicable Socialism*, in 1915. Many of the articles were detailed reports publicizing the work of Toynbee Hall, in the hope of attracting support for the various activities and programs there. But others elaborated the environmentalist argument, acknowledging that institutions such as the hall would need the assistance of the state to ensure a social climate that would promote an individual's best self.

In the essay "Practicable Socialism," which Barnett published first in

1883 in the *Nineteenth Century,* he argued that it was not enough to free the laborer and his family from the degrading habits of dependent charity. This the Whitechapel Union, by enthusiastic application of cos principles, had in the main accomplished. And yet what was the result? The abstemious hardworking laborer, earning twenty shillings a week, could feed, clothe, and house himself and his family; but he could do precious little else. "Pleasure for him and for them is impossible; he cannot afford to spend a sixpence on a visit to the park, nor a penny on a newspaper or a book. Holidays are out of the question, and he must see those he loves languish without fresh air and sometimes without the doctor's care, though such air and care may be the necessities of life. The future does not attract his gaze and give him restful hours. . . ." Nor was the worker earning forty shillings a week much better off. "There can be for him no quiet hours with books or pictures, while his children or friends make music for his solace. He can invite no friends for a Christmas dance; he can wander in the thought of no future of pleasure or of rest." With an eye to cos orthodoxy, Barnett argued that it was not enough to say that these men were hardworking and thrifty. "The saddest monument is, perhaps, 'the respectable working man,' who has been erected in honour of thrift. His brains, which might have shown the world how to save men, have been spent in saving pennies; his life, which might have been happy and full, has been dulled and saddened by taking 'thought for tomorrow.'"[21]

Toynbee Hall had been founded, in part, to carry men such as these beyond mere respectability and worthiness to consciousness of their best selves. But what Barnett was now admitting was that the task, because it meant tackling the environment as well as the individual, was too big for institutions such as Toynbee Hall to handle unassisted. If proper air and care were necessities of life, without which the spirit could never expand, if fears about the illness and impoverishment of old age kept workingmen and -women from any sense of the enjoyment of life, then though a Toynbee resident might introduce his East London neighbor to the pleasures of art or music, the effort would end as no more than an empty gesture. The state needed to provide an environment that would foster the growth of the human spirit. Provision by the state of the "means of health, education and recreation" would be proper provision of "'needs, not wants,'" Barnett wrote in the introduction to the 1894 edition of *Practicable Socialism.* "Practicable" socialism did not mean jobs for all regardless of their willingness or abilities to work, any more than it meant indiscriminate relief to those without work.[22] What it did mean was providing an environment that would make men and women anxious to work well at whatever their particular job might be, by affording them a measure of present comfort and enjoyment and the promise of a future that held more than simply misery.

In an article on "Distress in East London" in 1886, Barnett reminded his readers that Arnold Toynbee had demanded "an intellectual basis" for the moral fervor of those who wished to relieve poverty. In attempting to establish such a basis himself, Barnett came to believe that its best expression might well be state-dispensed services that would guarantee all English men and women the chance of a happier, healthier life. He wrote, rather surprised, to his brother in 1889, of the degree which his own ideas had come round to that conclusion. Returning from a meeting to establish a privately maintained dispensary, he remarked that he had once been "keen for such a place," and that even now he was willing to acknowledge its usefulness.

> But the whole system is such a muddle. Who is to get the advice free and who is to pay? All these supplementary charities must vanish someday—medical, educational, relief will have to be free. There is no law to discriminate desert except the law which lets the weakest starve and that another law set in humanity contradicts. Free schools, free doctors, free books . . . are plainly in my platform.[23]

Although in 1886 the Charity Organisation Society abandoned the classification "undeserving" in its administration of relief, it did not abandon the principle which that potent term expressed. "Not likely to benefit"—the euphemistic substitute—continued to mean that *present* character remained foremost among the criteria employed to weigh the potential benefit of any program of social betterment. Before they took a chance on what men or women might become, cos administrators demanded to know what they had been. Barnett was willing to argue that all were at least "deserving" of a healthy and pleasant environment; that slums and disease were genuine hindrances demanding the intervention of the state. If men or women were failures at the time, one should put them in an environment designed to bring out their best selves and see what happened. If they prospered, well and good; if they remained failures, then—and only then—they could be called "undeserving" and treated accordingly.

By the mid-1880s, the Barnetts had begun to make public their dissatisfaction with the limitations of cos policy. Barnett complained that the society was too willing to limit its goals to a kind of soulless respectability: "The outcome of scientific charity is the working man too thrifty to pet his children and too respectable to be happy." By the time the society's secretary, C. S. Loch, came to address a Toynbee Hall "smoking conference" in 1891, the atmosphere was hostile. "Mr. Loch's Society was the subject of attack on all sides," the *Toynbee Record* reported. "'Too much business and too little heart and soul' fairly summarizes the criticism."[24]

As Barnett continued to urge his practicable solution to social problems, his quarrels with the cos grew sharper and more specific. Because the society could not accept the environmental thesis upon which he grounded his proposals, it could only reject the proposals themselves. Barnett's search for ways to transform the Poor Law into a creative instrument led him into frequent clashes with society spokesmen. In 1887, at a Mansion House conference on the unemployed, he proposed that state funds be used to train able-bodied men "of good character and of apparently solid determination" as farmers, at a country settlement, and under regulations that would not force them "to conform to rules which are suggestive of the workhouse." During the period of their training, their wives and families would receive relief; at the end of the period, they would be offered fixed tenure on a plot of land either in England or the colonies.

Barnett elaborated upon the suggestion in an article for the *Nineteenth Century* the following year, arguing that such a scheme would make of the Poor Law an educational rather than a merely deterrent instrument. He acknowledged that critics would attack him for making relief something more than punitive.

> The arguments of its opponents are based . . . on the assumption that ineligibility or disagreeableness must be the condition of every offer of relief, so that applicants may be "deterred." Is mere disagreeableness a deterrent worthy of a civilized community? In a barbaric state it may deter wrong-doers to take an eye for an eye; in a civilised state such a punishment is considered brutal, and the wrong-doer is treated as one to be educated.[25]

Loch would have none of it. He confided to his diary that the article was "a queer medley," a muddle of deterrent dogma and Carlyle that provided nothing like proper supervision and regimentation. As Barnett predicted, he declared that the scheme might work only if the trainees "were treated like vagrants," the "question transferred to the police authorities," and the period of training viewed as "quasi-penal." But he admitted to himself that the public would probably oppose the wisdom of such strict enforcement; hence, best to drop the idea. Barnett had already encountered this kind of resistance. He wrote in disgust to his brother of a meeting with "a lot of cos folk" to discuss training farms. "They were just impossible—refusing to do anything except to clothe themselves in the dirty rags of their own righteousness. *They* were on true principles, the public could subscribe or not, they did not care, they would not hold meetings, etc., etc."[26]

Four years later Toynbee Hall sponsored a conference on problems of East London unemployment, chaired by Barnett, and including as participants Sidney and Beatrice Webb, Scott Holland, Sydney Buxton, the member of Parliament for Poplar, and three representatives from the cos, Loch among them. Their investigations confirmed the fact of both temporary and permanent unemployment on a large scale in the East End. The recommendations of the majority included the prohibition of indiscriminate doles, the collection of reliable statistics to facilitate the administration of relief schemes, and the provision of a number of temporary jobs, financed from both public and private sources, to assist those who had lived a settled life in London for at least a year.[27] The cos members resigned from the committee before it had completed its report, objecting in particular to the proposals that public funds be used to help pay for the scheme and that public officials be party to its administration. Barnett complained that on every occasion when reformers suggested using public money allocated for relief of the poor to effect change, the society's only response was outworn dogma. To a proposal to place London hospitals under a central public authority, the cos answered (as Barnett wrote exasperatedly), "The one thing worse than the present confusion [is] municipal control. The poor die for want of skilled medical care, they are demoralized by begging for hospital letters, they are contaminated by the atmosphere of waiting rooms, but at any rate the relief they get is not State relief. . . ."[28]

When in the 1890s a variety of commissions and committees, both public and private, undertook investigations of the problems of old age,

Barnett joined forces with Joseph Chamberlain, Charles Booth, and others in recommending a system of state-financed pensions, and again drew the society's fire. He favored payments of five shillings a week, to begin at age sixty-five. Such a system would assist a workingman to do what Barnett had maintained in "Practicable Socialism" he could not do at present: "to think of a time when work will be done and he will be free to go and come and rest as he will." Without the necessity of "pleading or patronage," he would acquire "a sense of stability to [his] life" which would, in turn, increase both his energies and responsibility. To those who argued that such a scheme would discourage thrift and encourage pauperism, Barnett replied that "they save most who have some possession."[29] He was concerned to improve the quality of life old people were leading and insisted that for a great many a decent, humane existence was possible only by means of state assistance. In the society's opposition to pensions, Barnett complained, there was "no sign of consideration how changed conditions of the time, . . . the new sense of inheritance of divine rights, would affect the receipt, and does affect the refusal of such relief."[30]

This criticism had been voiced in an invited paper, subsequently published, at a meeting of the society's council in 1895, during which Barnett took the membership to task for its devotion to dogma rather than to living principles. "'Independence of State relief,' and 'saving,'" he charged, "thus become the idols, the visible form, the expression of the principle that 'dependence demoralizes.' They are defended as an idol is defended by its priest."[31] Loch, replying to Barnett's outspoken charge, taxed him in turn, with a history of inconsistencies.

With Mr. Barnett progress is a series of reactions. He must be in harmony with the current philanthropic opinion of the moment or perhaps just a few seconds ahead of it. Then having laid great stress on a new point, he would "turn his back on himself" and lay equal stress on the point that he had before insisted on. Thus, he was at one time in favour of suppressing outdoor relief and promoting thrift, now he favours outdoor relief in a new guise and depreciates thrift. Before he praised the virtues of personal charity. No sooner did personal charity organise itself to fulfill a new function in the community, than he slighted it, and chided those who did not wish to extend State provision in the very department of work where personal charity could be made most effective.[32]

When Henrietta Barnett included Loch's rejoinder in her biography, she prefaced it by remarking that his anger had led him to depart from the "high ground of public policy for that of personal attack."[33] Though the attack was certainly personal, it undoubtedly struck many listeners as pertinent to the debate. "In considering criticism," Loch had said, "it is worthwhile to consider also the character of the critic." And given what Barnett had just said, it was an easy enough matter to suggest that his attack on outmoded dogma was nothing more than a personal defense of the shifts and changes in his own position toward the role of the state over the past twenty years.

Barnett's rhetoric, scarcely less heated than Loch's, though not as directly personal, was in part to blame. At one point he had challenged the council to say "whether a pension from all the community is necessarily more degrading than one from a neighbour," implying that he had forsaken entirely his insistence upon individual connection as the basis of any enduring social reform. He believed, in fact, that assistance from any source—individual or institutional, local or national—had the capacity either to degrade or to uplift; its effect would be the result of the motive of both giver and receiver. A dole bestowed by the rich man as a sop to his conscience, taken up by the poor man as an excuse for idleness, did only harm. Poor relief, administered by the state in the last resort to solve a social problem and accepted by paupers as their unhappy fate, worked no positive evil, if distributed evenhandedly, but it certainly did nothing to bring men and women closer to a consciousness of their best selves. Old-age pensions, awarded by the state to ensure at least an opportunity for human development to all its citizens, and accepted as such, were an important, positive means toward the goal of community.

Here, indeed, Barnett's position had changed during his years in the East End, as he increasingly confessed the inability of individual connection by itself to provide a proper environment for the growth of the human spirit. More willing than the Charity Organization Society to see at least a spark of worthiness in all men, he abandoned the harsh certainty of "deserving" and "undeserving" as he campaigned for a practicable minimum of "needs." In a speech to workingmen in 1894 he declared: "There is a danger even in thinking of [the poor] in a lump and treating them by rule. Each differs from the others and all have powers of growth. The loafer is a man with capacities of thinking and loving." Thus the need for an environment in which those capacities would be given a chance, its creation in large measure the task of the state. Arnold Toynbee had insisted that "where people are unable to provide a thing for themselves, and that thing is of *primary social importance*, then . . . the State should intervene and provide it for them"; Barnett could argue that he was doing no more than putting that principle into practice.

Yet the state was only one—and a less important—means to community. The other remained the individual. "No machinery will ever by itself develop energy in the loafer or self-restraint in the weak. Only individual care will succeed."[34] In their introduction to the first edition of *Practicable Socialism* the Barnetts declared "the truths with which we have become familiar" as those upon which they and their fellow workers at Toynbee Hall were willing to take their stand: "the equal capacity of all to enjoy the best, the superiority of quiet ways over those of striving and crying, [and] character as the one thing needful."[35] Read in the light of that declaration, Barnett's attitude and proposals regarding unemployment, poverty, and the state did have a consistency, not only with themselves, but also with the intellectual traditions of which they partook.

Though Toynbee Hall professed a belief in the efficacy of "quiet ways," its mission and achievements were widely chronicled, not least by the Barnetts. In addition to their own articles and speeches, two collections of essays—*The Universities and the Social Problem*, published in 1895, and *University and Social Settlements*, which appeared three years later—furnished evidence of the extent to which Toynbee Hall's example had led to the spread of Barnett's ideals and the establishment of other settlements in London and elsewhere. An appendix to the latter book lists twenty-four London houses and ten elsewhere in England and Scotland, and an article on American settlements notes the affinities between Toynbee Hall and Hull House, a relationship of which the Barnetts were particularly proud.

Many of the other English settlements were sponsored by the universities and their individual colleges, probably the best known being Oxford House in Bethnal Green, founded in 1884. Unlike Toynbee Hall, Oxford House was a mission as well as a settlement, established by Church of England clergy and laymen in the belief that the parish church should be the focal point of community life. "The principles of the Oxford House," its 1892 *Annual Report* proclaimed, "are, and will continue to be, first and foremost the belief in Christianity as the starting point of all civilising effort, and second, the recognition of the power and efficiency of community work under religious sanctions." Although J. G. Adderley, one of the first heads of the house, later wrote that there was no antagonism between the two institutions, there was unquestionably tension. This was largely the result of a willingness on the part of Oxford House proselytizers to characterize Toynbee Hall as unacceptably secular and of the hall's defenders to label Oxford House as narrowly sectarian. Henrietta Barnett insisted that her husband suffered "a deep, a very deep, pain" at the implication that Oxford House was needed because Toynbee Hall was not sufficiently religious.[36]

Most Nonconformist houses were, like Oxford House, and unlike Toynbee Hall, a combination of settlement and mission. The activities of the Wesleyans' Bermondsey Settlement, founded in 1890, consisted primarily of religious work, according to its first warden, Scott Lidgett. The Congregationalists' Browning Hall Settlement in Walworth was directly affiliated with a nearby chapel. When the residents of their second settlement, Mansfield House in Canning Town, dedicated a memorial stone to T. H. Green in 1896, the denominational *British Weekly* was perturbed, remarking that "every Settlement worth the name must be in a real sense a Christian mission" and implying that a settlement subscribing to Green's watery theism was clearly less a boon to its neighborhood than a threat. In fact, Mansfield House under its first warden, Percy Alden, and its secretary, Will Reason, came closest in practice to Barnett's own definition, encouraging conversion to a kind of nondenominational higher thinking rather than to the dogmas of a particular sect. The most self-conscious attempt to put the precepts of Green into practice occurred at University Hall, founded in 1890 by his disciple and proselytizer, Mrs. Humphry Ward. Its initial failure was primarily the result of its divided location: a lecture hall in Gordon Square, built as a temple to Elsmerian brotherhood, and a residence for settlement workers in the nearby slums of St. Pancras. Once the enterprise was combined into the Passmore Edwards Settlement in 1895, its fortunes improved.[37]

These and other settlements founded in the 1880s and 1890s, whatever their denominational commitment, undertook much the same sort of community work as did Toynbee Hall: men's clubs, boys' clubs, work on parochial relief committees, and crusades on behalf of better sanitation and housing for the poor. Both Browning Hall and Mansfield House supported the principles and programs of advanced social reformers. The public campaign for old-age pensions was launched at Browning in 1898.

Mansfield established a lodging house for the homeless and was the first settlement to provide free legal advice to the poor.

The majority of the residents at all the London settlements were, like those at Toynbee Hall, recent Oxford and Cambridge graduates. In little more than a decade after its coinage, "university settlement" was firmly established in the lexicon of contemporary social reform. And the essays in the two volumes published to celebrate its precocious coming of age demonstrate the degree to which the Toynbee Hall ethos had emerged as accepted gospel. The social investigator Arthur Sherwell declared in his article "Settlements and the Labour Movement" that "the real and vital significance" of settlement work "lies in its suggestion of a spiritual idea, a new human relationship, the co-operation of all classes of society in a fellowship of sympathy and service that shall give head to the interests of all while preserving the freedom of each." The reform-minded Conservative Sir John Gorst, a frequent visitor to Toynbee Hall, reminded readers of the need to reestablish the paternal bond that had joined rich and poor together in preindustrial communities:

> The congregation of the wage-earning classes in districts of their own is a product of modern civilisation. In olden times, whatever the distinction of classes, rich and poor lived side by side. The master constantly beheld the homes of his men, and was a witness of the events of their social life. In affliction the men could appeal to the sympathy and help which human beings will usually accord to prevent visible distress. The railways have altered all this. Both parties have left the spot on which their livelihood depends: the rich, for luxurious homes far removed from the sight of misery and contact with the poor; the poor, for districts inhabited almost exclusively by those whose means are scanty, and in which very few persons of culture or leisure are to be found.

The solution to this unnatural separation was connection of the sort advocated by Barnett and attempted by settlement residents. Many of the writers referred especially to the need for so-called one-by-one relationships between rich and poor. Personal service was "the note of the new philanthropy," Sir Walter Besant declared: "not money, but yourselves." Maud Corbett of the Cheltenham Ladies' College Settlement, Mayfield House, pleaded: "We must be ready to hear their stories, and try and understand their difficulties and their burdens,—in fact, to try and put ourselves in their places, not being content with merely a pleasant friendly feeling with the people, but trying to go beyond—to dig deeper, as it were, to give them something that will make a *real* difference in their lives." Connection after this fashion could not help but encourage a rebirth of genuine community. Percy Alden of Mansfield House spoke for all in declaring his belief that the settlement had a unique opportunity in this regard. "It comes into a district that is chaotic and disorganized, and proceeds to weld into one harmonious whole the broken, and often antagonistic, fragments of local life. It gives the people of the district an ideal to work for, and calls forth reserve force which is always to be found even in the most apathetic and poverty-stricken locality."[38]

Though the writers proclaimed, along with Barnett, that settlement workers came into the neighborhoods of the poor to learn as much as to teach, they insisted with him that disinterested, university-trained men and women had a special obligation to assume the responsibilities of leadership within the communities they were reshaping. Discussing the role settlements might play in the intelligent local administration of the Poor Law, Scott Lidgett of Bermondsey House remarked that when a community was denied the presence of "the educated, the prosperous, and the leisured," it too often passed into the hands "of men with lower aims, or at least less competent." Residents were particularly suited to fill the vacuum. Activated by a kind of classless "consecration to social service," they would possess none of the negative characteristics of either middle- or working-class leadership, proving themselves "neither stingy and selfish administrators whose only object is to save the rates, nor noisy demagogues whose great desire is to win popularity with the multitude." As a kind of model neo-governing class they could be expected to display not only a "trained intelligence" but also "the leisure and the knowledge to follow out carefully the consequences of various policies offered to them."[39]

The essayists agreed generally that it was important to encourage working men and women to manage their own affairs. Yet, like Barnett, they hesitated at the threshold of democracy. "A persistent effort should be made," Alden wrote, "to induce the working class to put forward candidates of their own who can be trusted, and who are intelligent, and the University Settlements should encourage such candidature: but while a sound public opinion in that direction, which takes a long time to create, is being formed, a man of university education, if he be thoroughly progressive, will do good service."[40] The essayists believed with Barnett that settlement workers stood in relation to their poor neighbors as fathers to their children. Alden, quoting the early nineteenth-century social reformer Sir Arthur Helps, provided what might have been the motto for both the writers and the work their articles described and celebrated: "Never is paternal government so needful as when civilisation is most advanced."[41]

Toynbee Hall was now no longer just an ideal or a place: it had become a movement. Once it had, Barnett began to question the success his experiment had achieved. He feared the implications of a movement, too easily equated with nothing more than the machinery which he had always professed to distrust. In his own essay in *University and Social Settlements*, Barnett declared almost plaintively that "Toynbee Hall is not what it seems. . . . Imitators who begin by building lecture-rooms and by starting schemes for education and relief, make the same mistake as those who followed our Lord because He made the sick man take up his bed, and not because He forgave sins. True imitation is when half-a-dozen men or women set on social service go and live among the poor. . . . Toynbee Hall is really a club, and the various activities have their root and their life in the individuality of its members."[42]

The sort of creative drift that was the focus of the hall's efforts and activities frustrated men who wanted clearer direction and the more readily attainable goals that other settlements espoused. Cosmo Gordon Lang, Balliolite clergyman, future archbishop of Canterbury, and Toynbee resident for a time, left the hall for the certainty that Oxford House seemed to embody, a place where "they were rather loyally accepting something old and tried and sure and bringing it as a gospel, a good gift, to the people." When compared with the gospel of other settlements, Toynbee Hall's seemed vague enough to preach but too vague to practice with any feeling of sustained success. C. R. Ashbee, who left frustrated and angry, later caricatured Barnett as "the Reverend Simeon Flux" in his novel *The Building of Thelema*, published in 1910. Flux, proprietor of "the great tea-cum-service-cum-politico-economico-religious punch and judy show" refused to stand for anything definite. "Perhaps it was more honest of him . . . not to do this, but it lost him the love of the younger generation, who looked to him for leadership."[43]

A former resident, Henry Nevinson, remarked of Barnett in his memoirs that he was never afraid "to lead a revolution against himself."[44] And by 1900, Barnett was prepared to acknowledge the need for a significant change, if not a revolution, in the direction of the hall's activities and purposes. While he never ceased to preach the importance of one-by-one connection, he recognized that the hall would have to rely on something more than that dogma if it was to survive. His willingness to change course marks not only his ability to face facts but also his readiness to grant the need for the machinery of the state, along with the imperative of individual connection, to solve the problems of social distress. In an article entitled "Social Reform," which appeared in the *Independent Review* in 1903, he wrote:

> The generation of reformers which is leaving the stage has played its part. The condition of the people is vastly different from what it was twenty-five years ago; but still, every human observer of the present condition is full of anxiety. The people, because of their improvement, have more ability to criticize what is done; reformers, weary of their own ways, disillusioned, perhaps, by the results of their own efforts, are tempted to say "reform is vanity"; and all classes—rich and poor alike—with more leisure and more opportunities, inclined to seize on pleasure with an avidity which astonishes onlookers.[45]

Barnett would never admit that "reform is vanity." He was too much the optimistic child of the nineteenth century for that. Instead, he set about to discover a new solution to the old problems and a way in which Toynbee Hall might be put to the service of that new solution.

When Toynbee Hall was founded, one of its stated purposes had been "to inquire into the condition of the poor and to consider and advance plans calculated to promote their welfare." It was an objective upon which Barnett focused far less in the early years of the hall than he did upon that of individual connection. What inquiry there had been had come in response to particular campaigns—opposition to indiscriminate giving by Mansion House funds—or as part of larger investigations only tangentially connected to the activities of the hall—Charles Booth's survey being the most notable example. During the 1890s, however, Toynbee-centered inquiry and investigation had begun to play a larger part in the hall's yearly programs; the 1892 conference on unemployment was an indicator of the direction into which new energies were to flow.

In his essay on settlement work in *University and Social Settlements*, Barnett had included "demand for more information," along with "distrust of machinery" and "growth of the human spirit," as one of the three causes behind the settlement movement. "A generation which had breathed something of the modern scientific spirit was not content with hearsay knowledge and sentimental references; it required facts and figures—critical investigation into the causes of poverty and personal knowledge of the poor."[46]

The use of Toynbee Hall as a center for the gathering and analyzing of social information and for the manufacturing of schemes for social reform was both a logical and appealing solution to the malaise Barnett and others sensed. This change did not require surrender so much as retrenchment. Barnett never disavowed his belief in the primary goal of a community of best selves, achieved through the one-by-one efforts of a disinterested elite. He could continue to preach, as he did, the virtues of connection while encouraging work which, although always a part of the Toynbee Hall agenda, had never enjoyed the prominence and priority it was now to receive. Residents, who had suffered for their lack of anything more than a tenuous personal relationship to the neighborhood in which they lived, would be well served by that detachment when it came to acting as social observers. As settlers, they were in the community but rarely of it, a disadvantage when the goal was connection, an advantage when it became analysis. Once they left the neighborhood—and the presumption, based upon patterns of residence, was that they would remain but a short time—they would take with them facts and experiences of invaluable future use in terms both of their own public careers and of the national interest.

The change resulted for a time in a heightened reputation for Toynbee Hall. One could more easily grasp the utilitarian potential of social inquiry than comprehend the vague if nobler purposes of connection and a community of best selves. Recruitment to residency would become a simpler matter when the relationship between present pursuit and future occupation could be so clearly enunciated. "I used to be afraid of sending my men to you," Henrietta Barnett claims Jowett remarked to her at the end of his life, "not knowing what you would do with them; but now I safely send them, for you are ambitious for them. A man's career should be his first concern."[47] Had it been Barnett to whom Jowett was confiding, Barnett might justifiably have retorted that he had always been ambitious for them, and that he had assumed that Jowett had been ambitious for them in the same way. The quotation, whether apocryphal or not, makes the point. By 1900 Toynbee Hall had begun to gain a reputation as training ground for bright, young, reform-minded civil servants. Did it, in the process, lose the soul with which Barnett had initially attempted to endow it? An answer, which the remaining chapters have been written to provide, is important not merely as part of the history of Toynbee Hall but for an understanding of the way in which its ethos endured well into the twentieth century.

4

CHALLENGES TO THE
TOYNBEE ETHOS

The refocusing of the purpose and activities of Toynbee Hall after 1900 took place both as a consequence of Samuel Barnett's conscious determination and in response to more general challenges to the Toynbee ethos arising in the first decade of the new century. Barnett's hopes for community and connection were thwarted not only by the particular experiences of settlement life and work. They were confronted also by countervailing attitudes and philosophies. Pessimists declared that the magnitude of twentieth-century urban problems would condemn any attempt to achieve social regeneration; optimists argued that the goal remained attainable, but not by the means Barnett and his followers had championed.

A sense that the uncontrollable was upon them—urban decay, imperial decline, material heedlessness—at one time or other clouded the pronouncements and predictions of even the generally optimistic. The intensity of gloom one discovers in the writings of the Edwardians testifies to the degree of their uncertainty, their fear that, having begun to discard the solutions their Victorian predecessors had attempted to impose, they might be left without any solutions whatsoever. Often they wrote as if exhausted by their repeated failures to solve social problems.

Samuel Hynes has argued that the most compelling literary image of the Edwardian poor emerges, not in the sort of realistic novels in which George Moore and George Gissing portray the late-Victorian underclass, but in H. G. Wells's *The Time Machine*, which describes a breed of "evolved underworld creatures" called Morlocks. "The poor were no longer simple, dependent inferiors to be dealt with in a district visitor manner; they were a mysterious and frightening new type."[1] The authors of a pessimistic collection of essays published in 1901, *The Heart of the Empire*, edited by the gloomy Liberal C. F. G. Masterman, warned of the threat of an emerging "town type, . . . stunted, narrow-chested, easily wearied; yet voluble, excitable, with little ballast, stamina or endurance—seeking stimulus in drink, in betting, in any unaccustomed conflicts at home or abroad."[2] The journalist P. W. Wilson, writing in the same volume, concluded with a jeremiad on cities and the kind of existence they bred: "children who . . . struggle precariously to a pasty-faced puberty (and who) are obviously born with half a brain, which half is saturated in youth with all the filth—pictorial, verbal, and dietary—that a rotten civilisation can devise."[3]

Comparing the essays of these recent Cambridge graduates with the writings of the previous generation of social reformers, one is constantly aware of the melancholic note that distinguishes the point of view of a man like Masterman from that of men such as Green, Toynbee, and Barnett. The diagnosis of both generations is much the same. "A background to life—some common bond uniting," Masterman wrote, was what "the masses" must find in order to prosper: "Some worthy subject of enthusiasm or devotion behind the aimless passage of the years—some spiritual force or ideal elevated above the shabby scene of temporary failure."[4] It was proving difficult for these men themselves to discover a "worthy subject of enthusiasm," however, let alone to transmit one to the masses. The experience of the past twenty-five years suggested to them that the various solutions proposed and then implemented by their predecessors had been of no avail. They had little use for model housing—"a vested interest . . . in overcrowding to the acre."[5] They disparaged the work of clubs, well-meant efforts which resulted in the undermining of home life.

Nor could they endorse university settlements. "I cannot believe," Masterman wrote, "that this is the machinery destined to bridge the ever-widening gulf between class and class." Masterman observed that the poor wanted nothing more than to be left alone, and he appeared to conclude that they might just as well be granted their wish. "It is doubtful if much personal interference can be of any practical service. The effect of our meddling is similar to the effect of the preaching of Western morals in the East. The old faiths are destroyed. The new faiths are not assimilated." So much for the positive power of connection. Masterman, along with his fellow essayists, professed to trust in some sort of muted progressive hope. But he did confess himself anxious, "as I believe all the thinking men of today are anxious, when they realize the forces which are making for decay."[6] The anxiety did not encourage Masterman and those who thought as he did to seek new solutions. Aside from a half-hearted wish that the Church might once more assert its social and moral authority within the community, the essayists in *The Heart of the Empire* had relatively little to propose—far less, certainly, than was contained in the programs outlined by the Barnetts in *Practicable Socialism*.

Lamentation of this sort was by no means the only note struck by the articulate Edwardian middle and upper-middle classes. If others expressed fear, as they often did, it was more a fear that their particular solutions would go unheeded, rather than that solutions—no matter whose—would ultimately make little difference. Though the dominant Edwardian chord may have remained major, however, minor subdominants abounded. And we shall fail to understand the Edwardian challenge to Toynbee Hall unless we acknowledge the degree to which those subdominants might strike a response in the minds of socially conscious men and women. There was a temptation to say, as "decent" men were saying, as Robert Elsmere refused to say: though we have tried and failed, we have at least tried. And then to say no more.

Meanwhile, three powerful positive challenges arose to confront directly the tradition of which Toynbee Hall had become the exemplar. The first declared that the nation's primary responsibility was to increase its national efficiency by means of widespread centralization. Its proponents, though arguing the importance of community, redefined it in national rather than local terms, thus denying its function as a focal point for individual connection. At the same time, though they relied for the implementation of their centralizing reforms upon a disinterested elite, they insisted that their elite possess a degree of expertise that made of it something very different from the amateur urban governing class that was Barnett's beau ideal. The second challenge, embodied in a revived and radicalized Christian Socialist movement, argued that Toynbee Hall was a practical failure and its philosophy of social regeneration a muddled irrelevance because neither was specifically Christian or militantly socialist. The third challenge was that of a handful of sociological theorists, who insisted that idealists' unwillingness to separate what *ought* to be from what *is* only confused their attempts to reform society. Sociologists argued as well that the notion of community, as articulated by thinkers like Green, possessed little utility as a concept and little relevance as an end, because it ignored the intermediate institutions of family and class and because it refused to acknowledge the degree to which social organization was prey to irrationality—again, *ought* as opposed to *is*.

National efficiency became the goal of an increasing number of worried social reformers after 1900. Not only was Britain's less than triumphant management of the war in South Africa a cause for growing concern. The government's 1904 *Report of the Inter-Departmental Committee on Physical Deterioration*, which contained statistics concerning the large number of city-bred volunteers turned down for military service (eight thousand of eleven thousand in Manchester), seemed to establish irrefutable evidence of human waste and inefficiency. Germany appeared as both enemy and model. Its rapid industrialization was understood to have been the result of an extraordinarily efficient use of national resources, human and otherwise. If it posed a serious threat to Britain's economic and political hegemony, it represented a challenge as well. The report's implied imperative was that Britain respond by instituting a regime of efficient management upon the community of the nation, a regime that might require the sacrifice of a certain degree of personal liberty, the discarding of traditional assumptions, the drastic modification of venerable institutions. Reformers defined government as machinery, to be designed and manned no longer by amateurs, talented though they might have been, but by expert technicians. Their task was to use that machinery in a way that would rid the nation of social and economic waste and make it again a keen, effective competitor among the nations of the world.

The goal of national efficiency attracted advocates across the political spectrum. When in 1902 the Fabian socialists Sidney and Beatrice Webb assembled an informal dining club, The Co-Efficients, dedicated to propagandizing on behalf of more vigorous government intervention, had no difficulty in persuading Conservatives like Leo Amery and Liberals like Edward Grey to join them.[7] Their schemes received theoretical support from the writings of a growing band of economic and social thinkers. Alfred Marshall, the Cambridge economist, though a cautious interventionist, nevertheless recognized the dangers inherent in a society built upon as unstable a foundation as the unskilled "residuum," and he was prepared to lend the weight of his position as a professional economist to proposals for centralized social reconstruction. In his evidence submitted to the Royal Commission on the Aged Poor in 1893, he proclaimed himself an environmentalist, convinced of the direct relationship between a healthy, productive citizenry and an efficient nation.

> The problem of 1893 is the problem of poverty. . . . A man ought not to be allowed to live in a bad home, . . . extreme poverty ought to be regarded, not indeed as a crime, but as a thing so detrimental to the State that it should not be endured; . . . everybody who, whether through his own fault or not, [is] in effect incapable of keeping together a home that contributes to the well-being of the State . . . should, under the authority of the State, pass into a new form of life.[8]

Marshall's pronouncements were particularly reassuring to centralizers because of his reputation as an expert, a man who was making an academic profession of economics. John Maynard Keynes in his memoir of Marshall calls him both a scientist and a "preacher and pastor of men." But Keynes makes it clear that Marshall's achievement was his ability to give the discipline of economics a stature in its own right, rather than as one of the moral sciences. "After his time," Keynes writes, "economics could never be again one of à number of subjects which a Moral Philosopher would take in his stride. . . . He was the first to take up this professional, scientific attitude to the subject, as something above and outside current controversy, as far from politics as physiology from the general practitioner."[9] This is not to suggest that Marshall saw no link between the principles he was discovering as an economist and the causes he was promoting as a social reformer. On the contrary, he believed that "the possibility of progress depends in a great measure upon facts and inferences which are within the province of economics: and this it is which gives to economic studies their chief and their highest interest."[10]

Because the facts and inferences had been derived scientifically and as a consequence of professional experimentation and theorizing, reformers could summon them to their aid as professional and expert. When Marshall testified as to the effects of increased expenditure upon the aged poor, he was not just another concerned witness speaking out in favor of a pension scheme. He was disinterested in the sense that settlement workers were presumed to be; but he was professional as well, in a way that they were not. As such, his word was more difficult to refute, and his position encouraged those anxious to increase the role of the state.

The arguments of other writers, inhabiting a kind of borderland between economics and social theory, served much the same purpose. J. A. Hobson and L. T. Hobhouse, for example, on the staff of the *Nation* during this period, both contributed substantial theoretical support to campaigns for immediate programs for increased centralization. Marshall was an expert with a sharply tuned individual conscience. Hobson was an expert whose theories, relating economics directly to larger social issues, suggested that individual conscience might be an irrelevant (albeit worthy) anachronism. His theory of underconsumption led him to insist that those with large unearned incomes must be made to surrender their excess wealth for the efficient functioning of the community as a whole. If the state were to impose a minimum wage and to assume control of private monopolies such as mines and railways, the poor would in time become more active consumers, more goods would be manufactured, and unemployment could be vastly reduced. "Taxation, or State assumption on equitable terms, of properties whose increasing values are due to public activity and public need" was the most direct and effective way to raise the general standard of consumption.[11]

Hobson's concern for consumers was a concern for community, which he defined in a way that Green, Toynbee, and Barnett had not. When the latter three used the term, they meant either a particular locality or, in a wider sense, an agglomeration of individual best selves. If the state had a role, it was to assist individuals as they pursued their goal of self-fulfillment. The state served the individual, and not vice versa. Hobson understood community not only as a national rather than a local phenomenon but also as a complex organism of interconnected parts. Individuals were subordinate to their roles as producers and consumers; producers were, in turn, subordinate to the needs of community as a whole. And community was directly dependent upon the state for its productive and efficient functioning. "The most important duty of state craft," Hobson wrote in 1910, was, on the one hand, "creating the conditions most favorable to the absorption of 'surplus' by individual producers in proportion to their capacity to use it" and, on the other, "the application of the remainder of the surplus to the direct use of the state for public services." No simple task: "the performance of this work . . . involves on the part of the State a careful calculus of the respective requirements of the State and of the individual," toward the goal of "progressive efficiency."[12]

L. T. Hobhouse was as concerned as Hobson was to establish an efficient community as the end toward which the means of increased state power might be directed. He rejected idealism of the sort Green espoused, largely because it seemed to him to inhibit a clear, precise understanding of the necessary relationship between individual and society. "It is scarcely too much to say that the effect of idealism . . . has been mainly to sap intellectual and moral sincerity, . . . to soften the edges of all hard contrasts between right and wrong, truth and falsity, to throw a gloss over stupidity, and prejudice, and caste, and tradition, to weaken the bases of reason. . . ."[13] Hobhouse could not accept Green's assurance that individual and community good were identical. Perhaps in an ideal world; not in the actual. Hobhouse's solution was to urge "that the national good is not the good of the individual as such but the good of the whole of which he forms an integral part."[14]

Hobhouse defined rights according to this general social good.

> It it were well for society as a whole to destroy every right of private property tomorrow, it would be just to do so, and the owners would have no right to object. . . . If, therefore, any right to any form of property or freedom no longer serves a good social purpose, it must go. And whatever tenderness we show to the interests of individuals, remember that we do this, too, in the name of common welfare.[15]

Hobhouse cut through Green's late nineteenth-century ambivalences to establish a central, unequivocal role for the state. He advocated that the state extend itself so as to protect personal rights—"particularly in the economic sphere," and to organize public resources, by means of increased taxation, in support of educational programs and national insurance. The purpose of taxation was to recapture for society "the element in wealth that is of social origin, . . . all that does not owe its origin to the efforts of living individuals." Money derived in this way to benefit the community was not money taken from Peter to pay Paul. "Peter is not robbed. Apart from the tax it is he who would be robbing the state."[16]

Possessed of both authority and wealth, the state could proceed to establish a minimum standard of life for all its citizens, guaranteeing to them economic conditions "such that the normal man who is not defective in mind or body or will can by useful labour feed, house and clothe himself and his family. The 'right to work' and the 'right to a living wage' are just as valid as the rights of person or property. That is to say, they are integral conditions of a good social order." Such a minimum would act as a tonic to the workingman and his family. Though Hobhouse would in all likelihood have rejected the notion of a best self, his state-imposed minimum would provide the worker with a sense of security, without which there would be little incentive to improve either mind or spirit. "He would have a basis to go upon, a substructure on which it would be possible for him to rear the fabric of a real sufficiency. He would have . . . a brighter outlook, a more confident hope. . . ."[17]

Hobhouse insisted that despite his dedication to the principles of efficient centralization and state intervention, he was a liberal, not a socialist. "The general conception of the State as Overparent is quite as truly Liberal as Socialistic."[18] Others willing to call themselves socialists spoke very much as he did, using the concept of a national minimum as a way of defining community and insisting on the state as the proper authority to insure that minimum. In doing so, they too challenged the precepts of the Toynbee Hall tradition. Sidney and Beatrice Webb were as concerned as Hobson and Hobhouse to preach the subordination of the individual to the community. In *The Prevention of Destitution*, their apologia for a national minimum which was published following Beatrice's service as a member of the commission to investigate the administration of the Poor Law, the Webbs declared poverty a national disease which threatened the healthy and efficient functioning of the nation. They attacked the waste of underemployment, declaring that an employer who laid off his work force in times of recession was acting in a way as detrimental to the national interest as he would were he to "turn all his machinery into the street to be rained upon, so that it was found rusty and unserviceable when new orders came in."[19] Such industrial habits would cease only when citizens understood the importance of putting community interests ahead of their own. "It is of comparatively little importance, in the long run, that individuals should develop life to the utmost, if the life of the community in which we live is not thereby served. . . . A society is something more than the sum of its members; . . . a social organism has a life and health distinguishable from those of its individual atoms."[20]

The Webbs defined community, as did Hobson and Hobhouse, in

terms of the nation. They believed its activities should be directed toward the service and protection of consumers, as well as producers, thereby to a large extent turning their backs on the implications of class which lay at the center of more orthodox socialist doctrine. They saw community as a complex network of agencies and institutions, both private and public, which together would bind and sustain the people of England, producers and consumers alike, as they worked to create a more efficient—and therefore more effective—society. Schools, health programs, old-age pensions, unemployment insurance, and systems of labor relocation and retraining would not only function together to guarantee a decent minimum for all but would operate as well to encourage the development within the community of "far finer shades of physical, moral, and spiritual perfection."

The Webbs thus defined their state in two ways: as a complex piece of machinery designed to produce a more efficient society; and as an effective instructor in the arts of community preservation and reinvigoration. In its latter role, the state would assume the task assigned by Barnett to individual members of the disinterested elite. As a teacher, the state would demonstrate and enforce the lessons of responsibility that Barnett believed could only be effectively taught one by one. The Webbs opposed compulsory national insurance programs that placed little obligation upon their beneficiaries: "The state gets nothing for its money in the way of conduct," Beatrice Webb complained in her diary in 1909.[21] The Liberal party's 1911 insurance schemes demanded too little. "The member drawing sick pay is not required to subject himself to any hygienic regimen, to go into hospital; . . . and the man drawing out-of-work pay is under no restrictions as to conduct and under no necessity to be so very energetic in discovering a new situation." The existing workmen's-compensation provisions drew the Webbs' fire as well. "There is nothing to ensure that the incapacitated workman, or the widow, does not lose or squander the sum handed over by the insurance company . . . and eventually become as dependent on Poor Law relief as if the commission had provided nothing at all." Instead of unconditional payments they recommended state grants-in-aid, to be administered by trade unions in a way to ensure that payments resulted in right conduct.[22]

Theories and programs which insisted on increased centralization, such as those propounded by Hobson, Hobhouse, and the Webbs, threatened the assumptions that had inspired Toynbee Hall. They altered the dimensions of community, transcending the localism that Barnett had believed necessary in order to achieve connection. Despite his willingness to admit an increased role for the state, he had continued to try to bring community to life in a particular place. Centralizers argued, however, that the urgency and interconnectedness of social problems demanded solutions across an area far greater than that of a few slum neighborhoods. Those solutions would more often than not be general and nationwide, rather than specific and local. The energies of reform, which Barnett had hoped to generate by means of human connection in Whitechapel and in a number of similar communities throughout the nation, and which he had hoped to see flow outward until they touched and reinforced each other, would flow instead from Whitehall downward, first to cities and then into neighborhoods. Centralizers redefined community, treating the local and concrete as irrelevancies, if not stumbling blocks, to their plans for a revitalized and efficient community on a national scale.

Centralization and the increased need for knowledgeable experts, which planning and administration encouraged, prompted a redefinition of disinterested service that further challenged Toynbee Hall perceptions. Again, the change had to do with dimension. The disinterested Toynbee Hall resident was expected to spend his time cultivating connections with local working-class residents, in order that both he and they might better understand each other and work together toward mutually beneficial ends. That the resident might more often find himself in the role of teacher rather than learner was a circumstance accounted for by his more clear-sighted (because more disinterested) ability to ascertain those ends. His own personal relationship with the men and women with whom he lived would, in turn, encourage them to make his goals their own.

Once the dimensions of reform began to be perceived as national rather than local, distance made connection an impossibility. The disinterested resident, armed with little more in many cases than an amateur's willingness to deal with workers and their families as fellow human beings, was of no use in a growing bureaucracy that understood disinterestedness as the expertise of the social technician. To the degree that Barnett was prepared by 1900 to accommodate the work of social investigators and planners at Toynbee Hall, he was reflecting this movement toward impersonal—and away from personal—elitism.

The reformers who preached the need for further centralization argued for a professional body of trained experts to design and staff the machinery of intervention. The professionalism of men like Marshall had helped establish this new tradition. Hobson wrote of "specialists" who would "take over much of the legislative work so badly done or so badly left undone by our elective assemblies of legislative amateurs," and of the need for an improved educational system to train them.[23] The Webbs were not afraid to leave as much decision making as possible to men and women educated for their particular bureaucratic task. Beatrice Webb, who never disguised her mistrust of "the average sensual man," was equally unimpressed by the notion of an elite composed of dedicated amateurs. Despite steps taken earlier in the nineteenth century to professionalize the civil service, of which the Northcote-Trevelyan reforms of the mid-1850s were the most notable, she and others remained convinced that too much government still rested in the hands of well-meaning incompetents. "We do not want clever school boys at the head of our great departments," she wrote in 1896. "We want grown men, 'grown up' *in the particular business they have taken in hand* . . . behaving towards their profession as the great civil engineer, lawyer or medical man behaves."[24] Efficient, effective government must depend upon "the professional expert," someone who would "add to its enormous advantages of wholesale and compulsory management, the advantage of the most skilled entrepreneur."[25]

The prospect, then, was a heady one: entrepreneurial service as disinterested expert on behalf of the nation as a whole. Like that unfolded to the young men of Oxford by Green and Toynbee, it evoked the ideal of duty to a community which, though it transcended class, nevertheless remained divided, between those who defined the responsibilities of citizenship and the rest whose task it was to act in accordance with those definitions. But its increased dimension, its insistence upon rigorous professionalism, as well as the sense of urgency for the national condition of England that it projected, imparted to this new assignment a vitality that had drained from the old.

An insistent vigor unquestionably infused the thought and activities of certain Edwardian Christian Socialists, whose challenge to Toynbee Hall was as direct as that of the centralizers. The immanentist principles that Charles Gore and Scott Holland set forth in *Lux Mundi* had found expression after 1889 in the work of the Christian Social Union (csu), an explicitly Anglican and vaguely socialist organization of which Holland was the first secretary. Its establishment had come on the heels of the Lambeth conference of 1888, which had proclaimed the urgency of social questions and the need for Christian answers to them. The union's conscious denominationalism and moderate interventionist stance were reflected in its stated objectives: "to claim for Christian law the ultimate authority to rule social practice; to study in common how to apply the moral truths and principles of Christianity to the social and economic difficulties of the present time; and to present Christ in practical life as the living master and King, the enemy of wrong and selfishness, the power of righteousness and love."[26]

Because of its founders' belief that the national Church had a particular social task to discharge, the union's generally elitist membership was limited to Church of England communicants. The Church, Gore wrote, was "specially bound to think for the whole nation," and the union specially charged to awaken the Church to that duty, "which, if it wished to claim the names of Christian or Catholic, it could not ignore." For this reason, "it limited its membership to Church people. Only Church people, it felt, could awaken the Church. Only Church people, sharing the same sacramental system, could awaken their fellows to the real meaning of their baptism, their confirmation and their holy communion."[27]

Gore believed that denominationalism, by intensifying commitment, could sharpen the attack upon contemporary social evils. In a 1905 address at the csu annual meeting, he criticized those whose belief in the importance of tolerance had lost them their proper share of righteous zeal.

What we want is *in*tolerance—a blessed and holy intolerance; a determination in the heart of men, in the heart of us because we believe in God, that these things shall be changed, as they can be changed. . . . What you want [is] not to believe less particularly about God, but more particularly about God. It is the vagueness of people's belief about God that does them harm. . . . So long as you have vague, slack ideas, . . . you may go on tolerating; but if you hold a definite creed and know that you believe it really, then you must want things changed.[28]

Whether or not Gore had Green and Barnett in mind as he spoke, he was declaring that agnosticism and ecumenicalism hindered an effective crusade for social change. Reformers must surrender to the necessity for deep and abiding conviction, grounded in a faith that could be translated directly into social action. Without that spiritual engine, they would too readily tolerate half measures and therefore half solutions.

The union established branches throughout England which encouraged and undertook a variety of reform activities: surveys of sweated workshops, campaigns for further factory regulation, and slum clearance. A CSU settlement house—named Maurice Hostel to commemorate the work of the mid-century Christian Socialist F. D. Maurice—was founded in Hoxton in 1898. Probably the union's most effective effort was its organization of consumer boycotts of stores that refused to pay union wages. A monthly review, the *Commonwealth,* founded in 1896 with Scott Holland as a coeditor, published articles and reports sympathetic to the union's programs and purposes.

Despite Gore's insistence upon wholehearted commitment, the CSU was not explicitly socialist. Though it professed the sort of practicable socialism that meant opposition to unregulated laissez-faire capitalism, it assiduously kept its distance from doctrines such as worker control or state ownership. The union's Christian Socialism thus often seemed to bear as hierarchical a stamp as Barnett's did. Holland spoke and wrote of the duties of stewardship, of property held in trust by men responsible both to community and God for its beneficent use. Arthur Winnington-Ingram, a CSU stalwart who was successively bishop of Stepney (1897) and London (1901), attributed the growth of what he called "bitter Socialism" to "the want of Christian Socialism . . . and the forgetfulness, by the moneyed and leisured classes, of their stewardship."[29]

Ernest Aves once remarked that Winnington-Ingram had succeeded because he was "attractive and safe." The same could be said of the CSU, sixteen of whose members were appointed to episcopal sees between 1889 and 1913.[30] Its safeness increasingly frustrated a number of Churchmen far less frightened than the union of the implications of a truly socialist creed. Gore himself wrote Holland in 1906 that the organization "had done its bit" and had better "acquiesce in being Academic and leave the Socialists to make a fresh start."[31] Others had by that time formed a rival organization, the Church Socialist League, insisting that the Christian Socialist movement could effect significant social change only if it gave to the term "socialism" as orthodox a definition as it gave to "Christian."

These men were part of a tradition of radical High Churchmanship with roots in the East London ministries of men like L. S. Wainwright, vicar of St. Peter's, Wapping, who, contrary to the principles of both the Charity Organisation Society and Toynbee Hall, continued to dole out food and money to the poor, believing indiscrimination preferable to starvation. They were rebel priests, enacting the lessons of Christ's ministry as literally as they could and without regard to the consequences in terms of their own livelihoods. Their outspokenness meant they occasionally lost their jobs; unlike most Church of England clergymen, some shared first hand the experience of unemployment with the workingmen and -women they served. Undoubtedly the most famous of these radical clergymen was Stewart Headlam, curate of St. Matthew's, Bethnal Green, socialist, founder of the Church and Stage Guild—organized to defend the reputation of actors and dancers, and of their professions—and persistent thorn in a succession of episcopal sides. Others included C. L. Marson, who served as Barnett's curate at St. Jude's in the early 1880s; A. H. Stanton, rector of St. Alban's, Holborn; Robert Dolling, at St. Saviour's, Poplar, at the turn of the century; and Conrad Noel, whose father wrote *The Red Flag* while serving as groom of the Privy Chambers. Noel preached in his youth to labour churches in Manchester and Bradford, later moving as gadfly curate from one London parish to another until settling finally at Thaxted in Essex.

In 1877, Headlam had founded the Guild of St. Matthew, which until the 1890s succored a good many socialist High Churchmen. But Headlam's willingness to stand bail for Oscar Wilde, and his frequent use of the guild as little more than an instrument for his own crusades, cost it membership. Not until 1906 and the founding of the Church Socialist League (CSL) did the Christian Socialist Left possess an organization capable of responding effectively to what Noel described as "that mild and watery society of social reform," the csu.[32] The league's membership was more eclectic, both socially and geographically, than that of the union. Its founders were northern clergymen: W. E. More and Algernon West of Newcastle; T. C. Gobart of Darlington; P. E. T. Widdrington of Halton, a Lancashire mill town. They took pains to separate their organization from the csu. In the first issue of their monthly journal, the *Church Socialist*, they declared themselves champions of "the ordinary economic

Socialism of all Socialists, which we believe to be economic justice." The editors, taking a self-conscious swipe at the union, proclaimed: "We do not expect to be popular, or to have the enthusiastic support of many of the great in the land."[33]

The policies of the league insured the accuracy of the prediction. At the annual conference in 1912, the executive committee introduced a successful resolution welcoming the unprecedented labor unrest of the past year "as indicating the Revolt of the People against industrial injustice and social wrong and their determination to achieve better conditions of labour and life." The conference affirmed as well "the duty of the Church to abandon its profession of neutrality and openly to further the revolt."[34] The league's special and urgent mission was to convert Churchmen and -women to the fact that socialism, more clearly and directly than any other creed, embodied the political and economic implications of the Christian faith. "To us in the League," Widdrington wrote, "socialism is the most notable attempt in the history of the world to work out the Christian virtues of faith, hope, and love in the spheres of politics and industry."[35]

This brand of Christian Socialism was a tougher and more insistent faith than that of Toynbee Hall. The league's commitment to "economic" socialism, like Gore's equally wholehearted commitment to theological "intolerance," reflected a pugnacious willingness to follow the example of secular socialist organizations like the Social Democratic Federation and the Socialist League, to dogmatize in a way that was foreign to the thinking and to the actions of the less strident, more gentlemanly, intellectual traditions of Balliol. There were other differences as well. Though the Christian Socialism of Gore and Holland reflected the immanentism that lay at the heart of Green's philosophy, "immanentism" to a devout member of the Church Socialist League meant something more than Green's "Christ within us." It meant living as nearly as possible as Christ himself had lived—within the world, yet in rigorous, constant opposition to most of its self-destructive assumptions. Christ's miracles, Headlam wrote, "were all distinctly secular, socialistic works: works for health against disease, . . . works taking care to see that the people were properly fed, . . . works showing that mirth and joy have a true place in the life here."[36] The kingdom of heaven, Noel insisted, is a kingdom not of this world—that is, a kingdom in opposition to the present ways of the world. But it is a kingdom "'in' this world, . . . thrust like leaven into the ages." Those who profess to work on behalf of the

100

Church "must seize every opportunity of interfering with the world," until its "warring, factious kingdoms" have been transformed into "the commonwealth of God and His Christ."[37]

Immanentism of this sort meant responding immediately and fully as one compassionate Christian to another, without concern for a "scientifically" calculated list of future consequences. Charles Marson, a CSL priest, in a pamphlet that bitterly attacked what he called the "new charity," by implication condemned as well the disinterested elite that believed it knew best how to respond to the needs of the poor. Marson told of his desire to assist a starving woman whose husband was a drunkard. He sought the advice of a "lady representative of the 'new charity'" who instructed him to withhold assistance, since the wife's need was "the one inducement the husband has to deny himself. If you rush in and relieve her now, you kick away the one and only ladder he has to the better life." Marson retorted:

> I swallowed it all down and lay awake thinking of the sublime duty of hardening one's heart. At last I could stand it no more. . . . "This woman must be saved." So I jellied and blanketed and pampered the woman all I could, and more. The unexpected followed—the husband ceased to drink; he in turn helped me all he could. Mr. Loch and Miss Octavia Hill's theories vanish into thin air. Care and love begot care and love; a responsibility shared was not diminished, but felt deeper.[38]

When immanentism was defined as *sharing* responsibility rather than *assuming* responsibility, one by one came to mean something other than the didactic relationship it meant to Barnett. Marson, who had served as rector of a parish near Romney Marsh noted for the benevolence of its local squire, objected to the "model" relationship he found in place. "My heart aches and burns here at the degradation of village life. These poor folk are swirking and sweating to produce £1,500 a year for one person, and similar sums for others, and their own children go short and half-clad, and they none of them have time to read, think, dance, play music or games."[39] Other Christian Socialists echoed Marson's uneasiness and distaste. Percy Dearmer, one of the movement's leading publicists, recorded in his diary the discomfort he felt when confronting "the idea of our setting up as heaven-appointed guides,—by virtue of what? Our learning! And this in the face of the gospels."[40] A laywoman, writing

"Against the District Visitor" in *Commonwealth*, attacked the principle upon which Toynbee Hall's apologists had based their argument for its foundation. "If the ideal . . . for the country was 'a resident gentleman in every parish,' for the town it was 'a squire's daughter in every street.' Both are in their way, quite honestly, beautiful ideals. But they are feudal, *not Christian;* . . . and they are intensely unsuited to do the work that needs to be done today."[41] Present-day, reform-minded Churchmen, Headlam complained, "will do almost anything for the people except one thing, and that is, they won't get off their back—and they will never get off their back until the people themselves shake them off."[42]

Such injunctions proclaimed that these radical Christian Socialists were prepared to welcome democracy to a degree Toynbee Hall was not. They preached an optimistic "Catholic democracy," arguing that God, by manifesting His immanent spirit throughout the entire body of the Church, had imparted not only its blessing, but its rewards—including that of full citizenship—equally to all. Dearmer wrote that the Church had been attempting to establish "a Christian democracy ever since the Divine Democrat of Nazareth founded her, and set a handful of working men to preside over her interests." And Headlam declared his hope in 1907 that "the Education of the People will soon be in the People's hands; the land values, the result of the People's work, will soon be taken out of the hands of those who have monopolized them; and the Church, for so long regarded as the Church of the Classes, [will] be claimed as the Church of the People."[43]

Commitment to democracy meant that Christian Socialists were as disinclined to the idea of a didactic, elitist state as they were to the notion of a benevolent, authoritarian barony. What socialism is *not*, Headlam declared angrily, is "the regulating and licensing and managing the lives of the people by a set of bureaucrats."[44] William Temple, a young socialist despite the fact (or perhaps, in part, because of the fact) that his father had been archbishop of Canterbury, wrote in a 1908 article on the Church and the Labour party that "the State is not external to the individual; it includes him." But it included all individuals as equals, with an equal role in the service of the community. "Public service," Temple argued—in response to the growing popularity of bureaucratic elitism—"is not service of the *other* members of society, but of the whole of society, the man himself included." The goal was neither efficiency nor the realization of one's best self. It was "brotherhood," a "mutual dependence binding all men to each other and to the body politic."[45]

The Christian Socialists' belief in the power of the Church to shape the national community to its ideals led them to accept social institutions as positive contributors to the general well-being in a way a man like Barnett could not. For him, class consciousness, because it stood between the desire of rich man to connect with poor man, thwarted community. The Edwardian Christian Socialists, on the other hand, appear to have come as close as any group of middle-class reformers to seeing the working class, its culture, and its institutions, as something positive, to be judged on its own terms and welcomed into the community on its own right. Headlam's campaigns to garner respect for actors and actresses suggest this, as do Noel's frank enjoyment of the London music hall ("with a few exceptions the comedians avoided indecent jokes, and when they were indecent they were also humorous") and Marson's delight in "the smell of cooked stuffs and petrol and the rush of life" in Soho.[46] One should not make more of this point than the admittedly slim, and generally negative, evidence will allow. It is in part because of what the Christian Socialists did not say that one can venture a tentative generalization. Their writings contained none of the patronizing, de haute en bas tone that found its way into Barnett's pronouncements despite his good intentions; they never insisted that workingmen and -women adopt the characteristics of a best self that accorded with upper-middle-class notions of what that best self should be.[47]

Christian Socialism's most potent challenge to Toynbee Hall was its buoyant, persistent optimism. The religious conviction that encouraged these men to dogmatize gave them a confidence that infused their writings with a vitality the apologists for university settlements could no longer match. When Headlam pronounced the magnificat "the hymn of the universal social revolution, which tells of the deposition of the mighty, the scattering of the proud, the emptying of the pockets of the rich"; when Dearmer declared that "everyone who says the Lord's Prayer proclaims himself a fellow-worker with God for a perfect social state," they were not simply articulating a creed but broadcasting an appeal whose aggressive certainty would contrast sharply and, in many young minds, favorably with the muted, muddled call to action that by 1900 or so was emanating from Toynbee Hall.[48]

The challenge to Toynbee Hall represented by the emerging discipline of sociology was potentially more destructive than that of centralism or of radical Christian Socialism. The latter two, if they contradicted.the Toynbee ethos at many points, still bore some relation to it. Those who advocated centralized bureaucracy and state intervention could be perceived as concerned for the future of community, albeit on a national scale; those who preached of Christ as a socialist, despite their distance from the Oxford idealists, nevertheless shared with them an insistent immanentism. Sociology, however, rooted as it was in the positivist understanding that change accords with the working of objective social "laws," stood by its nature in direct opposition to a philosophical tradition that understood social ends as the expression of a moral ideal, rather than a logical arrangement of scientifically verifiable "facts." What Noel Annan has called the English passion "for laying down how men ought to behave and how society ought to be reorganized in order that they may behave better"—the passion at the heart of the precepts of Toynbee Hall—had induced its proponents "to neglect new techniques for describing how in fact men do behave and how far reorganisations of society are capable of changing their behaviour."[49]

By the turn of the century, English men and women had gone some way toward remedying that neglect. True, as Philip Abrams has remarked in his study of the origins of British sociology, when the Sociological Society was established in 1903, some of its founders were more concerned to decide what they wanted sociology to do than to define what it was. "Ought" and "is" were not disentangled overnight. Nevertheless, as Abrams observes, a growing number of social investigators, who could trace their intellectual lineage back to the statistical societies of the 1840s and 1850s, were prepared to express a "distaste . . . for controversies of principle," along with a "faith that facts properly gathered would eventually speak for themselves."[50] Some, like the venerable positivist Frederic Harrison, continued to insist that sociology be defined not simply as the "tabulation of mere observations, unexplained or coordinated," that "the business of a real master science is to systematise laws."[51] Whether concerned with laws or simply with the collection and arrangement of data, however, sociologists increasingly insisted that moral considerations, if allowed to intrude upon either investigation or synthesis, would muddy their conclusions and irreparably taint the ultimate value of their work.

Thoughtful settlement workers, once they acknowledged their function as fact gatherers and social analysts, might ask themselves whether their new role as social scientists did not preclude their mission as connectors. Charles Booth used Toynbee Hall residents as assistants in the first stages of his survey of East London in the early 1890s and the hall itself as a center for the gathering and checking of facts. Booth, though a major influence in the development of sociology in England, was not himself a sociologist. Nor did he hesitate to claim that his investigations into the conditions of poverty were motivated by a desire to see them improved. But he insisted that the investigations themselves be as "scientific" as possible. Poverty, Booth's biographers have written, seemed to him attributable directly "to the working of some 'natural' law whose nature it was the function of science to reveal. The important thing was, therefore, to accept science and not oppose it, and to devote all one's energies to discovering its laws and living in obedience with them."[52] When Booth went to live among the poor it was not to improve them or to change them but to discover as much as he could, as an anthropologist might, about their lives and habits. His dedication to the principle of scientific inquiry did not prevent him from making *value* judgments: that a man or woman living in classes A or B ("loafers and semi-criminals"; "very poor") was worth little or nothing to society. Yet he endeavored to avoid *moral* judgments and the assessing of personal blame for the misfortunes he discovered.[53]

This point of view was not easily reconciled with an insistence upon the overriding need to cultivate a better self. E. J. Urwick, a Toynbee resident who became the hall's subwarden from 1901 to 1903 and was subsequently professor of sociology in the University of London, insisted that the resulting intellectual tension should be resolved by subordinating sociological method to idealist ends. In his book *A Philosophy of Social Progress*, published in 1912, he declared that behind his desire "to introduce students to the sociological point of view"—not, be it noted, to sociology—lay "the even stronger desire to show them that sociological science is and must remain a very partial aid to the understanding of our social life; that it is and must be subordinate to a philosophy of that life which passes boldly beyond the domain of any science." Urwick argued that it remained not only possible but necessary to connect sociological investigation to spiritual goals. "The analysis of the social person, the self, and the soul, has entitled us to assert that no aim is true which is not really spiritual—that is, which is not consciously directed to bringing nearer the attainment of the only absolutely good end, the realisation of the true individual as supreme over both society and self."[54]

To Hobhouse, argument of this sort led to confusion detrimental to both sociology and philosophy. He acknowledged the necessity for ethical judgment, as well as the fact that a sociologist cannot, any more than any other human being can, remain value free. But he insisted that sociologists separate actual conditions and ideal values, that they distinguish as clearly as they could between development—what has happened, and progress—what they would like to see happen. In an introductory editorial to the first issue of the *Sociological Review*, published in 1908, Hobhouse pronounced the clear and necessary distinction between political philosophy, whose concern is with what society ought to be, and sociology, whose subject matter is "the most general conditions of social life, the intimate nature of the social bond, and the problems arising out of the bare fact that distinct personalities form a social whole." Sociologists must avoid the temptation to confuse the two disciplines or to "pass from the one to the other without sufficiently clear consciousness of the step that they are taking. . . . Sociology as a science . . . has no concern with the right and wrong of human conduct, or with the good and bad of social life, but only with the nature and conditions of the social structure and the observable laws of its growth and decay."[55]

Hobhouse did not deny to the sociologist any more than to the philosopher the right to develop theories of social progress, as distinct from social development. Indeed, as Abrams remarks, Hobhouse's ideal sociologist was to be "a social philosopher and a social scientist, continually testing his science against his philosophy and his philosophy against his science."[56] Yet he could function in that way only if he began both tests with a certain understanding of his starting point. For a young Toynbee Hall resident, the injunctions, if he understood and heeded them, were therefore formidable: cease to suppose that you can function effectively as a social investigator unless you first accept the rigorous, objective standards of that discipline; or cease to assume that your prescriptions for a society that ought to be can come to pass in a society which you have observed only through the lens of your amateurish presuppositions.

The lens clouded scientific perceptions in two particularly significant ways. First, by centering its analysis of society upon the individual, Toynbee Hall tended to ignore those institutions such as family, work place, or class upon which social scientists were focusing an increasing amount of their attention. Toynbee Hall believed class interests too often stood between men as they were and men as they ought to be. Whereas sociologists might see class as a key element in the general social structure whose analysis was their primary concern, a Toynbeeite, intent upon moralizing directly from individual to society, saw class as a hindrance to that task and very little more. He might appreciate the work of Booth or of Seebohm Rowntree, whose survey of poverty in York was published in 1901, because of what it could tell him about individuals whom he had previously understood only as part of an undifferentiated mass. But his lens prevented him from seeing and therefore appreciating the degree to which Booth and Rowntree were themselves perceiving the institutions of family and neighborhood as dynamic elements in the shaping of social structure.

As Abrams has pointed out, neither Booth nor Rowntree was particularly comfortable with the language or technique of sociological synthesis. Yet "the shift of attention from the individuals to the family, . . . the meticulous analysis of household budgets," reflecting the direct and acknowledged influence of the French sociologist LePlay, show them capable of sociological perceptions denied someone like Barnett. Rowntree's success in conceptualizing poverty in relation to a social system and his ability to integrate case studies "with the influences of the ecological and economic setting of rural work" declare the importance of intermediate institutions and their relationship to structure in a way that directly challenged Toynbee Hall's understanding of social organization and the mechanisms of social change.[57]

A Toynbeeite's concern with "ought" rather than "is" kept him as well from a willing acceptance of the fact of man's irrationality. He grounded his understanding of human change upon the idea of rational man's freedom to transcend his immediate form to realize his best self. When, therefore, social scientists began to insist upon the need to study men and women as they are—as a psychologist, not a philosopher, would study him—they were charting what was to him at best a diversion. E. J. Urwick, for example, while prepared as a sociologist to acknowledge the power of the irrational and its manifestations as social habit and tradition, could not disguise his impatience in his writings with the manner in which they served to block social advance. "A progressive society," he declared in *A Philosophy of Social Progress*, "is one whose mind is more than tradition—ready to criticize and overhaul all social habits. . . . The distinction between habitual, customary, traditional ideas and feelings, and systematic thought and purpose, is the clue to the distinction between social tradition, or the social mind in its earlier form, and social thought, or the social mind in its later form."[58]

Psychologists argued, however, that it was not so simple to distinguish earlier from later forms and that exhortations to leave the earlier behind implied a foolish unwillingness to examine thoroughly the patterns of irrationality whose persistence in fact made the exhortation ultimately pointless. Such was the position of the political scientist Graham Wallas, who, as his biographer has written, believed that "the times demanded not still more idealism, but less."[59] Wallas wished to study human nature in order to achieve a science of politics that accommodated to the instinctive social behavior of men and women as they were. He put forward this view in an address in 1906:

> Unless he is prepared to study undismayed the nature of man as evolution has for the moment left it, the reformer who is also a politician will find his life one of constant and cruel disillusion. Even if, like Disraeli, he is against Darwin and on the side of the angels, he may learn, against his will, that his efforts to check the brutalities of Chinese indentured labour are only successful when they are backed by the instinctive hatred of the Western European man for the Mongolian racial type. He may recognize in the shouting crowd who applaud his election the same instinct which shocked him at a great football match. He may realize with disgust, but with understanding, the professional skill by which his agent and the agent on the other side work up the driving force of a great political contest, by playing on those factors in human nature which he most desires to forget.[60]

Wallas argued that it was foolish to be disappointed as settlement workers frequently were when men and women who had proved themselves rational as individuals managed to react in less than rational ways as members of their community. Group behavior was part of that intermediate ground which Toynbee Hall tended to ignore. Scientific study of the social phenomenon of group action would help men and women understand that the citizens of modern England acted as they did not because "'individually' they are thoughtful and temperate and 'collectively' blind and ferocious," but because "they are human beings, whose intellectual and emotional nature was evolved in contact with the restricted environment of the primitive world, and who have not yet learnt, if they ever will, either to educate . . . their faculties to fit their environment, or to change their environment so as to fit their faculties."[61] Though he devoted his efforts to an analysis of the irrational, Wallas by no means advocated its passive acceptance. Education, one of his major concerns, could temper irrationality, and must be made to do so. He was prepared to admit the power of an ideal—"the persistent preaching of some new and higher life"—to effect important change.[62] Like Hobhouse, however, he believed that the idealists' continued willingness to confuse what *ought* to be with what *is,* meant that their methods were impractical, their goals unrealistic, and their initial optimism misleading and therefore ultimately dangerous.

The challenge of social scientists such as Hobhouse and Wallas to the ethos of Toynbee Hall was fundamentally an intellectual one, demanding a thorough and difficult recasting of basic ways of perceiving the relationship between man and society, and a potentially painful rethinking of the purposes of social thought. It was an academic challenge, and one which, in that sense, corresponded to the campaign Mark Pattison had mounted against what he saw as a Jowett-inspired impulse to translate half-digested philosophy into immediate, ill-directed activity. The compulsion to be up and doing, Pattison had charged, too often masked a young man's unwillingness to think clearly and deeply about what it was he did and why he did it.

As social scientists argued the future direction of their profession in the early twentieth century, their disagreements echoed the divisions of that earlier debate. Urwick, not only heir to the tenets of Oxford but committed as well to the policies of ameliorationist "doing" that characterized the activity of Toynbee Hall, was the first director of the Department of Social Science and Administration, established at the London School of Economics in 1912. Urwick's definition of sociology as empirical rather than theoretical, as an applied rather than a pure discipline, was reflected in the department's title—the inclusion of the word *administration*—and its curriculum, grounded in analysis of statistics and governmental reports and emphasizing their direct applicability to the solution of social problems. The program suited men and women who possessed an intellectual heritage similar to Urwick's. A course in applied sociology, focusing upon practice at the expense of structure and theory, allowed students to learn a craft without the necessity of rethinking their fundamental assumptions.

Hobhouse, also on the LSE faculty, continued to argue against the tendency, promoting a curriculum that included courses on subjects such as the forms of family and social structure and the development of social control.[63] But enthusiasm for sociology defined and articulated in theoretical terms was a long time coming in England. A recent study has argued that Hobhouse was himself much to blame. He continued to espouse a Victorian evolutionary meliorism that eventually proved intellectually sterile, professing a "seductive biological model that promised approaching social harmony," at a time when society was strained by social conflict. Idealists preached social harmony as a goal. To the extent that Hobhouse described it as a fact, he was guilty of an even greater degree of wishful hypothesizing than were the idealists he criticized.

Philip Abrams suggests another reason for the failure of sociology as an academic discipline: that the nation's growing commitment to centralization was luring potential scholars away from the academy and into government offices. It is certainly true that a great many potential academic sociologists emerged from Oxford antithetical to the tenets of theoretical social science. Government service as social reformers allowed them to escape rethinking. Instead, they could apply a discipline to the solution of urgent national problems and thus avoid confronting and resolving the challenge which social science represented.[64]

Figure 1. Samuel A. Barnett
and Henrietta R. Barnett.

Figure 2. Toynbee Hall.

Figure 3. Toynbee Hall.

Figure 4. Toynbee Hall.

Figure 5. An evening concert, Toynbee Hall.

The Toynbee Record.

Vol. VI.—No. 2. NOVEMBER, 1893. One Penny.

Calendar.

1...W ...8.0 Elizabethan Literary Society: " Measure for Measure " by Mr. Wm. Poel.

2...Th...8.0 Smoking Conference: Mr. Percy W. Bunting on ''The Limits of Parliamentary Power."

2...Th...8.0 Toynbee Shakespeare Society: Reading of " The Comedy of Errors," with Notes, by Mr. J. M. Dent.

3...F ...8.0 Mr. Robin Allen, Lecture on " Wordsworth."

4...S ...8.0 Saturday Popular Lectures: W. M. Conway, M.A., F.R.G.S., " Climbing in the Himalayas."

4...S ...3.0 Students' Union ; Visit to the National Portrait Gallery, Bethnal Green Museum.

4...S ...7.30 Pupil Teachers' Debate.

5...S ...8.30 Sunday Evening Lecture: Miss Townsend, " Matthew Arnold."

6...M ...8.0 Toynbee Natural History Society: Paper by Mr. A. J. Chitty on " Beetles."

6...M ...8.0 First Meeting of Reading Party : " The Elements of Political Economy," F. F. Liddell, M.A.

7...T ... St. Jude's Congregational Party

7...T ...8.0 Party to Lower Chapman Street Boys.

7..T ...8.0 A. O. F. Court Garibaldi.

8...W ...8.0 Library Readers' Union : Paper by Mr. C. T. Folkard, on " State Interference with the Hours of Labour."

9...Th...8.0 Smoking Conference.

10...F ...8.0 Mr. Robin Allen : Lecture on " Hood."

11...S ...8.0 Saturday Popular Lecture : Col. Sir Colin Scott Moncrieff.

11...S ...8.0 East London Antiquarian Society: Excursion to St. Botolph, Aldgate.

11...S ... Students' Union: Visit to South Kensington Museum.

12...S ...8.30 Sunday Evening Lecture : Rev. Philip Wicksteed, " Wordsworth."

13...M ...8.0 Toynbee Literary Association : R. G. Tatton, M.A., on " The Late Master of Balliol—Benjamin Jowett."

14...T ...8.0 Meeting of Toynbee Camera Club.

15...W ...5.0 Sanitary Aid Committee.

16...Th...8.0 Smoking Conference.

16...Th...7.45 Toynbee Travellers' Club: Miss Hughes on " Ancient Athens : the Acropolis and Lower City."

17...F ...8.0 Mr. Robin Allen : Lecture on " Rossetti."

18...S ...8.0 Saturday Popular Lecture : Canon Scott-Holland.

18..S ...8.0 Students' Union Conversazione (Members of Science Classes).

19...S ...8.30 Sunday Evening Lecture.

22...W ...8.0 Library Readers' Union : Mr. George Turner, on " Emerson."

23...Th...8.0 Smoking Conference.

25...S ...8.0 Saturday Popular Lecture.

25...S ... Students' Union : Visit to the Parkes Museum.

26...S ... Sunday Evening Lecture : T. S. Peppin on " Marlowe."

27...M ... Toynbee Philosophical Society : Miss M. S. Gilliland on " Prof. James' Theory of the Self."

27...M ... East London Antiquarian Society : Mr. H. S. Blakeman, " With the Canterbury Pilgrims, April 17th, 1388."

28...T ...7.45 Toynbee Travellers' Club : Miss Jane Harrison on " Greek Vases."

28...T ...8.0 Toynbee Economic Club : Mr. C. J. Dawson on " The Employment of School Children."

30...Th...8.0 Smoking Conference.

Figure 6. Toynbee Record calendar, November 1893.

TOYNBEE HALL, 28, COMMERCIAL ST., E.

UNIVERSITIES SETTLEMENTS ASSOCIATION.

Warden: The Rev. CANON BARNETT, M.A.
Chairman of the Council. VISCOUNT PEEL.
Secretary to the Council: Mr. ERNEST AVES, M.A.
Hon. Treasurer: Mr. P. M. MARTINEAU.
Secretary: Miss COKER.

Toynbee Hall Education Committee — *Hon. Secs.,* Mr. J. E. Monk. and Mr. T. H. Nunn

Clerk: Mr. D. J. Chubb. *Registrar:* Mr. W. Bruce.

Toynbee Hall Entertainment Committee. *Hon. Sec.,* Mr. E. L. Matthews, B.A.
Evening Classes for Men ... ... *Hon. Sec.,* Mr. P Duncan, B.A.
Afternoon Continuation Classes for Girls. *Hon. Sec.,* Miss Townsend.
Elizabethan Literary Society ... *Hon. Sec.,* Mr. J. E. Baker.
Toynbee Shakespeare Society ... *Hon. Sec.,* Mr. E. J. Martin.
Toynbee Literary Association ... *Hon. Sec.,* Mr H. F. Wyatt, B.A.
Toynbee Antiquarian Society ... *Hon. Sec.,* Miss Mason.
Toynbee Natural History Society ... *Hon. Sec.,* Mr. R. Paulson.
Adam Smith Club ... ... *Hon. Sec.,* Mr. J. Lovegrove.
Toynbee Economic Club ... ... *Hon. Sec.,* Mr. H.W. Pyddoke, M.A.
Toynbee Library Readers' Union ... *Hon. Sec.,* Mr. D. I. Freedman, B.A.
Toynbee Travellers' Club ... ... *Hon. Secs.,* Mr. Bolton King, M.A. and Mr. F. V. Turpin.
Free Students' Library ... ... *Librarian,* Mr. C. F. Newcombe.
Students' Union ... ... *Hon. Secs.,* Miss Wild and Mr. J. Spencer Hill, B.A.
Old Students' Association .. ... *Hon. Secs.,* Miss Ina Hickling and Mr. T. S. Widdowson.
Toynbee Orchestral Union ... *Hon. Sec.,* Mr. T. S. Widdowson.
Toynbee Nursing Guild ... ... *Hon. Sec.,* Miss M. M Wills.
Leonardo Sketching Club ... ... *Hon. Sec.,* Mr. S. Hancock.
Students' Residences at Wadham and Balliol Houses ... ... *Censor of Studies,* Mr. C. Jackson, M.A.
Ambulance Brigade .. .. *Hon. Sec.,* Mr. H. L. Jones.
Poplar Economic Club ... ... *Hon. Sec.,* Mr. W. G. Martley.
Pupil Teachers' Scholarship Committee ... ... *Hon. Sec.,* Mr. T. S. Widdowson.
Pupil Teachers' Association: Girls — Division I.—Members' Branch — Division II.—Hon. Members' do. — *President,* Mrs. Barnett. *Hon. Secs.,* Miss Townsend, and Mrs. R. Hepburn.
Pupil Teachers' Debating Society: Boys' Division ... ... — *Hon. Secs.,* Mr. F. Prichard and Mr. E. B. Sargant, M.A. *Registrar,* Mr. P. Abbott.
Argonauts Rowing Club *(for Teachers)* *Hon. Sec.,* Mr. S. Dickinson.
Women's Co-operative Guild ... *Hon. Sec.,* Mrs. Rye.
Court Garibaldi, A.O.F. ... ... *Treasurer,* Mr. T. J. Hull. *Secretary,* Mr. R. Stoneley.
United Order of the Total Abstinent Sons of the Phœnix... ... ... *Gen. Secs.,* Messrs. T. Wilson (Adults) T. V. Mills (Juveniles).
Lolesworth Club (34, Commercial-st.) *(For Men and Women).* *Hon. Secs.,* Mr. E. J. Picking and Mr. R. W. Kittle.
Sydney Club .. *For particulars. apply to* Mr. R. W. B. Buckland.
Old Rutlanders' Club ... „ „ Mr. R. W. B. Buckland.
Old Northeyites' Club... „ „ Mr. Cyril Jackson.
Dalgleish Street School Club „ „ Mr. A. H. Grenfell.
Dempsey Street School Club „ „ Mr. F. H. Cobb.
Whittington Club ... „ „ Mr. Ernest Morley.
Whittington Chambers „ „ Mr. W. Tourell.
Whitechapel Sanitary Aid Committee *Hon. Sec.,* Mr. A. J. Ball.
Cadets: St. George's-in-the-East Cpy. 1st Cadet Battalion The Queen's... Mr. H. W. Nevinson, Captain.
Whitechapel Fine Art Exhibition ... *Hon. Sec.,,* Mr. H. Kemp-Welch.
Co-operative Education Committee — *Hon. Secs.,* Mr. Ernest Aves, M.A., and Mr. E. L. Matthews, B.A.

Figure 7. Toynbee Hall committees, clubs, and associations, October 1896.

TOYNBEE HALL,

28, COMMERCIAL STREET,

WHITECHAPEL, E.

University Extension Lectures on LABOUR QUESTIONS.

"Labour and the Law."

W. H. BEVERIDGE. M.A., B.C.L.

Tuesdays at 8 p.m., beginning Oct. 10th.

1. The Labour Contract.
2. State Regulation in the Past.
3. The Claim to Combine.
4. The Claim to Combine (*cont.*)
5. The Claim to Personal Safety.
6. The Claim to Compensation.
7. The Claim to Live.
8. The Claim to Live and the Claim to Work.
9. The Interests of the community and Compulsory Arbitration.
10. The State and Labour.

"Social Aspects of Industry."

R. H. TAWNEY, B.A.

Fridays at 8 p.m., beginning Oct. 13th.

1. Before the Factory.
2. The Factory System: Division of Labour.
3. The Factory System: Machinery.
4. The Factory System: Concentration of Capital.
5. Trade Unionism.
6. The Factory Acts.
7. Profit Sharing.
8. Home Industries.
9. The Factory and the Citizen.
10. The Factory and the Citizen (*cont.*).

FEE for the two courses (20 lectures) 1s. Inclusive Fee for these two courses and a course on "CITIZENSHIP," by Graham Wallas, on Fridays, beginning January (30 lectures altogether) 1s. 6d

The first lecture of each course may be attended without fee. Each lecture will be followed by a discussion class.

PRELIMINARY MEETING, FRIDAY, OCTOBER 6,

AT 8 PM

Mr. GRAHAM WALLAS will deliver an address on "Francis Place, the liberator of Trade Unionism from the Combination Laws."

The curriculum

Figure 8. Advertisement for Lectures on Labour Questions by W. H. Beveridge and R. H. Tawney.

5

TOYNBEE HALL AND THE NEW CENTURY

It is useless to rail at the times," Samuel Barnett wrote his brother in the fall of 1901. "I daresay they are in labour with a new birth, but it is hard to know death throes from birth throes."[1] Like so many upper-middle-class social critics and reformers, Barnett remained confused by the new century, often alarmed, sometimes exhilarated. Events in the years after 1900 did little to assuage his protracted anxieties about the dangers inherent in the democratic temperament. Writing in the *Saturday Review* of the unruly celebrations that marked the end of the Boer War in 1902, Barnett deplored "the rough boisterousness of drunkenness" and "rude demonstrations of high spirits" that one had come to expect from the residuum but that now, unhappily, appeared to mark the behavior of the working class as a whole. "The effect on the observer is that he is looking on at an immense accession of the 'respectable' to the standards of vulgar life." What was to Barnett particularly discouraging was his sense that this decline might well be indirectly attributable to that one reform upon which he and fellow workers had set such store to improve standards of conduct: the introduction of compulsory state education. "Manners have deteriorated and there is only too much reason to ascribe the deterioration to a flashy unnutritious kind of teaching which has fostered the conceit of the half-educated prig, . . . the superficial, thin, perky, insolent creature whose exploits of last Monday we are told are the expression of English feeling at the termination of the war."[2]

Like Masterman, Barnett grew increasingly fearful of the new town breed. He believed, as he always had, that its infecting presence was in large measure the result of the indifference of the rich. Unabashed indulgence.in needless luxury, as disturbing a phenomenon of the new age as was rampaging vulgarity, encouraged the always present inclination of the privileged to turn their backs on social duty. "Luxury," Barnett argued in a 1911 lecture, "is the enemy of freedom; . . . it lowers the capacity of its own followers and clouds the capacity of all whom its glory dazzles."[3] Though he took occasional encouragement from particular events—welcoming, for example, "the rising sun" of the Labour party[4]—Barnett found the direction and pace of English life and thought after 1900 reinforcing the fears and doubts that had helped to determine his attitudes and outlook in the last quarter of the nineteenth century.

Of the three major challenges to the Toynbee ethos, that which insisted upon centralization and a greater role for the state was the one to which Barnett was able to respond most positively. The Barnetts were well acquainted with the Webbs and their work. And though their goals were not the same—an ideal state on the one hand, an efficient state on the other—the means to their differing ends often coincided. Beatrice Webb included the Barnetts at dinner parties designed to win converts to her Poor Law reform schemes and sent Barnett a draft of her report. Barnett in turn found his earlier commitment to practicable socialism leading him progressively toward support for the idea of a national minimum. He voiced increasingly enthusiastic adherence to specific state-managed programs enacted by both Conservative and Liberal governments after 1900.

As one of the nation's most highly regarded authorities on the subject of poverty, its causes and remedies, Barnett played an active part in the protracted public debate on Poor Law reform that took place with the appointment of the commission in 1905 and that increased in interest following the publication of majority and minority reports four years later. He generally favored the schemes propounded by the Webbs. He approved of their proposal to abolish local boards of guardians, thereby placing the management of poverty at a farther remove from the democratic process. "The same . . . body which is responsible for the health, for the education, and for the industrial fitness of some members of the community should be responsible in like manner for all the members, whatever their position."[5]

Barnett was prepared to advocate a series of measures in concert with the reformed administration for poor relief which would establish something like a decent minimum for all members of the national community.

He continued to urge the establishment of farm colonies as a means of combating unemployment. And he defended unemployment insurance and old-age pensions against the charge, still leveled at them by upholders of Charity Organisation Society dogma, that they would encourage thriftlessness. Barnett argued, as other centralizers were arguing, for larger, more disinterested units of organization and control, despite the fact that reform of this sort tended to undermine the one-by-one localism he still espoused.

Support for the Webbs' recommendation that local boards of guardians be abolished reflected this desire to move decision making from the hands of special interests, whether the short-sighted parsimony of shopkeepers or the unreasonable profligacy of the unemployed, and into the hands of officials who could be expected to implement "a more scientific expenditure of the rates."[6] In an article drafted in 1900 urging the abolition of locally elected school boards, Barnett attacked the parochialism and special pleading that he maintained had become more and more characteristic of board deliberations and implementations, very much as Sidney Webb was to do at the time of the passage of the Education Bill two years later. Barnett supported the placing of education (as well as poor relief) in the hands of county councils. "A vote now taken on such a body . . . on the question whether secondary education should be brought within everyone's reach would get, I believe, fairer discussion than on the School Board where many members would think at once how the proposal would affect the interest in which he was concerned."[7] Here again, as so often in the past, was a plea for disinterested decision making.

Although Barnett continued to believe that the most effective education resulted from one-by-one connection, he sympathized with the increasingly popular notion of a less than personal state as moral instructor. "Laws and their administration," Barnett wrote in 1911, could be influential either in securing or in hindering morality. The task of government, therefore, "included the consideration of how far laws are helpful or prejudicial to industry, rectitude, and honesty, and how far a policy, by lowering the national ideal, may introduce strife and jealousy."[8] Reviewing the reports of the Poor Law Commission, he declared that their recommendations needed to be measured against questions that reflected the roots of his support for state assistance to the poor: "Do they make it possible to relieve needs without demoralizing character?" Do they respond, that is, to concern for right behavior? "Do they stimulate energy without raising the devil in human nature?" Do they respond, as well, to a concern for social order?[9] Barnett praised both reports for their determination "to elaborate a system founded on the principle that the method of relief must always be directed to the *restoration of the individual*" and for their recognition that relief must be subordinated to treatment.[10]

Authoritarian impulses continued to persuade Barnett that the state might have to require a minimum standard of behavior from men and women who persistently refused to undertake their responsibilities. There was an increasing shrillness to his language as he campaigned for the subjugation by the state of this dangerous "residuum". These were people who, by their refusal to cooperate in the interests of community, had proved themselves incapable of self-respect and therefore unworthy of programs designed to promote that all-important social virtue. These were the social incorrigibles who had been offered a chance and had refused it. An unrepentant and unregenerate pauper, Barnett declared,

> feels himself to be ill-treated, so he is always discontented; he thinks every man's hand is against him, so he is against every man. The sudden death of all confirmed paupers—it is a terrible thing to say of men and women—would be a great economic gain and hardly a social loss. Paupers are not free men nor desirous to be free men, and their presence is a blot on a Nation called to establish freedom.[11]

In a 1903 article, Barnett labeled these "the unemployables." Without specifying their number, he argued that it was large enough to represent a threat to social health with which the state would have to deal. "They are the means by which contagion—moral and physical—most rapidly spreads." Only the state had the power to segregate this class, and thus prevent general infection. Armed with a magistrate's order, officials should be empowered to commit "wilful vagrants and stubborn idlers" to "schools of restraint." Though Barnett wrote that inmates would receive "not punishment but the training to fit them for work," his discussion leaves little doubt that he expected their incarceration would be a lengthy one and the chances of their rehabilitation small.[12]

Barnett's hopes encompassed the centralizer's goal of efficiency while transcending it. "National efficiency is what we all desire," he wrote his brother, "but how is it possible till individuals have some motive for efficiency which will inspire and guide the conduct of each." Several years later he wrote: "There is plenty of sense but no passion. . . . Figures and passion must go together." Deprived of vision, the centralizer would never succeed in reaching a goal worthy of his efforts and the nation's real interests. Barnett wrote critically of "the modern reformer": he "has no illusions. He is not on his way to a promised land, and so his doings in the desert will not fit himself or his nation for a higher calling than that of enjoying milk and honey."[13] Once on the path toward a worthy goal himself, however, the reformer need feel no compunction about using the state to compel others to march behind him toward the promised land of ideal community.

An increasing willingness to see the state respond to the needs of its individual members encouraged Barnett to continue calling himself a practicable socialist. Yet both his beliefs and personality kept him apart from the radical Christian Socialism of the early twentieth century. Practicable socialism extended no further than centralization and increased taxes. The socialism professed by the Church Socialist League, however, implied far more in the way of economic and social reordering than Barnett was contemplating.

Nor could Barnett sympathize to any degree with the sort of radical immanentism that resulted in the dramatic anti-Establishment confrontations characteristic of the public careers of Christian Socialists such as Stewart Headlam and Conrad Noel. Barnett's personality encouraged him to prefer permeation to confrontation. He moved among important people in a way that advanced Christian Socialists considered suspect; he was of the world as well as in it to a degree most of them were not and did not want to be. His persistently cautious appraisal of the abilities of the urban poor and his consequent pessimism as to their potential as citizens in a democracy reinforced his belief in the necessity of a disinterested ruling class—all this at odds with Christian Socialism's professed desire to share rather than assume responsibility. The premium Barnett continued to put upon disinterestedness marked his separation as well from the immanentism of those who insisted that the true measures of a necessarily zealous Christian commitment were a passionate, and immediate, concern for the plight of the poor and a readiness to break the rules of scientific charity to come to the aid of a fellow human being.

He was no zealot. Charles Gore's declaration on behalf of intolerance would have seemed at best misguided, at worst perverse, to a man like Barnett, who had made a conscious decision to free Toynbee Hall from what he believed to be the debilitating confines of Anglican denominationalism. Writing to his brother at the beginning of Toynbee's fall season of activities in 1899, he remarked on the degree to which changing attitudes had made that decision of his appear old fashioned. "It is curious how thought has changed. . . . When we started, 'undenominational' was a popular word. Now one wants a word to express the inclusion of many striving denominations." Toynbee Hall, he concluded, was no longer undenominational, but rather "multi-denominational"; and he was not particularly happy to see the change.[14] Barnett was no more sympathetic to the insistent denominational demands of the Church of England than he was to those of other churches. Accustomed to viewing the Church as an institutional impediment to his goals, he would find it difficult if not impossible to share the Christian Socialist's insistence that it be understood as a necessary spiritual engine for social regeneration.

Barnett met the challenges implied in the developing discipline of sociology by ignoring them. To have responded to its implications with some sort of closely argued defense of his own beliefs and goals would have required him to compose a philosophical treatise beyond his capabilities and apart from his concerns. He was a doer, and his continued commitment to doing was an indirect response of sorts to sociologists such as Hobhouse who insisted that sociology concern itself with theory as well as with analysis to aid social amelioration. As we have noted, Toynbee Hall began to redirect its efforts and to encourage just that sort of analysis at the end of the century. In an article in the October 1904 *Toynbee Record*, Barnett declared the pressing need "for more accurate knowledge of social conditions." Society, he wrote, "needs facts as to children's underfed and ill-fed bodies, facts as to working men's use of their leisure, facts as to infant mortality, as to the necessity for casual employment. . . . Society, in a word, needs the knowledge necessary for scientific treatment by philanthropists and public bodies."[15] To that degree he was prepared to support the sort of surveys Booth, Rowntree, and now others such as E. J. Urwick, the former Toynbee subwarden, were engaged upon. And to that extent, therefore, Barnett was committed to the promotion of social science.

Yet he regretted Booth's lack of some sense of higher purpose. "By faithful obedience to his own right he is higher than most men. If his own right could be transfused by, say, Christ's spirit, how high he would be."[16] He feared, in other words, that Booth's obsession with what *was* would inhibit the usefulness of his inquiry as an indicator of what *ought* to be. Hence when the volumes of Booth's survey began to appear, Barnett's appraisal was based upon his perception of the extent to which they would result in social betterment, not upon an appreciation of their contribution to the methodology of social investigation and analysis. Writing in response to a proposal in 1903 for a survey of Sheffield, Barnett remarked that "the gain of Booth's and Rowntree's work has been . . . a certain modification of public opinion. The facts, disputed or not, are preparing the public mind for reforms and for efforts. Perhaps this is the best result of any work." He was less convinced of the worth of surveys by lesser-known investigators, his wife reports, because the youth and obscurity of their authors would keep them from public notice, thereby decreasing their potential as instruments for "social betterment," whatever their worth as scientific investigations.[17]

Barnett's general willingness to ignore the challenge of sociological theory is by no means surprising. He was a man in his late fifties and early sixties, whose life's work had been the expression of a mind formed by the tenets of men like Arnold, Green, and Toynbee. His interest in irrationality and habit was to minimize the former and alter the latter. He could not be "objective" as a social scientist was prepared to be objective, since his goal was not analysis but social progress toward an ideal. Insofar as the analysis of others assisted in that progress, he was prepared to encourage it. But to treat it as an end in itself was to subvert rather than to assist the goal Barnett had set both for himself and for his country.

Despite the challenges mounted by the new century to the basic tenets of the Toynbee ethos, and despite his own willingness to countenance further centralization, Barnett's articles in the years before his death in 1913 continued to reflect his determined adherence to the set of beliefs that had inspired his original programs for reform in East London. He remained convinced that programs of social amelioration, whether public or private, were best understood as gifts from rich to poor. "The gift without the giver is bare," he wrote in a 1912 article on the virtues of "up-to-date" charity. "When the giver's thought makes itself felt, the gift is enriched."[18] The exercise of personal example, set before the needy recipient by a sensitive and persuasive giver, was the most valuable gift a reformer could give.

Barnett's unwillingness to forego the doctrine of one by one compelled him to continue a persistent enemy of class, or of any institution that he believed might impede individual connection between rich and poor. He never ceased to lament "the absence of that inspiration which creates a feeling of common membership" that kept Edwardian England apart.[19] The founding of Hampstead Garden Suburb in 1908, a project initiated and sustained in its first years by Henrietta Barnett, was another attempt, made in the light of the Toynbee Hall experience, to provide a setting that would encourage communality through neighborly connection. Toynbee Hall, Henrietta subsequently wrote, "acting as the meeting place of rich and poor, old and young, learned and ignorant, had created transfiguring friendships. So how much more would be possible when the artificial machinery to effect introductions could be saved, and relationships be naturally born of neighbourliness." With the lowest rent set at 11*s*. 6*d*. per week, only the most steadily employed and highly paid working-class families could afford housing in Hampstead Garden Suburb, not to mention the daily fares to and from work. Nevertheless, Henrietta Barnett insisted that the suburb had succeeded during its first years not only in bringing all classes together but in breaking down the barriers separating them.

> No sort of difficulty has arisen, and the often expressed fears have proved groundless. Indeed, the result of the admixture of all classes has been a kindlier feeling and a richer sympathy, as people of varied experiences, different educational standards, and unequal incomes feel themselves drawn together in the enjoyment of good music, in the discussion of social problems, in the preparation by their children of such a summer's day festival as "The Masque of Fairthorpe," or to enjoy the unaffected pleasure of the public spaces and wall-less gardens.[20]

The suburb, according to Mrs. Barnett, had as its aim "the development of human understanding, whereby spiritual forces are given freedom."[21] In fact, it was in conception an earthly paradise in celebration of the hopes and goals that the Barnetts had espoused over the past quarter-century. Managed by a board of directors whose first chairman was Lord

Crewe, the suburb boasted an institute, an art scholar, a music scholar, "a residential club-house for working ladies," family accommodation for workhouse children, and an assortment of convalescent and retirement homes, as well as a variety of houses and flats. Its location adjacent to Hampstead Heath imparted the sort of healthy countrified air congenial to spirits never fully reconciled to urban existence. No noisy streets, no corner parks, no music halls—no working-class culture. Instead, good music, discussion, and "The Masque of Fairthorpe."

Hampstead Garden Suburb thus afforded a second chance to do what Toynbee Hall had not succeeded in doing: to impose one particular culture upon a community. Consider, Henrietta Barnett wrote, the didactic value of gardening:

> father working, mother watching, children helping, the land yielding with that generosity which under any climate seems to follow spade labour and personal interest. The pennies would not be needed for "sweeties" as the "goosgogs" [gooseberries] are enjoyed; the pickles will give place to the lettuces; the hastily obtained indigestible "relish" to the "vegetables we growed," and which is worth more than all the material advantages, the family will be able to take its pleasures together—the pleasure of preparing for, and tending, watching, hoping and wondering about "the kindly fruits of the earth" which they will enjoy and deserve to enjoy "in due season."[22]

Barnett remained as determined as his wife to preach the remaking of working-class culture to accord with his image of what ought to be. To protect future generations from low-mindedness, in their own interest and that of the community, was the task of that dedicated, disinterested elite in which Barnett continued to put his faith. The birth and rapid growth of the Labour party fed his anxieties about the incapacity of an uneducated working class to govern intelligently. A government in the hands of the Labour party, he predicted, would, despite an earnest faith in its own purpose, "be 'brutal' in its disregard of all issues it did not understand." Today's worker—tomorrow's Labour party supporter—possessed "less superstition but also less idealism" than his Victorian counterpart. "He is a closer prisoner of his senses, and is inclined to mock at offers of knowledge which will give him nothing more to taste, to touch, or to see. But without this knowledge, he can neither satisfy himself nor add strength to the nation."[23] Hence the continuing need for disinterested authority. "We would give to everyone the high thing which he does not want," Barnett proclaimed in his introduction to *Towards Social Reform* in 1909.[24] His declaration then was a measure of how little his own vision had altered during his forty years as a reformer.

Debate continued during the early years of the new century concerning the proper purposes of settlement work—whether, indeed, settlements any longer had a legitimate purpose of any sort. E. J. Urwick, midway through his term as subwarden of the hall, in 1902 wrote a dispassionate and discouraging assessment of what the "Settlement Ideal" had come to represent. Like Barnett himself, Urwick recognized that to many people a settlement house meant nothing more than organized doing by short term, temporarily committed residents within a depressed urban community. The tendency to trust to machinery to produce the effect of accomplishment was, Urwick wrote, the natural result of a compulsion to prove to subscribers that they had invested contributions wisely and of the need to put transient residents to work as quickly as possible. The easiest way to make use of "the raw material of newcomers," Urwick observed, was to set them to work as "machine hands . . . in an established organisation of some sort devoted to a definite end, and existing independently of the irregular few of human agents who have to try to give it life."

Yet the essence of the ideal, Urwick continued, was "undifferentiated helpfulness"—connection by another name—"entering into natural relations with the people of all kinds around us" for the purposes of "larger sympathy" and "mutual understanding." Settlements, "founded as a protest against reform by machinery, . . . have themselves become centres of machinery, and the machines are running away with the inventors. As settlers, we too are becoming institutionalized, and our doings show the same taint." Urwick was particularly critical of the degree to which settlements isolated residents from the very people they had hoped to know better. "An hotel has not neighbours, nor has a palace." Residents living at Toynbee Hall for no more than six months or a year were little different in Urwick's opinion from lodgers at a comfortable inn.[25]

Urwick's own solution was to do as other dissatisfied residents had done before him: to leave the hall—in his case, with three others for a flat in Limehouse. His departure highlights Barnett's increasing difficulty in attracting and keeping the young recruits who, a generation previously, had been inspired by the goals of community and connection. It was progressively difficult to find the dedicated self-sacrificing university man, tutored in idealism by Green or Toynbee to understand life's purpose, and determined, like another Robert Elsmere, to pursue that purpose. Volunteers there were, but without the depth or intelligence of old. Or so it seemed to Barnett, as he journeyed up to Oxford and Cambridge to seek residents. He placed the blame for the decline of a proper spirit on the public schools and the universities, which failed to turn philistine boys into high-minded young men. Writing to his brother in 1900, he complained that universities were no more than "expensive schools with a schoolboy's ideal." He understood the power of public-school attitudes and ideals to shape life at Oxford and Cambridge. Thomas Arnold's professed goals had inspired Green not only as a Rugby schoolboy but also as a Balliol undergraduate. Now a new credo, grounded in philistine athleticism, appeared to have replaced that of godliness and good learning. Barnett ridiculed the notion that football was a test of character. "Schools or universities ought to develop a character which would defy the tyranny of games. . . . The public school boy rules the colleges and the dons," he complained in a letter from Oxford. "He is the 'finest product of the times' and because he is so strong looks down on other boys. . . . There is no one to check this spirit. Jowett who was in with the great could do so, but no one has succeeded him."[26] (Caird, as devoted to what Barnett considered the proper ideals as Jowett, was master of Balliol still, but apparently not sufficiently "in with the great.")

Barnett may well have been correct. The Balliol mode was the expression of a faith, but it was undoubtedly a fashion as well. So long as apologists like Green, Toynbee, and Jowett remained to set the style, many young undergraduates would find it a compelling one. It had never been the only style, though. Once the great worthies had departed the scene, other fashions—athleticism, aestheticism—would catch the undergraduate fancy. Bright, serious-minded students, meanwhile, though inspired by such as Caird or Sidney Ball, would be likely to translate that inspiration into a dedication to the cause of reformist centralization. Like most young men, they would be inclined to reject solutions that had inspired their immediate predecessors, which, perhaps for that very reason, appeared now as outmoded and therefore untrustworthy. Barnett continued to proselytize. But "the experience is so old and so new," he wrote his brother. "The men look as they did twenty years ago and yet the world is another world." Oxford had changed; its undergraduates had changed; the world into which Barnett was inviting them was changing. And the "early ideal," Urwick declared, was no longer of much use. "The texts are worn too threadbare to cover any more sermons; the phrases which inspired the Settlement movement twenty years ago will not serve our purpose today."[27]

As evidence of decline, Urwick and other critics cited the fact that the educational programs that had been the focus of the hall's earlier attempts at individual connection and improvement now no longer attracted members as they had in past years. Barnett's letters to his brother in 1901 and 1902 are a litany of decline: "The lectures are badly taken up and I fear this is our last year of the University Extension Service"; "It seems impossible to get people to lectures. We have twenty-two when we used to have a hundred"; "Education work is failing and failing."[28] The *Record* noted in 1902 that the lack of interest in university extension courses could be explained in part by the increased number of School Board evening classes, an increase for which the hall had campaigned. "But the result is far from satisfactory. The more popular education progresses the more should the need be felt for advanced education."[29]

That feeling was to have been inculcated by residents eager to assist Whitechapel working-class men and women in their pursuit of better selves. But after 1900 Whitechapel provided relatively few participants in Toynbee Hall's programs. By 1905, of the 644 members of Toynbee clubs and societies, only 25 were residents of Whitechapel. Sixty-seven were from the borough of Stepney; 261 from some part of north-east London; 449 from across the city; and 195 from the suburbs.[30] Wadham House and Balliol House continued to draw their residents from the ranks of salaried white-collar clerks and technicians. Anxious to establish their middle-class credentials, their assertiveness in doing so may have been one reason why workingmen were having less to do with the hall, and why, in turn, the hall was becoming each year an ever more thoroughly middle-class institution.

William Beveridge, a resident from 1903 to 1906, made a wry note of the social pretensions of the Balliol House residents in a letter to his mother. "It was originally hoped that the artisan might come there, but as a matter of fact the artisan is conspicuous by his absence and the men are most superior and educated people—second-class Home Civilians, electrical engineers, elementary and secondary school masters, etc.—all of whom one addresses as Esq.!"[31] By 1913 Balliol House had closed its doors, victim, according to one former resident, of "additional facilities offered by the railways in travelling to and from the suburbs and the increase of similar houses in other and more attractive parts of London."[32] Wadham House and Balliol House had provided comfortable and relatively inexpensive living quarters for clerks and school teachers. An appreciation of their convenience, as much as a commitment to the goal of connection, had undoubtedly persuaded men to settle there. Whatever the degree of that commitment, it was apparently not strong enough in most cases to resist the prospect of accommodation in the suburbs or in the "more attractive parts of London."

Determined to assert their middle-classness, these students would have been particularly hard to convince of the virtues of connection. A young graduate of Balliol College, however much he might desire to cross class boundaries for a time, knew full well that he could recross them without difficulty and find himself on familiar upper-middle-class turf once more. A young Balliol House resident clutching desperately at his clerkship and his aitches did not enjoy the luxury of that certainty. If he made use of Toynbee Hall it was to advance himself, and not the cause of community, by means of connection. The more Toynbee Hall manifested this self-directed spirit of lower-middle-class endeavor, and its accompanying determination to keep even the skilled artisan at bay, the less its appeal would be to the working-class men and women of East London.

An atmosphere hostile to notions of community would encourage Toynbee Hall to retreat from the neighborhood into which it had come as a connector. Withdrawal of this sort was facilitated by Barnett's decision to emphasize the hall's role as a center for the work of upper-middle-class social analysts and investigators. The change increased all the more the distance between hall and community, and consequently the lack of interest in, or in some cases the hostility of the neighborhood toward, the settlement. George Lansbury reflected on this with some bitterness in his autobiography:

> The one solid achievement of Toynbee Hall, and the most important result of the mixing policy of the Barnetts, has been the filling up of the bureaucracy of government and administration with men

and women who went to East London full of enthusiasm and zeal for the welfare of the masses, and discovered the advancement of their own interests and the interests of the poor were best served by leaving East London to stew in its own juice while they became members of Parliament, cabinet ministers and civil servants.[33]

Probably the clearest manifestation of the change in the direction of the hall's activities was the prominence given to the deliberations of the Enquirers' Club, founded in 1904 "for purposes of social enquiry and discussion." J. A. Salter, himself a junior civil servant and resident at the time, describes the club's membership as "for the most part young civil servants. We would invite someone of distinction and special knowledge of social problems to be our guest for the evening, and, after an opening exposition (all being comfortably seated in arm-chairs in the drawing-room), submit him to comment and cross-questioning. . . ." Programs in subsequent years included Beatrice Webb on "Methods of Social Investigation," Beveridge and C. S. Loch on Poor Law reform, Urwick on boy labor, and Margaret Macmillan on school clinics. The Enquirers perceived themselves as more than a discussion group. The club began issuing reports in its first year, one on "The Homeless Man" and another on "The Boy in Industry," and continued to do so for several years afterward. By 1910 the Enquirers, with sixty-four members, had prepared a variety of surveys and had examined the problem of London's municipal government, recommending its consolidation into a single administrative community. The *Toynbee Record* printed and supported its conclusions, as well as summarizing investigations of various governmental commissions which bore on the work the club was undertaking.[34]

Soon after Beveridge's arrival at the hall, he was instrumental in organizing a Committee on the Unemployed, which undertook inquiries into the state of employment at the time; the success and failure of various former schemes of relief, including public works, emigration, and labor exchanges; and the drafting of recommendations of its own. In December 1903 the committee resolved to establish a local labor exchange, and to enroll employers as participants.[35] Activities of this sort increased the tendency on the part of residents to consider themselves expert advisors to the community in which they were living. Election campaigns offered them an excellent chance to tell their neighbors what their inquiries had convinced them were the policies and programs most necessary for the general improvement of East London. In the borough council election of 1903, a statement signed by the residents outlined a platform that included more health inspectors, more open spaces, cooperation with the London County Council, and more evening meetings—this last in order to allow *both* professional and workingman representation on a council at present dominated by shopkeepers and publicans. Toynbee had all but surrendered its pretense of not officially endorsing candidates; and its candidates were almost invariably residents from the middle and upper-middle classes. In the 1903 race there were three "connected with Toynbee itself," as the *Record* put it: one a resident of the hall and two residents of Balliol House—all three successfully returned.[36]

Additional opportunities to put expert analysis and recommendations to work for the benefit of the community were afforded by committees such as the Stepney Council of Public Welfare, an organization founded in 1903 by Barnett to coordinate local relief efforts and to propagandize, in the face of COS opposition, for further legislative reform and intervention. Beveridge served as the council's municipal secretary, and under its auspices conducted a survey of Sunday trading laws as they affected the ability of local workers to enjoy a day's vacation from work. Though his report did not result in any immediate reform within the borough, it did contribute to the more general debate on Sunday trading which culminated in the appointment of a Parliamentary Commission on the subject in 1906.[37]

In so doing, it reflected the desire of its author and his fellow analysts at Toynbee Hall to see their work there applied beyond the confines of Whitechapel and Stepney. E. F. Wise, a resident and chairman of the Stepney council's industrial committee, worked in 1906 with fellow residents Clement Attlee and T. E. Harvey to assist a Toynbee associate J. J. Mallon in a survey of sweating in the clothing and paper-box trades in East London. Again, the study resulted in no immediate local changes for the better, but it did help lay the investigative groundwork for national regulation of sweated industries under the Trade Boards Acts of 1909.[38] A resident and council member, C. B. Hawkins, put his Toynbee training to use in a survey of poverty and industry in Norwich, which appeared in 1910. Urwick had edited *Studies of Boy Life in Our Cities* in 1904; H. R. P. Gamon, another resident, published *The London Police Court Today and Tomorrow* in 1907. Toynbee Hall had been founded to bear witness to the virtues of neighborliness. The focus of these books expressed the degree to which that purpose had changed after 1900. Their authors did not go to Whitechapel to befriend and serve its citizens but to learn something there which might be of benefit to the whole nation.

Salter, in his account of the founding of the Enquirers' Club remarks that though its discussions and investigations were "instructive for ourselves, . . . Toynbee Hall and the East End got no very direct benefit."[39] The Enquirers were apprentices, learning their craft as social investigators and reformers in the workshop of Whitechapel, but always with the assumption that as masters they would practice their skills in the precincts of Westminster and Whitehall. Robert Elsmere no longer served as a model. Instead, the pattern to follow was that established by men such as William Braithwaite, graduate of New College, Oxford, who during his residency at the turn of the century was already a civil servant with the Inland Revenue, and who served as Lloyd George's chief assistant in the drafting of the National Health Insurance scheme after 1910. In the Parliamentary elections of December 1910, three former residents and eleven associates were returned, a fact reported with evident pride by the *Record*.[40]

Nor could Barnett himself refrain from a bit of a boast as his protégés thrust themselves onto the national scene. Unconscious perhaps of the extent to which his delight in their success as important people conflicted with his continuing commitment to the idea of connection with the unimportant, he wrote off to his brother following Beveridge's decision to leave the hall in 1905 for a position with the *Morning Post*: "Beveridge has been made leader writer . . . at £500 a year, so he has got home." And of two other residents: "[Henry] Maynard is Secretary of the new Central Body on the Unemployed Fund. And [T. Hancock] Nunn (private) is on the Royal Commission on Poor Laws. Toynbee men to the front."[41] If Jowett had worried, as Henrietta Barnett reported, about Barnett's ambitions for his young men, his spirit could now rest easy.

While Toynbee men prospered in the world beyond Whitechapel, the hall languished. Barnett resigned his position as warden in 1906, assuming a canonry and then a subdeanship of Westminster. He reported to his sister-in-law two years later that the hall was "flourishing very much," hence his conviction that he was "well away" from its direct management.[42] Yet under his successor, T. E. Harvey, the history of the hall's activities and programs increasingly expressed the now explicit confusions as to its purpose: was it to be a settlement or a social laboratory? Harvey attempted to keep it both, though his own sympathies lay with the efforts of the analysts who continued for a time to make use of Toynbee Hall as an observation post. His "Prospect and Retrospect" for the year 1909–10 found him struggling still to keep the old ethos alive and conscious of the difficulties he faced in doing so:

> In the past Toynbee Hall has stood for fellowship in the search after knowledge, in the quest for Truth, in the service of man for man. To spread something of that spirit should be the aim of all of us, and as we make this our object we feel that whatever our difference of view or work may be, we are all fellow-labourers. So, despite the difficulties in the way, let us go forward together up the hill, our faces toward the light.[43]

The vacuity of Harvey's rhetoric suggests the truth of Urwick's assertion that the texts had become too threadbare to cover any more sermons. His wardenship was no more effective than his rhetoric in rescuing Toynbee Hall from its decline. Following his resignation in 1911, one further attempt was made to paper over institutional divisions by appointing Maurice Birley, whose interests lay in redirecting the hall's activities toward settlement work, as warden, and Alexander Carr-Saunders, a young civil servant, as subwarden. The result was further confusion. In May 1913, at the time of Samuel Barnett's death, his wife was lobbying Alfred Milner, chairman of the hall's trustees, to fire Birley, "a nice man . . . but a poor creature without power of organising or attracting or keeping men."[44] A month later both Birley and Carr-Saunders resigned, Birley to take up residence in Limehouse, Carr-Saunders to join J. A. Salter and other residents and former residents in drafting a statement in support of their understanding of what the hall should now become.

The statement argued against any attempt to continue the educational and recreational work "which can as well or better be pursued elsewhere." It urged increased participation by residents in local affairs; not, however, in order that they might connect their lives with those of their neighbors, but so as to "obtain a grasp of the inter-relation of . . . classes and their mutual reactions." Experience of this sort would prove "of inestimable value to him who seeks to know the worth of the theories and proposals for social reorganisation that are afloat at the present day." By encouraging this kind of work, the hall would appeal to "a better type of man. . . . The type of man we require is repelled by the idea of the ordinary Settlement, and if he has ever heard of Toynbee Hall, he does not distinguish it from his College Mission, with which he possibly intends never to have anything to do."

The signatories proposed that the hall increase its efforts to work in concert with other institutions: trade unions, Friendly Societies, the Workers' Educational Association, and the like. And they declared it should devote more attention to the work of centers for social analysis in other countries—the Musée Social in Paris, for example, or similar institutions that could provide information concerning "labour troubles in America or the new experiments [in social legislation] in Australia." Finally, they advised that the hall oppose recent suggestions to move deeper into East London, to a neighborhood more receptive to the programs of a genuine settlement. One great advantage to its present location was its accessibility to and from the world beyond working-class East London. "The most important work of Toynbee Hall is the opposite of parochial; we might almost describe it as national. Toynbee Hall is admirably situated from the point of view of the wider aspects of its work. It is easy of access from all parts of London; to move the institution further East would be . . . a sacrifice of the greater to the less important aspects of its work."[45]

The greater work no longer corresponded to the ideal of personal connection and local community that had inspired the foundation of Toynbee Hall. In an appraisal of the work of settlement houses written in 1914, Werner Picht, a young German social worker who had lived at Toynbee for several months in 1912, argued that the nondogmatic spirit of Oxford had not proved strong enough to inspire dedication to its goals for more than a generation or so. Effective settlement work continued to be accomplished by Church missions, "organisms with a soul, such as can only be developed from a community of life, never from an organisation"—organisms such as Barnett had hoped to bring to life. But Toynbee Hall had become something else: a "political Settlement, . . . more interested in questions of public life than in that of individuals." It had begun as an institution determinedly ecumenical and nondenominational, standing "for the idea of humaneness." Though it had "inherited this ideal in its purest and intensest form," Picht wrote, it had sustained neither the ideal itself nor the resulting spirit, "which takes unlimited interest in the individual and never asks itself whether it would not be more productive to give one's time to reforms of administration by which thousands could be helped."[46]

Picht's analysis was a fair and accurate one. Yet to say that Toynbee Hall had abandoned its original goals is not to say that the tenets of the faith ceased to direct the thought and work of young Edwardian social reformers who had felt its influence at Oxford and at the hall before they moved further into the world. William Beveridge and R. H. Tawney, though they outgrew Toynbee Hall, worked as reformers in a way that revealed their continuing debt to the perceptions and goals which had brought it into being.

6

WILLIAM BEVERIDGE: "BENEVOLENT, BOURGEOIS BUREAUCRAT"

William Beveridge, born in 1879, was the son of a conscientious district sessions judge in the Indian Civil Service and his equally conscientious and radically minded wife. Henry Beveridge's devotion to his work owed more to a sense of duty than to any particular love of the bench: he was by nature a scholar, not a judge. Yet he refused to leave India for the sake of his family's health, despite his wife's urging, until the death of their youngest child in 1890 brought him home to England and an early retirement. By that time Annette Beveridge had had more than enough of the East. She had gone out in 1873 to campaign for the emancipation and education of Indian women, but found herself disillusioned by the unresponsiveness of her pupils and the contempt with which their husbands and fathers continued to treat them. A consequent conviction of the superiority of Western ways, coupled with struggles to keep her children well and to provide them with what she deemed a suitable education, persuaded Annette of her duty to raise the family at home. She and Henry eventually settled near Haslemere, whence William was dispatched first to Kent House preparatory school at Beachy Head, then in 1892 to Charterhouse, and finally in 1897 as a mathematics exhibitioner to Balliol.

Charterhouse, which at the time of Beveridge's attendance had succumbed to a particularly severe infection of athleticism, did not suit the rather delicate William, although he managed to win appointment as head of the school. "I cannot remember a single intellectual pleasure or the dawning of the faintest intellectual or literary interest," he wrote later, his comment a measure of the degree to which public schools, as

Barnett had perceived, were betraying their high-minded Victorian legacy. Annette commented once that wherever he had gone, he would have "been with the minority," his intellectuality casting about him "an air of exclusiveness" that those of "ordinary working powers" could admire, perhaps, but not get very close to. She nevertheless wrote him after he had left school "that since you have got over some smarts, the uncongenial surroundings may have been of preparatory use to you."[1] The observations suggest she understood her son well. Beveridge remained a private, prickly person, chary of personal relationships and with few friends. Perhaps, as Annette suggested, Charterhouse helped teach him the art of suffering fools—something he ultimately learned to do, though never gladly.

For a year or so at Balliol his shyness kept him from making friends, after which he grew into Oxford life in a way that had been impossible for him at school. Friendships came in time: a difficult and occasionally stormy relationship with Arthur Collings Carré, a Balliol classicist; easier emotional ties to Richard Denman and R. H. Tawney, both historians and both concerned with questions of politics and social reform. In letters home, Beveridge, who first read mathematical moderations and then greats, worried regularly about his standing as a scholar, whether he was working as hard as he should, and what course of study he might most profitably pursue—the characteristic concerns of a conscientious late Victorian at Oxford, liberated from self-consciousness into the life of godliness and good learning Charterhouse had denied him.

Liberation for the serious-minded Beveridge, however, meant freedom to discover an ethical basis for the duties he increasingly believed it should be his business to undertake. Here Edward Caird was of help to him. After three years at Balliol he could write his mother that attendance at Caird's lay sermons was one of the great privileges of membership in the college. He defined the master's particular contribution as an ability to be "both philosophical and practical on these occasions." Beveridge acknowledged that other Victorians had succeeded in "swallowing [their] difficulties and getting on without any philosophy in the Master's sense"; T. H. Huxley, whom Beveridge much admired, was a case in point. Yet how much better if one could follow Caird in his attempt "to reconcile our consciousness of ethical standards in ourselves with the wickedness . . . of the world around us." Caird's purpose was "to make us feel at one with the whole universe in aim and end," a goal which Beveridge declared he admired as an ideal, though he could not be sure that its realization was "absolutely essential to my practical welfare."[2]

What *was* essential, apparently, was some purposeful social philosophy. As a proper Balliolite, Beveridge was impatient with the notion that one could treat religion as a subject for philosophical debate rather than as a basis for moral commitment. He was attracted not only to the thought of men such as Caird and Green but also to the essays of Huxley and the novels of George Eliot, who—as he remarked in a paper delivered in 1901—was to be admired above all for her "absolutely serious and relentlessly moral vision of life."[3] Responding to his sister Jeannette's inquiry as to his own religious beliefs, he replied in a long letter in 1898 that he believed in a God whose "chief function . . . is to suggest noble thoughts to men and influence the world through them," assisting them, that is, to realize a community of best selves. Those men and women through whom God worked in this way would manifest a commitment that might strike some as fanatical, a state of mind Beveridge declared himself prepared to admire as necessary for the advancement of mankind. "I really think," he wrote again to his sister a few months later, "that no man can do really progressive work who has not the idea carried to excess. It must be rather excessive to counterbalance all the conservative forces of society which tend to retard the carrying out of the idea. The man must have one great ideal to aim at, to a certain extent excluding all else, and his convictions must be very strong."[4]

Beveridge, wary of the emotional and irrational, was constitutionally incapable of fanaticism. Even so, his gradually acquired, increasingly certain convictions produced in him a strong-mindedness as to what he wished to do with his life: something, he wrote his mother, that would prove "directly useful" to society.[5] In his autobiography he claimed that it was Caird who had inspired his commitment to a career as a social reformer. "'While you are at the University,' said Edward Caird . . . to me and to others, 'your first duty is self culture, not politics or philanthropy. But when you have performed that duty and learned all that Oxford can teach you, then the thing that needs to be done by some of you is to go and discover why, with so much wealth in Britain, there continues to be so much poverty and how poverty can be cured.'"[6] Beveridge's biographer, José Harris, argues correctly that in attributing his commitment almost entirely to Caird's direct influence and intervention, Beveridge was oversimplifying. She points out that, despite his admiration for

Caird, Beveridge possessed a mind basically out of tune with the abstract philosophical explorations that preoccupied the master. She notes as well Beveridge's more than passing interest in natural science—his fascination with questions of scientific theory, his methodical, meticulous, patient habits of mind and research—as further explanation of his desire to be a scientist of society. And she remarks that his final determination to undertake a career as a social reformer, in 1903, came just after the emotionally jarring suicide of his friend Carré and that the decision may have been, in part, a response to that crisis.[7]

Granting those qualifications, however, there remains the fact that at Balliol, under Caird, Beveridge's instinct and predilections were stimulated and nurtured in an intellectual atmosphere sympathetic to the course he had begun to chart for himself. If the words Beveridge puts into Caird's mouth were apocryphal, the sentiment they express was certainly characteristic of Balliol, even in the late 1890s, and one that would have naturally impressed itself on someone of Beveridge's mind and temperament.

A different sort of man might have understood the Balliol injunction as a summons to political life. Beveridge, though, distrusted politics: he once wrote his sister that he wished there was a truly "respectable" party, so that he might belong to it.[8] Even at Oxford he had begun to express a preference for the disinterested reform activity that Toynbeeites found appealing. He associated himself with the Liberal party, out of family habit as much as anything. But increasingly he began to spend his time with men such as Denman and Tawney, who could share his interest in social problems, their investigation and their cure. He began to attend the Oxford meetings of Toynbee Hall enthusiasts. He and Carré volunteered to shepherd a group of Old Northeyites around the town and to take them punting on the river. In October of 1899, Beveridge wrote his mother that he would "like to do something" for the hall, "but I seem incapable of teaching anything that is wanted except perhaps swimming." Despite these reservations, he found time to visit the hall the following January, writing an enthusiastic report to his parents: "I feel like an American tourist doing Whitechapel in two days, and spend the whole day practically tramping about."[9]

It took Beveridge another three years to translate his desire for a "directly useful" career into a full-fledged commitment to the work of Toynbee Hall. Following a first in greats in the summer of 1901 he stayed on at Oxford, uncertain as to whether he should enter the Home Civil Service, compete for a prize fellowship, or study for the bar. His mother had the previous year attempted to discourage the idea of the Home Civil: "The pay is too small for saving and the pension a pittance." Instead, she introduced the idea of partnership in a "good house of business" and then a political career at mid-life, citing Joseph Chamberlain as an example. Beveridge responded that he was not set on a civil-service career himself, but that it seemed the only way "in which I could turn my University education to practical advantage." He deprecated the idea of a businessman's life; Balliol had not educated him to that end. "Certainly the habits induced by the system and life here are highly deleterious of business capacity." He remarked that the making of money was of no importance to him—reflecting the antimaterialist, disinterested sentiments that Oxford so successfully bred into affluent upper-middle-class young men, who never doubted the availability of enough income to live comfortably, and who had been taught to despise the desire to live luxuriously. "Up here . . . I have never wanted for money and shall do without much of it with great satisfaction." [10]

In the end, Beveridge settled without great conviction for the law, persevering despite the shock of Carré's death in January 1902 and the admonition of his tutor Edward Jenks, the legal scholar, that "a certain excitability" made him a less than suitable candidate for the bar. [11] He moved to London and into the Temple flat his friend Denman had been sharing with Carré. In the fall of 1902 he won the Stowell Civil Law Fellowship at University College, Oxford, which provided him with a £200 annual stipend and permitted him to continue residence in London but did little to increase his waning enthusiasm for the course he was pursuing. With both Tawney and Denman he engaged in "directly useful" pursuits, such as interviewing the parents of candidates for the Children's Country Holiday Fund and managing a South London boys' club. In a letter to his mother the previous January he had reiterated his belief that "what perhaps is most of all demanded from Tutu's [his sister Jeannette] and my generation . . . is a consideration of the big modern social problems."

In January 1903 Beveridge wrote that he had given up altogether the idea of practicing law, and for reasons that reflected his impatience to get at "the big problems." He argued that the law was no more than an intellectual exercise to the average barrister: "he in no way leaves the world either better or worse than it was." Beveridge's attack on the law read like the manifesto of an already dedicated and disinterested social reformer.

> My repugnance really includes . . . the idea that law as profession is both worldly in the extreme and remote from reality; it has nothing to do with any real problem or difficulties and does not go about slaying any dragons. . . . I believe it is a perfectly just simile to compare the bar as a life to the solving of endless chess problems with the chance of a prize [a judgeship or a political career] at the end. . . . I suppose power is the thing that everyone deserves to exercise. I too—but it is just that sort of power which rests upon money and position that I should care very little about; the power of knowledge and experience seem the only thing worth having. . . . I think I may take it that the one thing in which I am interested wholly and completely is getting to know something about human society and working at some part of its machinery. (I avoid "social problem" because it always suggests "slumming" and drink and I mean something wider—simply the question of under what conditions is it possible and worthwhile for men as a whole to live.) I get no help in that from the bar except the possibility at 45 (more probably 50) of hastily snatching up and putting into action somebody else's situations.[12]

Power at the service not of itself but of "something wider"—the betterment of the conditions of national community—had now become Beveridge's clearly identifiable goal.

Throughout the spring of 1903, Beveridge battled with his parents over his decision. They had traveled to Florence with his sister, in the hope of hastening her recuperation from a serious operation. Now they did not hesitate to accuse their son of prolonging the process of recuperation by his heedless intransigence. At first his mother sympathized to the extent of agreeing "with your wish to do real and not parasitic work and do it with other men." From the beginning, however, his father argued fiercely in favor of a legal career of some sort, if not at the bar, then as a scholar. Beveridge would have none of it. "My interest in the law is neither historic nor scientific." He argued that in choosing a career, one must discover "what is wanted," which he defined in terms of an elitist's mission to learn what needed to be done for others and then to set about doing it for them. "The times seem stagnant; people seem to sit waiting to see in what direction things will move; and therefore now above all there seems need of an effort to make them move in a direction dictated by reason rather than by the line of least resistance." To move them, that is, not as a self-interested politician would, but as a true servant of the community must.

By April, Beveridge had begun to investigate alternatives: the Board of Education, a teachers' training college. He had briefly considered a residency at Toynbee Hall the previous summer. Now Barnett approached him again. On 18 April Beveridge wrote his mother and father that Barnett was looking for a subwarden, and he intimated the strong likelihood that he would take the job. Both parents responded immediately, heatedly and negatively. His father insisted that he make Bentham, rather than Barnett, his model. "If you can do anything in his wake you will do far more good than by [running] soup kitchens for the proletariat or trying to be social to people with whom you have little in common. . . . I don't think you are cut out for influencing horny-handed mechanics."[13]

Beveridge responded in a series of letters that made clear both his determination to pursue the course he had chosen and his reasons for doing so. To his father's suggestion that he follow in Bentham's path, Beveridge replied that there was little of that sort of work now left to do and that what there was amounted to no more than emendation. The reforms demanding attention at the present time were rather those "suggested by big underlying social questions." He cited trade-union law as a case in point, "on which there is certain to be early and bad legislation," in the wake of the Taff Vale decision of 1901 which had left unions liable for damages incurred by employees during a strike. "A reform of that sort is rather social than legal; it is the adaptation of law to a new order of society and is a matter neither for Jeremy Bentham nor the law lords— but for a combination of political philosopher and economist and (moderately learned) lawyer." It demanded legislation "guided by wide non-legal experience." His work at Toynbee Hall would put him "in a better position to have an opinion on this form of legal question by living the practical rather than the legal life."

That practical life, Beveridge insisted to his father, would not be a matter of soup kitchens or "genial smiles disposed on horny-handed mechanics. I am not going to Toynbee Hall to devote myself to such things."

As he then proceded to outline his own goals, he redefined the purposes of the hall to suit his own sense of the direction social work on behalf of community should take.

> If anyone ever thought that colossal evils could be remedied by small doses of culture and charity and amiability I for one do not think so now. The real use I want to make of Toynbee Hall and kindred institutions is as centres for the development of authoritative opinion on the problems of city life, an opinion based on the experiences of men of all classes such as Toynbee alone can really discover and supported by men of all classes.

Clubs and lectures were the means to this end, "an apparatus for the use of some central power in Toynbee which by its aid shall develop opinions (say rather convictions) and a policy *and express it.*" That expression, when it came, would because of its authority compel the attention of the nation. "I have a vision of Toynbee Hall speaking one day with a voice of thunder," Beveridge declared, "and I have a vision of myself . . . among others directing that voice's utterance." He emphasized that he was going to East London as a social scientist, that he wanted to view "the welfare of the state as a whole . . . in a scientific way. . . . I utterly distrust the saving power of culture and mission and isolated good feeling as a surgeon distrusts 'Christian Science.'" He declared himself as anxious as any scientist or physician to root out "destructive diseases" and to pursue the investigation of those diseases with "all the time at my disposal."[14]

Beveridge had emerged from Balliol with its stamp upon him. Yet as he undertook the subwardenship, his purposes were different from those Green, Toynbee, and Barnett had articulated in the 1880s. With his condemnation of the individual and subjective in favor of objective opinion and policy, he was declaring himself a member of the new generation of reformers, one of those whom Barnett recognized he must accept as a means of breathing new life into Toynbee Hall. At the same time, Barnett could not help wondering about the effect this determined young man might have upon the sensibilities of co-workers less ruthlessly "scientific" than he was, or about the ultimate influence of men such as Beveridge upon the institution of the hall itself. Ten days before he offered the job of subwarden to Beveridge, he wrote to express his worries to his brother. "He is very able—a whale for work—with definite views of filling up his life in social service. But not very patient of his tools, not a lover of the man in the fool." Barnett reasoned that Beveridge "might draw together a more intellectual set" but feared that he might also frighten off the current residents, "dear boys" who found pleasure in the sort of work for which Beveridge seemed to have so little use.[15]

Barnett swallowed his qualms and took Beveridge on his own terms. "You understand," he wrote him, "that you throw yourself into our object of meeting people in one another's service." The injunction was vague enough to accommodate the new subwarden's own understanding of his duties. Those, Beveridge wrote his father, involved the organization of meetings, interviewing, and letter writing, to be sure, but principally investigating and reporting. Barnett had pledged that he would not get lost in routine work. And, to placate his parents' worries that he might vanish into a "prospectless" dead end, Beveridge reassured them that, on the contrary, success in his work as Barnett's subwarden could very well prove the avenue to important advancement. He credited Robert Morant's rapid rise at the Board of Education to Barnett's willingness to speak up for him. "He got his chance simply because he was known to Canon Barnett to have done excellent educational work . . . and Canon Barnett knew great educational people. Toynbee is a force in the same way that Balliol is."[16] Whether or not persuaded by arguments of this sort, his parents, once convinced that they could not change their son's mind, capitulated without further rancor.

From the outset Barnett hoped that his new subwarden might serve as the catalyst necessary to keep the hall a flourishing institution. "If a young party gathered about you," he wrote Beveridge soon after his acceptance, "a new life might be begun just as the first 13 men made the life which has gone on for the last 19 years. Perhaps men now in Balliol or some in London could be found to come if you told them your own hopes." In the winter of 1904, the Barnetts left England for an extended stay in Italy, "much more for the sake of giving Toynbee the means of 'finding itself,'" Barnett explained to Beveridge, "than for giving us a holiday." He then proceeded to catechize Beveridge on the success of this experiment: "Are you men at the centre conscious of a policy? Do you see more clearly what there is to be done?" Barnett acknowledged that he had found it hard to withdraw himself and that "the experiment of leaving . . . has cost some anxiety." But "new times demand new men and new ways," and "if the place has the power of drawing in the enthusiasm of the time it will be more than repaid."[17]

Beveridge had meanwhile undertaken a round of activities that proved him the "whale for work" Barnett had perceived him to be. He sat on the Toynbee Hall Council and Finance Committee and acted as "censor of studies" for the men of Balliol House and Wadham House. He wrote for, and within the year assumed editorship of, the *Toynbee Record.* He taught and lectured. He traveled to Oxford and Cambridge in search of promising residents. He served a term as local school manager. He trained election canvassers. And, of most interest to him, through work as secretary of the Stepney Council of Public Welfare, member of the Central Committee of London Unemployed Fund, and organizer of his own local Committee on the Unemployed, he began to accumulate evidence about "the big problems" that had compelled him to forsake law in favor of social reform.

Beveridge found much of the work tedious. He was not—as Barnett had, again accurately, observed—"a lover of the man in the fool." Organizing and canvassing in local elections encouraged in him the distrust of democracy characteristic of so many elitist reformers. He recorded the dreary events of one London County Council election day in his diary: "Up at 7 a.m. and down to Committee Room . . . by 7:50 to find nothing and nobody . . . spent morning wrestling with three drunken carters . . . who wished to help but couldn't. Also in arranging the canvassing cards and weeding them. Very poor canvassing. . . . Very hard to get polling book manned. No carriages. Endless fights with small boys."[18] Far more to his taste was the work he undertook as editor of the *Toynbee Record.* Indeed, when he resigned as subwarden he boasted to his mother that his successful effort to remodel the paper was "the one really good thing I have done for Toynbee Hall." The changes he instituted were a reflection of the hope he had earlier expressed, that the hall might speak to the nation rather than merely to its own East London constituency. Beveridge started by altering the format, so that it was no longer an expression of "Canon Barnett's idea that each number . . . should contain something representative of every resident and all the activities of the place," a policy that had resulted in "a chaos of notes all too short to convey any information or any impression save of general good intentions and amiability." Instead, he began to pare the notes and "edit the 'gush' severely," replacing them with "specialist articles of some scientific value" that would be read with interest by men and women keen to learn what research and experience by East London investigators could teach them about social conditions and their solution. By the end of his first year as editor, he had increased the size of the journal to sixteen pages and had introduced regular lengthy articles each month on "subjects of general social interest," such as underemployment and the treatment of casual laborers. He was also reprinting reports of the Enquirers' Club on its investigations of the problems of homeless men and the employment of boys in industry.[19]

The *Record* came to reflect not only its editor's views as to the general purposes of Toynbee Hall but also his growing specific interests in the problems of underemployment and poor relief. His concern was consistently to use the opportunities the hall afforded him to investigate and analyze social and economic problems and then to publicize his conclusions as widely as possible. He organized his Committee on the Unemployed from among the residents of Toynbee Hall, Balliol House, and Wadham House not as an instrument for the alleviation of underemployment in the area but as a local "Royal Commission, . . . examining in particular the various schemes proposed in the past." He fell in enthusiastically with Barnett's proposal to remodel the Stepney Council of Public Welfare so that its primary function would be the issuing of quarterly reports "valuable enough to publish in the local papers and one or two special London papers (such as the *Westminster*)—so as to produce informed public opinion on local government."[20]

Beveridge's letters and diary make clear his preference for meetings among like-minded reformers, of the kind he organized at the hall in October 1904, to which he invited his friend Denman. The purpose was to hear Ramsay MacDonald, who was coming to explain himself and his views to a select gathering of barristers and journalists. "It ought to be really good to hear his position. It will only be a small private meeting of 10 to 20 people of the Masterman and P. W. Wilson type."[21]

This was not preaching to the converted, but it was instructing the potentially influential so that they might then go out and teach others. Beveridge took advantage of Toynbee Hall as a base for work of this sort, a place where he might serve his apprenticeship as social reformer and from which he might encourage others to consider the "big problems" as he was considering them. Once the apprenticeship was over, he lost no time in moving on. In October 1905 Fabian Ware, editor of the progressive Conservative *Morning Post*, offered Beveridge a job as leader writer, which Beveridge immediately recognized as a logical next step. He was tiring of the subwardenship, a fact Barnett had recognized the preceding year when he appointed a deputy warden to free Beveridge for outside work. Now he was anxious to put an end to his East End life altogether, to begin to speak as an expert to those in the West End who, once awakened as to need and instructed as to solution, could bring about desired change.

He was particularly pleased that the offer had come from a Conservative daily. "It is a great opportunity to preach to the comfortable classes doctrine which they couldn't stand for a moment in the Daily News or the Daily Chronicle [Liberal papers]." Barnett, according to Beveridge, supported the move wholeheartedly.

> Just think of the people I should see and the wisdom I, and the Canon through me, should pump into the comfortable public about Poor Law, trade union law, Unemployed, Garden Cities . . . everything in fact that isn't for the moment a burning party issue. . . . [Ware] wants to make "The Morning Post" an independent organ for moving the intellectual part of the wealthy classes. He believes them to be all patriots at heart, willing to do their duty in social matters if only it is brought home to them.[22]

Beveridge's purpose reflected his elitist's conviction that change could most effectively be accomplished by people like himself, who possessed what he had identified as "the power of knowledge and experience." He would put the knowledge and experience he had gained at Toynbee Hall (and would continue to gain through committee work) at the service of Ware's well-meaning if as yet untutored patriots, who would translate it into power for the benefit of the nation.

Beveridge did not plan to limit his activities to leader writing. One reason Ware's offer appealed to him was that it would leave him with time to lecture, investigate, and write on his own. He maintained a heavy schedule of public speaking engagements, taught a course for the university extension program on labor and the law, and attended A. L. Bowley's lectures on statistics at the recently founded London School of Economics, where he was himself invited to undertake a course on constitutional law and public administration, an offer he refused in order to proceed with a book on the unemployed. Much of the argument for that study, which was published in 1908 as *Unemployment: A Problem of Industry,* was derived from his work as a member of the Central London (Unemployed) Body (CUB), to which he was co-opted from the Stepney

Council of Public Welfare. The CUB, established to administer the Conservatives' 1905 Unemployed Workmen Act in London, was successor to the London Unemployed Fund, organized by Walter Long, president of the Local Government Board in 1904, as a means of establishing farm colonies to combat underemployment. The mandate of the CUB, however, was far broader. As Bentley Gilbert has described it: "They might aid a man to emigrate or to move from one area to another. They could establish labour exchanges and underemployment registers to bring employers and workers together. They could put men to work on their own account if no work were available with other employers and they could establish farm colonies to the end of returning men to the land."[23] Members of the CUB were primarily from the upper-middle class and, in Beveridge's opinion, included too many men and women whose concern was to promote more effective ways of distributing charitable assistance to the unemployed, rather than to discover the means of curbing unemployment itself. Nevertheless, the practical and theoretical knowledge that Beveridge gained from his work with the body, as expressed in leaders, articles, lectures, and ulitmately in *Unemployment,* in turn provided the basis for specific reforms which he undertook when he entered government service at the Board of Trade in 1908.

Beveridge's major contribution there was the planning and implementation of a national network of labor exchanges, established by Act of Parliament in 1909. His research had convinced him that exchanges represented the most effective means of reducing unemployment. They were predicated on the assumption that "the problem of industry" was not a general scarcity of work but an inability on the part of industry to bring together the appropriate worker with the appropriate job. Staffed by trained civil servants, they would serve as an efficient means of directing redundant workers into new industry, while reducing the number of surplus workers in casual trades.

Beveridge was named the first director of the labour-exchange department at the Board of Trade. By the end of 1913, 430 exchanges were operating in the United Kingdom. During the years before the First World War, workers and employers made use of them in increasing numbers, with the result that the age-old custom of "tramping" in search of work from one part of the country to another was all but abolished. Yet though the exchanges encouraged the mobility of labor, they created no new jobs. Statistics suggest that they played little role in reducing of the number of able-bodied paupers; hence they did not begin to solve the problem of decasualization in the way that Beveridge had both hoped and expected.[24] The exchanges proved effective to some degree in areas and in trades where unemployment was traditionally low. Overall, however, for every applicant before 1914 who received a job, three were turned away.

During these years, Beveridge worked hard as well to assist in the birth of a system of national unemployment insurance. Throughout the periods of planning and legislative maneuver, he acted as unofficial assistant to another former Toynbee Hall resident, Hubert Llewellyn Smith, the permanent secretary of the Board of Trade. Only industries in which unemployment was cyclical rather than chronic were selected for coverage: building construction, shipbuilding, engineering, vehicle construction, ironfounding, and sawmilling. Because of the trades covered, and because of the generally low level of unemployment between 1911 and 1914, the new apparatus was not stretched as it later was during the years of depression that followed the war. Nor was it used, as Beveridge urged that it should be, as a tool to enforce decasualization of dock labor by means of compulsory registration.[25]

In a report he wrote for the Board of Trade assessing the effect of both the Labour Exchanges Act and the Unemployment Insurance Act during the first years of their operation, Beveridge expressed himself as less than satisfied with the use being made of the machinery he had helped to create. The unemployment of those who had made claims under the Insurance Act had been, for the most part, of very short duration. "To a large extent," he wrote, "it would be regarded as changing of employment rather than as unemployment." And here the exchanges, to which the unemployed went to register for benefits as well as to apply for new positions, had been of real use. Even so, the overall situation gave little reason for more than cautious optimism. Despite the encouraging statistics which showed that "the numbers of employed men losing work each week have been balanced and more than balanced by the numbers of unemployed men regaining work. . . the whole picture thus presented by the statistics of men falling out of employment and men remaining unemployed is that of a constant irregularity of employment even when employment is at its best, a ceaseless shifting from job to job, a recurrent loss of productive power and of wages in the interval between one job and the next." The answer was more efficient use of the exchanges, which, despite his insistence to the contrary, appeared to become something close to a panacea in Beveridge's mind. "It seems clear that much could be done and needs to be done, towards reducing unemployment by shortening these unproductive periods, in other words, by hastening, through the Labour Exchange Organisation, the passage from employment to employment."[26] With the confidence of the seasoned, disinterested bureaucrat that Beveridge had by now become, he was urging that the programs he had fashioned be given a chance to prove themselves the sort of "directly useful" reforms he had advocated since his apprenticeship at Toynbee Hall.

To what extent did Beveridge's pursuit of the directly useful reflect an adherence to the precepts and goals he had encountered at Balliol and in Whitechapel? We have seen him, a newcomer to the hall, disparaging "small doses of culture and charity," his negative gloss on Barnett's faith in one-by-one connection. Nevertheless, in a generally sympathetic article written in 1907 for the *Oxford and Cambridge Review*, he observed that the success of the settlement movement could best be judged not by examining "the social, charitable, and educational activities which often appear the be-all and end-all of its existence" but by studying the lives of the men who had daily lived the real work of the settlement.

> It would be a record of what A. B. accomplished towards instituting the principles of clean collars and no grumbling into a hundred members of a rough boys' club, or raising the average attendance at an elementary school; of how C. D. during many years made corrupt appointments or corrupt contracting impossible or infrequent upon some small public body; of what E. F. did to secure the better administration of the Poor Law or the Public Health Acts, to revive apprenticeship, or to awaken a serious demand for University Extention Lectures.[27]

Beveridge was not usually as sanguine about the efficacy of individual effort as this catalogue suggests. The unqualified endorsement may have been the result of an unwillingness to speak out against Barnett's ideals publicly. Privately he deplored, as he had at the beginning of his subwardenship, the fact that connection too frequently deteriorated into patronizing, do-gooding philanthropy of the worst sort—"doing things for other people and other people's children," he described it to his mother; "all that is worst in social reformers."[28] Not that Beveridge's attitude toward Toynbee Hall and its purposes was entirely this simple or this negative. He had come to study social problems, and it was as a social laboratory that he primarily continued to regard the hall. He had not hesitated to use it, with Barnett's blessing, as an avenue for his own professional advancement. While there, however, he learned to admire Barnett greatly—"his everlasting youthfulness and infinite sanity"—and through Barnett he came to see Toynbee Hall as a practical expression of the social conscience that Balliol had implanted in him and that he never lost. After a trip to Oxford in 1904 to talk with undergraduates about settlement work in the East End, he wrote his mother that he had concluded in the course of those conversations that places like the hall

> represent simply a protest against the sin of taking things for granted, in particular taking one's own social position or conditions for granted. No man can really be a good citizen who goes through life in a watertight compartment of his own class . . . in my own case of less than a fifth of the State to which I belong. Toynbee Hall provides therefore a sort of general culture in political and social views. It doesn't neccessarily lead all men to one particular view. . . . One might not become a specialist in any one social subject; one would at least be in a position of having seen all sorts and conditions of men to have reasonable views on all social proposals. A protest against taking the structure of society for granted; . . . I feel that I have really got hold of a rather satisfactory phrase.[29]

The following year, Beveridge developed this particular theme more fully and explicitly in a paper he read to an Oxford literary society. In a lengthy discussion of the applicability of the thought of Plato and Aristotle to the modern situation, he argued that Oxford and Toynbee Hall together had helped him understand the way society might be restructured as genuine community. Beveridge observed that the ideas of Plato and Aristotle had been of little use during the past hundred years, when politics had been circumscribed by supposedly ironclad economic laws. Now Britain was within sight of a solution to the economic problems that had constrained her political objectives, a result of the growing willingness to use the state as a means of guaranteeing social security to all her citizens. There was once again, therefore, a chance to address "the ultimate questions as to the object of life, the end both for the individual and the state." Hence one could recognize afresh the enduring value of the thought of Plato and Aristotle as a "reminder that political speculation is not summed up in political economy." The state was now not simply "an association of tax payers but a community of workers in which all have their places large and small," and in which "the old distinction between private property and public property disappears, . . . to re-appear as a practical distribution of the total material dividend—part going to individuals in the general form of money to reward and stimulate their services, part going to provide the citizens at large with public services."

Freed from economic uncertainty, the men and women of Britain could once more consult Plato and Aristotle with profit as they addressed themselves "to the construction of ideals beyond economic needs." Beveridge chose to examine three of the philosophers' assertions with this end in view: that the object of life is not labor but leisure; that a worthwhile life for the few must be based upon unfree labor of the many; and that the individual has need of society in order to live "the highest life." Beveridge addressed the first two propositions together, arguing that the Greeks were wrong in supposing that the state could be satisfactorily divided into those who lived a life of cultivated leisure and those who were condemned to a life of incessant toil. He cautioned against applying the Victorian definition of work as virtue, "that toil itself is a good thing," as a rationalization for the degradation of modern workers into industrial drones. This "base doctrine" must give way to the realization of an "ideal modern state" which "somehow combines labour and leisure." The state must consequently "interfere with the ways in which men earn their livings," ruling out some ways altogether, "regimenting the lower faculties where this is required . . . to give the higher faculties scope."

To Beveridge, leisure meant more than the absence of economic servitude. It meant the chance for workingmen and -women to live not only freely but fully within a newly defined community. And those were the people particularly "for whom an ideal must be formed." With Green and Barnett, he insisted that "progress in society consists . . . in the transference of the fruitful struggle of personalities to ever higher and higher ground in the perpetual transformation of the aims for which . . . men contend; in the de-materialization of individuality." That transformation could not take place until individuals recognized their dependence upon society and their need to connect with their fellow human beings in their quest for best selves. To Beveridge, "the enormous accession of value" that one gains when bringing together "the study of Greek philosophy and the study of modern blue books" was "far the most important conclusion to which one is led by a return to Plato and Aristotle from the wilds of Whitechapel." His Balliol-born conviction that a community of interconnected, more than self-interested, individuals was a worthy goal had been strengthened by the practical knowledge, derived from direct experience as a student of society in East London, that such a community might now for the first time be possible.[30]

If Beveridge's experiences in Whitechapel had reinforced his dedication to community as an ideal, they had also convinced him that to define the task of recreating community as an earlier generation of Balliol-inspired reformers had, was to condemn the ideal to death at the start. His consistently vocal opposition to localism marked him in this respect an unapologetic member of the new generation. His intention as editor of the *Record* had been to address not the neighborhood but the nation. Reform undertaken on behalf of no more than a local community was reform imprisoned by parochialism. To Beveridge, connection as Barnett had defined it meant the trap of debilitating local conditions; as such it prevented achievement of the goal of liberation needed to realize a better life. He criticized the generally unsuccessful Unemployed Workmen Act of 1905, because it provided relief work only to those already resident in a particular district. "There is obvious danger of aggravating rather than reducing [the evil of underemployment] by measures of assistance which may tend to retain labour in places where it is no longer needed. There is a consequent necessity of accompanying any such measures by others facilitating the removal of men from congested areas."[31]

This was, of course, the function of labor exchanges, in Beveridge's mind a model of national community-directed reform. National programs such as this did not neglect the individual, Beveridge insisted; exchanges would not unnecessarily pry men and women away from the neighborhoods where they had lived and worked for years. But if, in order to earn a living, those men and women did find that they had to move, exchanges would see to it that the jobs to which they went were suited to their particular skills and abilities. Exchanges would thus serve particular men and women in a way far more useful and productive for themselves than any amount of localized attention. Here, then, was machinery which, by releasing workers from the debilitating fear of unemployment, would allow them the chance to do what Green had insisted all citizens must be free to do: "to make the most and best of themselves," within the community of which they were part.[32]

Beveridge hoped that community would not be prey to divisive class consciousness, here again reflecting the earlier concerns of his Balliol progenitors. Neither his purposes nor his temperament inclined him to investigate the nature and value of working-class institutions. He was impatient with the particular institutions and attitudes that seemed to stand in the way of the reforms he wished to effect, unwilling to acknowledge, as an anthropologist would have, the degree to which those phenomena might have to be fashioned into the schemes for reorganization he was proposing. He opposed the unrestricted freedom which he believed trade unions would be granted should the Liberal government repeal the Taff Vale decision, even though he respected the right of unions to engage in their "normal and most fully recognized" activities— by which he meant collective bargaining, official strikes, and peaceful picketing. In leaders for the *Morning Post* he supported the recommendations of the 1906 Royal Commission on Trade Disputes and Trade Combinations, which coincided generally with his own views. When the Liberals made it clear that they intended to press ahead with repeal, Beveridge argued against the decision as one designed to serve special interests to the detriment of community as a whole. By removing unions' liability for damages, the government was affording them the opportunity to do "without fear of the law anything they pleased." Repeal meant "a relaxation by the State of the conditions under which it will allow disputes to be conducted within its borders by the opposed associations of employers and workmen." It was, therefore, "a step backwards in civilisation and towards a less organised state—just as would be a proposal to give legal sanction to duels or prize-fights, or to allow certain persons to pick one another's pockets with impunity."[33]

Beveridge's concern to see the emergence of a less class-conscious state, a tangible embodiment of community, led him to look upon the advent of a separate Labour party as a mixed blessing. Though no one could legitimately oppose "the growth of Labour sentiment," he wrote, and although "the presence of Labour members in the House of Commons [was] to be welcomed by all friends of social reform," he warned that "no patriotic citizen can subscribe to the principle of class representation and class parties."[34] Generally, Beveridge accepted the Labour party, trade unions, cooperatives, and the like only to the extent that they encouraged social harmony among workers by assisting in the resolution of factious disputes.

Class institutions too often fostered sectional self-interest at the expense of communal purpose. In a 1906 lecture on socialism to the Oxford Social Science Club, Beveridge declared that the business of the state "is to make self-assertion and self-interest subserve the common good." Writing the following day to his mother, Beveridge admitted that what he had spoken of in his lecture as "a brand of socialism" might seem to others "disappointingly like individualism." This was because, along with the Toynbeeites, he understood the proper activities of the state as the activities of a community concerned to teach its individual members responsible behavior, in the hope that such behavior would eventually produce the sort of freedom that was not selfish agitation but disinterested obligation. The end of such a socialism, Beveridge had declared in words that echoed the precepts of Balliol, "is not the body but the soul. It laments not the millions of starved bodies, but the bodies soulless because starved. . . . It calls for social action to end once and for all the struggle for bare existence, to let a new struggle of ideas and ideals commence."[35]

Social action of this sort was the responsibility of the state. The individual's responsibility, in turn, was to respond to the lessons such social action taught by leading a productive life. To be a citizen, Beveridge asserted in a talk to the Sociological Society in 1907, one must occupy a "whole place" in the community. To be sure, the state had an obligation to help its members to attain that place. "Every place in free industry, carrying with it the rights of citizenship—civil liberty, political power, fatherhood, conduct of one's own life and government of a family— should be, so to speak, a 'whole' place involving substantially full employment and average earnings up to a definite minimum." But although citizens had the right to expect the state's help as they worked to secure and sustain their place, they did not have an automatic right to such a place itself or the privileges that accompanied it. Beveridge argued against state-guaranteed jobs (the Labour party's "right-to-work") on these grounds. A pledge of jobs for all would mean the acceptance as citizens of all born within the state. Yet "the intent of the state," Beveridge contended, "is not to make room for an indefinite number of citizens but *to see that all citizens it admits are healthy and happy.*"[36]

The social philosophy expressed in that declaration argued a community whose members were bound by a set of mutual responsibilities. Those willing to learn their social obligations were entitled to the rewards that willingness earned. Those unwilling or unable to do so, forfeited their rights. Beveridge insisted, for example, that the state should continue to disenfranchise paupers. "Many of the 'undeserving' unemployed," he wrote in the *Toynbee Record*, "undeserving that is of anything better than a rigorous Poor Law, are voters, to whom it would be ruinous policy to allow electoral control over any public relief agency by which they hoped to benefit." His argument was based on both his principle of citizenship and his concern for the disinterested management of the community. "Men who cannot in ordinary circumstances support themselves in independence are not citizens in fact and should not be so in right," he wrote; "disenfranchisement in this view is part of the 'stigma' of pauperism." Men out of work should be denied the vote even in those cases where underemployment was not the result of individual shortcomings but of trade depression, since "to let recipients of public relief elect its dispensers" was to ensure the perpetuation of indiscriminate relief to the detriment of the best interest of the community as a whole.[37]

Recipients of public relief could not achieve the disinterestedness required of citizens and therefore surrendered their right to the title. At the other end of the scale, Beveridge seemed to imply, were men such as himself, disinterested benefactors to the community of the nation, exemplifying citizenship in its highest form. He told the Oxford social scientists that he had little confidence in the ability of "the people" to make society function as it should, a predictable observation given the authoritarianism inherent in the view of society to which he was heir. "There is," he remarked, "an obvious though not inevitable opposition between certain democratic theories of 'freedom' and 'equality' and the gospel of authority and the subordination of the parts of the organic whole which forms the philosophic core of society." That opposition was bound to manifest itself in any society organized on socialist lines, since socialism as he defined it meant "the rule of the expert" on behalf of the community. Democracy, he delcared, "hates the expert—not indeed without cause but in general beyond reason," preferring instead what it liked to call "the practical man"—that is, the man without experience and knowledge of social problems and hence without reliable solutions to them.

He granted that in a democracy the expert must serve "as an administrator under practical men." But he worried that such a relationship would subvert the expert's objectively conceived plans. "Will a socialist democracy be content to trust sufficiently its experts? . . . Will it give its managers the degree of independence posessed by our judges?" Beveridge was inclined to doubt it. "The first requirement of justice is a consistent government, a remorselessly unsentimental government"—a disinterested government in the sense of one willing to put the "organic whole" ahead of self-interested parts. Practical men, however, were too often prey both to their personal ambitions and to the pressures of class and constituency. The result: "Democratic governments of today are weak, inconsistent, soft-headed—too generous to the appeal of the moment to be just."[38] To ensure justice, experts must do all they can to help democracy resist those appeals.

By the time he delivered those remarks, Beveridge had already cast himself as just such an expert, a role that suited him and that he found increasingly to his liking. He enjoyed the way "experts" managed to get things done, the way influence could be made to work for a worthy end. Dinner at the Webbs, he was able to write his mother in December 1906, was "always a liberal education." The Webbs did their best to bring together experts and practical men. It was at their table that Beveridge had his first chance to talk about labor exchanges with the future president of the Board of Trade, Winston Churchill, during the same dinner party at which the Webbs suggested that those they knew might be divided "temperamentally into A's (aristocrats, artists and anarchists) and B's (benevolent, bourgeois and bureaucrats)." Beveridge was delighted with the success he was making of his life among the Bs. When Churchill left the Board of Trade in 1911 and told Beveridge that his "future was assured and that he was very glad to have brought a man like ME into the public service,"[39] Beveridge believed he deserved the compliment. He was buoyed by the certainty that his expert's knowledge and planning promised to produce a considerable measure of lasting social change. In his essay on Plato and Aristotle he had written of the immortality that might come to those whose legacy was not merely "a memory but an influence."[40] Previously, the men and women who had achieved that sort of immortality had usually been As. Now Bs like himself, because of the important work they were accomplishing, would likewise remain a part of the community's consciousness after their death.

Beveridge disliked administration and the dulling effect bureaucracy produced on the minds of those who served it; at times he feared that his own mind was suffering the occupational hazards of a taxing and unedifying routine. The work of inspection and reporting that he was forced to undertake as director of the exchanges made him lament the days when "one was creating all the time." Yet the obvious pride he took in his work and the occasional excitement he derived from it were just as tangible to him as the boredom, and far more important. Beveridge believed that the exchanges and the insurance schemes proved the value of a disinterested elite to the community they served. Consequently, they deserved the pride he took in them, and in himself for having created them. "Yesterday was the big day of trial—the top of the climb," he reported to his mother on the morrow of the first payments under the Unemployment Insurance Act. He had visited a number of London exchanges which were being used to administer the program.

> Apparently it's been all right—or at least sufficiently all right. So I'm rather happy with myself. Three years to the day from the opening of the first Exchanges. . . . We must have paid something [like] 25,000 men in London yesterday. At one Exchange alone some 2,500 men came to sign the unemployed register each day, and 1,300 had to be paid yesterday. . . . Seeing the men lining up in a perfectly orderly way to get paid at Kilburn, and realizing that the same was happening at 1,400 other places all over the United Kingdom, and had never happened anywhere before, was quite impressive to my vanity.[41]

Here was a new kind of connection, not between one individual and another, but between the state and the thousands who were being taught to make use of it for their own good and that of the community. In place of the Toynbee Hall residents, transcending the impersonal machinery of reform through one-by-one relationships, stood a bureaucratic elite, whose particular concern was the perfection of that very machinery Toynbee Hall had disparaged.

Beveridge was a quintessential B: a benevolent, bourgeois bureaucrat who was determined, as he phrased it in *Unemployment*, to "banish disorganisation from the State."[42] And as a B he welcomed opportunities to perfect the machinery of social reform. Three weeks before the first payments under the Unemployment Insurance Act, he had written proudly to his mother that he felt

> like a giant refreshed, and ready to put the final touches to the unemployment insurance machine. It's really in its way rather impres-

sive to me to think of this machine which we've been furiously building for the last year, now standing ready (I hope) to start . . . for the first time into a life of which one cannot see the end. . . . And all this, once started, must go on like clockwork and with absolute continuity, for there will be a perpetual stream of applications for benefit, sometimes large and sometimes small, but never ceasing. Will the machine work? It's really almost as new in type as was the first steam locomotive, and of course one hasn't been able to make experiments and trial runs. Of course it will work, some how, but with how much or how little friction and partial breakdown and dislocation, one cannot tell. . . . I *think* the machine is well enough designed to stand the strain, but it's so large and complicated, and it's had to be designed against time, and not without some unnecessary hindrances to one's work and waste of time—so at times I can't help doubting whether it will really work at all.[43]

Whether or not this machine did work, Beveridge believed that no permanent solution to the social problems facing England would come without employing machinery of some sort. A machine, and only a machine, would make the difference. This confidence—faith, really—explains Beveridge's dogged devotion to labor exchanges, machines he considered even more vital than unemployment insurance to national well-being. It reveals as well the extent to which Beveridge's thinking, dedicated though he was to the triumph of an "organic whole," transcended the Toynbee ethos. There was, in fact, a good measure of positivism in Beveridge's thought. He remained committed to a general belief in social evolution, the ability of society to progress through successively higher stages.[44] With positivists he believed that facts, objectively gathered and arranged, would produce scientifically verifiable conclusions, and that those conclusions, in turn, were the only logical basis for successful reform. His argument for a single set of agencies to service the unemployed was grounded in part in his desire to see centralization replace the particular and personal with the predictable and uniform. "Insofar as scientific classification, impossible under the present system, lies at the basis of any proper treatment of the unemployed problem," he wrote in the *Morning Post*, "the reform is of the greatest importance."[45]

Barnett had preached the need to separate the sentimental from the personal, so that reformers might the more effectively retain the personal as the key to social transformation. Beveridge and those like him moved the argument a step further, arguing that one by one, even when shorn of sentimentality, could achieve almost nothing. Yet despite that important departure from the tenets of Balliol and of Toynbee Hall, Beveridge's compulsion to get at "the big problems" in a "directly useful" way was testament to his apprenticeship within the precincts of those two places. At Balliol, under Caird's tutelage, he had committed himself to a vision of community whose purpose was to encourage the living of "the highest life," dependent upon a state determined to provide what was needed in order "to give the higher faculties scope." Such a community would never come into being without the commitment of public-spirited servants whose disinterested and therefore clear-headed vision of "higher" and "highest" testified to their qualification as proper leaders. All this was as Green and Toynbee had preached. At Toynbee Hall, Beveridge discovered how best he could serve as a member of that disinterested elite. And he came to understand as well, in a way he could not have had he never set foot in Whitechapel, Balliol's lesson: "The sin of taking things for granted."

In his essay on George Eliot, Beveridge had observed that her remarkable imagination had compelled her "to resist to the last the scientific spirit which bade her classify and deal with types and not individuals."[46] Beveridge, whose mind was not equipped with such an imagination, was more than content to do the bidding of the scientific spirit. His goal remained the community that was Balliol's ideal; his means were a measure of the degree to which he was, in fact, redefining the shape—though not the purpose—of community in response to his own interests and what he understood as the interests of the nation.

7

R. H. TAWNEY:
EQUALITARIAN BRIDGE-BUILDER

Richard Henry Tawney's early years were patterned much as they were for his future brother-in-law William Beveridge. Like Beveridge, Tawney was born in India, at Calcutta, in 1880, where his father, a distinguished Sanskrit scholar, was principal of the Presidency College. Like Beveridge, he returned to England with his family when a small child, went to public school (Rugby), and on to Balliol in 1899. And, again like Beveridge, he worked at Toynbee Hall, residing there from 1903 to 1906 and for shorter periods in 1908 and 1913. But despite the similarities in their background and upbringing and their friendship which lasted until Tawney's death in 1962, the two were very different men, who read the lessons of their formative experiences in very different ways. Although both were exposed early in their adult life to the ethos of Balliol and of Toynbee Hall, they reshaped their common intellectual inheritance in response not only to the challenges of the new century but also to their sharply contrasting personalities, ambitions, and beliefs. What they did and what they professed in the years before 1914, and indeed throughout their lives, illustrates the degree to which the ethos, though transfigured, could nevertheless continue to impart a potent and varied legacy to twentieth-century England.

Historians must lament that Tawney was not the obsessive saver Beveridge was. What remains of Tawney's correspondence sheds very little light on his time at public school and university. His biographer, Ross Terrill, conjectures that the late Victorian rigidity and conventionality of Rugby did not sit well with Tawney. Terrill argues, however, that while at Oxford Tawney outwardly maintained the manner, if not the mannerisms, of a proper Arnoldian, displaying his lighter and more spontaneous side only occasionally and in the company of close friends.[1]

Undoubtedly, Oxford helped Tawney define his calling and his faith. He met and grew to know Beveridge. He joined the Christian Social Union. He formed a close and enduring friendship with William Temple, who came up to Balliol from Rugby a year after Tawney, and who at the time professed a confident belief in the immanentist Christian God of Scott Holland and Charles Gore. A 1914 passage from Tawney's commonplace book, written more than ten years after his departure from Balliol, reflects the extent to which he continued to derive his own faith from the theology of *Lux Mundi*.

> The special new and characteristic contribution of Christianity . . . is the statement that God became, or was fully expressed in, a particular historical individual as to whose life we possess records. The significance of this is immense. What it tells us is that the God who exists is like Christ. That is to say, it shows God not as universal, but as individual, not as infinite, but as limited and defined, not as principle but as man. . . . I think that the knowledge that God exists is a source of immense strength to man. But it is not by itself very helpful. What we want to know is what kind of God he is, and what he is like in ordinary human intercourse. This is what Christianity tells us.[2]

Tawney believed that to deny Christianity the historical conditions from which it arose, "the accidents of time and place," was to rob it of its essence, which was not God *in* man but *as* man.

Tawney accepted the principles of Balliol's sages, but as a corollary to Christianity, not, as had been the case for many of Green's followers, as a substitute for it. Although he was at the college under Caird, Tawney's beliefs appear to have come to him less from his exposure to the afterglow of Green's influence than from his later friendship with George Unwin, who occupied the first British chair of economic history at the University of Manchester, and to whom Tawney went for advice in 1911 when completing his first book, *The Agrarian Problem in the Sixteenth Century*. Unwin, the son of a Stockport railway clerk, had come to Lincoln College, Oxford, in the 1890s by way of a Wesleyan day school and University College, Cardiff. Tawney grew to admire Unwin both for the sort of man he was and for the set of beliefs he professed. According to Tawney, Unwin "glorified" Green. In a memoir that he wrote as a preface to

Unwin's collected papers in 1927, Tawney remarked that for a man with philosophical interests Unwin had arrived at Oxford "at the right moment, almost the last, perhaps, at which it could be said that any single school of philosophical thought was dominant there. Green had died eleven years before, but his was still the most powerful influence." Tawney maintained that what had drawn Unwin to Green was not the latter's metaphysics but his "teaching as to social obligation," particularly appealing to someone with Unwin's interests as an economic historian, "on the borderland where the universal and the particular meet."[3]

Tawney recognized early on that he wished to inhabit that same borderland and to tune his life to Unwin's admirable combination of the ideal and the practical. Hence Green's appeal for him. But though he could agree with Green and Unwin that idealism demanded the commitment of moral principle to the battle for a better society on earth, his Christianity drove him to acknowledge the further timeless battle to attain the Kingdom of God.[4] Green's philosophy helped him understand his obligation to engage in both struggles, adding an extra dimension to his already firm religious belief.

Whatever the exact stage to which Tawney's convictions had carried him by the time he left Oxford in 1903, it was far enough to impel him in the direction of Toynbee Hall. In his memoir of Unwin, who had lived in 1898 at the Congregationalists' Mansfield House, Tawney commented on the "mood of self-criticism" that had settled upon the movement at the turn of the century, a mood he almost certainly shared as he began his own residency. He wrote that the first impetus was spent. "What was the result of it all? What, indeed, was its object? Was not the whole conception which had prompted the foundation of colonies of young university men in East London unreal and artificial? Was it not a little naive to suppose that the barriers of economic conditions and social class would yield to the mere fact of physical proximity? Were not the residents in settlements trifling with desperate ailments?"[5] Regardless of these doubts, Unwin had gone to work at Mansfield House because of his belief in the need to improve educational opportunities for the poor. Tawney, with many of the same reservations, appears nevertheless to have perceived Toynbee Hall as a place where he could come to a practical understanding of how best to discharge that sense of "social obligation" he claimed had been Green's legacy to Unwin, and whose undeniable pressure he had begun to feel as well.

Tawney hoped to learn the same sort of socially useful lessons at Toynbee Hall that his friend Beveridge was learning. In an article he wrote for the 1904 *Annual Report,* he defended settlements on the ground that their "continuous collective existence" provided a valuable base from which "to gather information that may one day lead to combined action." This was Toynbee Hall as Barnett was now prepared to let others define it, and as Beveridge was insisting that it be defined. At the same time, Tawney wanted more from Toynbee Hall than Beveridge did. Although he had no desire to chase after Barnett's original goal of hierarchical community, he did share his belief in the need for connection. Arguing in the same 1904 article for a reform of higher education, Tawney wrote that settlements might lend valuable assistance to that cause by promoting the search for a "common basis" upon which it could rest—"common" in that it must appeal equally to the aspiration of both the middle and the working classes. The argument, as it begins, sounds deceptively like vintage Barnett: connection by means of attachment to a single culture. But Tawney almost immediately dispelled that perception by insisting that the words "common basis" should mean just what they said. Toynbee Hall's major purpose, he declared, "would seem to lie in the provision of a *neutral* platform where different classes may meet to thresh out *common* problems, and submit to be *permeated by each others' ideas.* . . . It is a centre where differing and often conflicting idealisms can grind each other into some practicable shape," a place where "rich and poor" can "meet to deliberate on matters which are the common concern of every citizen."[6]

Here, at the outset of his career as a social reformer, Tawney was declaring unequivocally what he would continue to declare throughout his life: his unwillingness to subscribe to the prevalent dogma of cultural hierarchy. Toynbee Hall must not be allowed to embody one culture in such a dominant way as to impose it upon another. Barnett had continued to define the hall as a distinctly *positive* force in that sense, as the aggressive manifestation of all that was "best" in an area that had known little but the "worst." By insisting instead on institutional neutrality, Tawney was denying Toynbee Hall and other settlement houses their role as cultural arbiters. He was saying that they could best fulfill their mission as connectors by bringing together people with disparate interests to "thresh out" those disparities, agree upon a "common basis" for practical action, and thereby achieve connection, all by means of something very much like genuine democratic debate. He was suggesting that all the participants in that debate, whatever their class or their experience, would bring to it something of genuine worth. And he was implying that the purpose of disinterested service was not to preach middle-class values to the working class and not merely to collect statistics and promulgate theories but to awaken in working-class men and women a sense of the contribution they could make to the community of the nation.

Perhaps because Toynbee Hall failed to define its mission as Tawney hoped it would, his time there does not appear to have been particularly satisfying. His commitment to the Children's Country Holiday Fund, which he had been engaged by Barnett to direct, was less than whole-hearted. "I find the literature on the subject somewhat heavy reading," he confided to Beveridge at the time he assumed his duties. "It has a monotonously benevolent tone." And a month later: "Who is the happy man who is going to guide me in the thorny paths of what Barnet [sic] magniloquently calls 'the policy' of the CCHF?"[7] Both policy and program were characteristic of late Victorian charitable enterprise. Over fifty local communities raised money and arranged accommodation to provide about thirty thousand children from working-class neighborhoods a fort-night's summer holiday in the country. Policy insisted that parents should wherever possible contribute toward their children's vacation. Visitors in-vestigated each family's financial circumstances, much as COS investiga-tors did. In an essay for J. M. Knapp's *Universities and the Social Problem,* which was undoubtedly part of the literature Tawney forced himself to digest, Cyril Jackson, the fund's secretary during the 1890s, testified that visitors were particularly instructed that their mission included the pro-motion of "independence and self-help." Sounding the recurrent theme of healthy country living, Jackson extolled the restorative benefits of fifteen days away from hot city streets. "What a haven of rest is the coun-try to the quieter mortals! and what a splendid playing-place for the en-ergetic, where you can hit a ball as hard as you like without fear of the stick from an irate neighbour whose window was too close to the bats-man."[8]

Nothing suggests that Tawney did not direct the affairs of the fund with competence, although he himself acknowledged in a 1906 letter to his friend E. J. Palmer that "I don't think administrative work is what I can do best."[9] He simply found it difficult to throw himself into an enter-prise whose aims and principles undoubtedly struck him as dated. "I disagree with the attitude of the COS toward many matters," he confided in the same letter to Palmer. Given that fact, it could not have been easy for him to manage the activities of a charity that had adapted COS methods to its own use. The one lasting benefit Tawney derived from his work with the CCHF was a personal one. On a visit to the fund's receiving center at Haslemere in Surrey, he met Beveridge's sister, Jeannette. Their marriage in 1909, if not precisely made in Toynbee Hall, nevertheless owed something to it and received its blessing. Barnett and Tawney's Oxford friend William Temple officiated at the service.

More congenial to Tawney's ambitions for himself and for Toynbee Hall were the classes he taught there during his residency. Most of them related to questions of politics and economics, designed in a way to encourage working-class students to speak up about their own experiences. His course on "The Social Aspects of Industry," which he offered in 1905, included sessions on trade unionism, profit sharing, and "The Factory and the Citizen." He, Beveridge, and a third resident, H. R. Maynard, together lectured on industry and politics. Beveridge recalled in his memoirs that he and Maynard were in no doubt that Tawney must give the final talk, entitled "The Real Governors of England."[10] Outside the classroom, Tawney investigated the minimum-wage question, work that was to bear fruit in his later study of trade boards. He also collected information about the problems of boy labor and about the pros and cons of work colonies for the unemployed. In an attempt to effect the kind of connection the hall was supposed to foster, he and Beveridge joined a Bethnal Green workingmen's club. As Beveridge duly noted, however, "we did not find the club a way into East London at all. Over shovehalfpenny we got friendly there with a very pleasant young man—I think he was a postman—and talked of meeting again and seeing his home. But when we came next he wouldn't speak to us. He must have inquired about us and decided that we were not his class."[11]

After two years as a resident, Tawney had come to the conclusion that Toynbee Hall was not providing him with "a way into" the world he wanted to be part of or the calling he wished to follow. In September 1905, he wrote Beveridge that "teaching economics in an industrial town is . . . what I ultimately want to do." Though there was just such an opening at Cardiff, he worried that he could not work up sufficient lectures in the month before term began. He had talked the matter over with Barnett, who encouraged him to make the move, largely because he recognized how uncomfortable Tawney had grown in his current work. "His approbation," Tawney wrote Beveridge, "is much more damping than his opposition would be. After saying several nice things about my character—he remarks 'if you were satisfied with your life in Toynbee Hall and the C.C.H.F. I should say "stay on." But as you are not I am inclined to advise you to try for Cardiff.'"[12] Tawney decided in the end to stay on, while continuing to search for a suitable way out.

A year later he accepted a temporary position as assistant to the economist William Smart at Glasgow University, where he remained for a little over a year, forming in that time a close friendship with his fellow assistant Tom Jones, the future cabinet secretary. Tawney supplemented his £50 salary by writing for the Glasgow *Herald*, whose management was soon after him for lacing his reports with ironic asides—"holding up its hands in horror at my depravity," he reported delightedly to Beveridge.[13] He undertook one further journalistic assignment, following Beveridge for a brief stint as leader writer for the *Morning Post* in 1908. But by that time he had begun to settle with increasing enthusiasm into the work that was to engage the major share of his energies until 1914 and to inspire in him the sense of commitment he had hoped to feel ever since he had left Oxford: the teaching of north-of-England working-class men and women in small tutorial classes sponsored by the Workers' Education Association, an organization to promote working-class higher education founded in 1903.

Tawney was in no doubt during these years that he could discharge his sense of social obligation best as a teacher. That conviction grew as he worked to refine his definition of the moral society and recognized, contrary to the Toynbee ethos, that the definition must encompass a democratically minded and genuinely independent citizenry. Yet, like Green and Barnett, Tawney judged a society according to its willingness to address moral issues and conform to ideal ends. That proposition lay at the center of his thinking and writing in the years before the First World War. It was the constantly reiterated theme of the commonplace book he kept between 1912 and 1914. In May of 1912 he set out the "Plan of a Book" designed to illustrate the proposition that "Modern Society is sick through the absence of a moral idea," because "under present arrangements men are used not as ends but as means."[14]

That same conclusion was the theme for an article or a speech entitled "The New Leviathan," which appears to have been written at about this time. Tawney analyzed the degree to which a "mechanistic" way of addressing society's problems was preventing their solution by denying society a moral basis. Were one to ask Englishmen "if current institutions and ideas fail to satisfy the deepest parts of man's nature," honesty would force them to answer yes—and that the failure lay in the subordination of humanity to economic convenience. They would assert that the present industrial system was inconsistent with the principles of liberty and justice, since it compelled human beings to live as "hands" and not as citizens. Once men could be made to discard that notion, they could proceed to the task of creating a moral society. "It is no good trying merely to go a little faster: it is no good taking a motor car or organising one's journey carefully, if the road to which one is confined never leads to one's destination, if no conduct based on our accepted assumptions can produce satisfaction."[15]

There is a forthrightness to Tawney's prose that echoes the boldness of militant Christian socialism. Yet his argument remains rooted in Christian idealism that was a logical extension of Green. Men were concerned in a general sense that humanity was being subordinated to the industrial system in a way that precluded the possibility of community. But they would not understand what must be done to achieve community until they enjoyed a clear perception of their direct relationship to an immanentist deity. "As a child of God and heir of eternal life, [man] has rights which are superior to the claims of the temporal order of which he is visibly a citizen." Men and women "do not dislike 'ill-gotten gains' because they are socially disadvantageous [e.g., discourage honest industry] but because they contradict [the belief] that the world should be carried on on a principle which they recognize, to award service to service, and not service to violence or mere cunning."[16] Green made a similar point, as we have seen, when addressing the question of wage negotiation in his *Lectures on the Principles of Political Obligation*. Attacking the same sort of dualism that Tawney found repellent, Green deplored the injustice of a contract over which the worker had no control whatsoever, imposed by agents who had "for the most part no moral objects in view at all."[17] Green, however, appeared content to rest the blame on the employer. Tawney, by implication, blamed employees as well for their failure to understand what justice meant and for their willingness, therefore, to acquiesce in its denial.

"The problem," Tawney noted in his commonplace book, "is to find some principle of justice upon which human association for the production of wealth can be founded." Before the French and industrial revolutions, that association had rested upon prescription and privilege, more recently upon what was falsely termed "individual choice and consent" but was really privilege once again, redefined now in terms of the explicit economic relationship between master and man.[18] Tawney insisted that real change would not come until justice was defined as equality. Equality was the ideal at the center of Tawney's moral community. Inequality was the untenable consequence of social organization that permitted the privileged to use "other people, not as human *personalities*, but as *tools*. . . . It is only when we realize that each individual soul is related to a power above other men that we are able to regard each as an end in itself."[19]

For Tawney, the greatest evil of modern society was not poverty but the fact that the poor, born equal to the rich, had no chance to enjoy the liberty their innate equality implied: "the opportunity for self direction." It was no surprise that without this opportunity they fell prey to "irresponsibility and recklessness." Like the Toynbeeites, Tawney believed that poor people must come to possess "the *will* not to be poor." But unlike them, he believed that this will would never be theirs until those now in power granted them "the control of the material conditions on which their lives depend, that is set them free."[20] "Equality," "liberty," and "freedom" did not appear frequently in the lexicon of Toynbee Hall. Barnett tended to define equality as a consequence, not a condition, of the achievement of one's best self. Tawney turned the notion around, insisting that unless the present inequitable system of dependence and subservience was first abolished, unless all people enjoyed equal status as ends not means, no one, rich or poor, was likely to realize the best that represented everyone's potential.

These sentiments encouraged Tawney to disparage elitist disinterestedness as a false ideal which led the rich to believe themselves especially fitted to rule, while subverting the confidence and independence of the working class. "The difference between the standpoint of the upper classes and of the working classes may be summed up as follows: the former think they make the laws becuse they [are] the best educated, most leisured, most civilized class in the community. The latter think the upper classes are civilized, intelligent, and leisured, because they have the power to make laws."[21] He recorded a conversation with Beveridge in his commonplace book in which the latter put the case for hierarchy: "the well-to-do represent on the whole a higher level of character and ability than the working classes, because in the course of time the better stocks have come to the top." Tawney would have none of this. One class ruled another because of its position of economic dominance rather than because of its better stock. Was Norman stock superior to Anglo-Saxon? If prosperous peasants were at the "top" in the fifteenth century because of their stock, how did one explain their decline a century later? Tawney grounded his answer in his current studies of the sixteenth-century agrarian problem. Breeding had nothing to do with it, economic and political power everything. "A new and very profitable method of using land paid the upper classes . . . better than the traditional system of agriculture"; since they were "almost omnipotent in administration they could have their way, with the result that the bulk of the peasantry were impoverished. . . . If 'stock' is the only thing that matters, how does a 'stock' which flourishes in one set of economic conditions become degraded in another?"[22]

It was Tawney's refusal to acknowledge one stock as better than another that led him to oppose the belief in a hierarchy of cultural values so characteristic of Balliol and Toynbee Hall. If workers understood the world in a different way from that of their masters, who was to call them wrong and their masters right? "A great many poor people are 'inefficient.' This means that they do not correspond to a standard of efficiency erected by their masters, the rich. Why the devil should they?"[23] The purpose of a decent standard of living for workers was not, as Barnett insisted, to allow an elite the opportunity to impose its culture of best selves upon them but to enable them to develop and enrich a culture of their own. Once able to resist the debilitating threat of poverty, they could far more easily cultivate ways of their own devising to achieve cultural as well as economic independence. "It is in proportion to its possession of such resisting power," Tawney declared in a speech in 1914,

> that a class is able, when some larger protective apparatus than the family is needed, to build up its own institutions with its own habits and ideals, to interpose a whole network of personal relationships between the individual and either the offensive intrusion of sympathetic outsiders or the bare machinery of bureaucracy, to make him superior to exceptional misfortune by establishing the routine of life upon a rock, to maintain its self-respect by making other people respect it.[24]

In rejecting the hall's notion of disinterested elitism Tawney did not, however, reject its ideal of service. He believed with Green that freedom meant more than the liberation of individuals to pursue their own interests. Freedom imposed a duty to serve the community. But here again activity was to be reciprocal rather than hierarchical, all classes performing equally useful and important functions for each other. The present economic system made it almost as difficult for the rich as for the poor to undertake their social responsibilities. Factory master, like factory operative, was trapped by the "logic" of enlightened self-interest. By encouraging him to ignore justice, that logic prohibited his understanding of duty. An employer with an eye to nothing more than his profits would never understand that justice might serve his own as well as his workers' best interests. "It is not until he has felt the hunger for justice in himself that he is capable of understanding that others will respond to his just treatment of them." [25]

Those words implicitly endorse the Toynbeeite goal of connection. Tawney believed that somehow the rich must be compelled to commit themselves to the ideal of justice and thereby fulfill their social duty. "They have got to be *disciplined* into being servants of the public. We must recover the idea of the landlord and employer as being a *post*, an *office*." [26] Neither Tawney's dedication to equality nor his rejection of elitist authority prevented his belief in a particular mission for the economically privileged. Those perhaps most suited to undertake "bold social experiments," he confided to himself in 1912, were "those who have leisure, have had opportunity to develop their faculties, have learned from history to realize that there are golden moments in the life of mankind when national aims seem to be bent for some noble purpose, and men live at peace in the harmony which springs from possession of a common moral ideal." The sentence which follows suggests that Tawney saw himself as just such a person. "I would ask them to think not of the misery of many today, but of the possibilities of joy and energy which every man knows to be in his fellow [man] because he seeks them in himself." Several months later he was at work once more defining his particular task, and in doing so, reiterating his determination to connect.

Every community should have a body of bridge-builders, pontifices, a very good name, for the bridge-builder is the real priest. These are the beavers of society, unobtrusive gentle animals, yet with sharp teeth and bright eyes, eyes to see where piles must be driven, what stout timber must be felled. . . . It is said that the devil builds bridges and I certainly think that social bridges are not built by men without any devil in them. But he is a good labourer devil, a lubber friend who does more work than most of the Saints in the Calendar.[27]

The consequence of bridge-building, however, was not the sort of connection that resulted in the teaching of moral purpose by pontifices to an unenlightened poor. Connection, for Tawney, was the union of all classes in the pursuit of communal goals. His definition encouraged him, but for reasons different from those of Barnett and Beveridge, to de-emphasize class antagonisms, to insist instead upon the importance of a kind of democratic fraternity that transcended class. While acknowledging the value of a distinct working-class culture, he believed that its purpose was to contribute to, rather than divide, the larger culture of the community. This sort of classless connection helped Tawney define his particular brand of socialism. As his biographer correctly discerns, "for Tawney, democracy was not a path to socialism, but a *part of socialism.*"[28] Unlike the Fabians, Tawney argued for a socialism that placed Beatrice Webb's "average sensual man" at the heart of governmental deliberations and decisions. At the same time, he differed from orthodox Marxists, defining democracy as something other than proletarian rule. Nor could he rely with the Marxists upon a future determined by the operation of inexorable economic laws. The future was to be shaped instead by the determination of a clear-sighted democratic citizenry prepared to direct its political efforts to the ends of equality and justice.

Tawney kept his distance from socialist organizations. Although he joined the Fabian Society in 1906, his democratic idealism left him with little sympathy for the socialism it espoused. The Fabians' "science of means," Tawney complained, resulted in nothing more than a tidying of the room, it "open[ed] no windows in the soul." Rather than trust democracy to accomplish their reforms, they spent their time trying to "trick statesmen into a good course of action," without recognizing that maneuvers of that sort were doomed to nothing better than partial success, so long as society remained content with "the same spiritual diet."[29]

Although Tawney's idealism compelled him to profess a bolder socialism than the Fabians, he shared their belief in the positive virtues of a strong state. Tawney's complaint was that the Fabians would not use the power of the state to push beyond a policy of national minimum and achieve genuine economic equality. "Intellectual socialism," as he called it, failed to address "the problem of inequality based on economic privilege, which is . . . even more than poverty, the great blot on modern society." Without "a large transference of property rights," democracy would be defenseless against economic tyranny. Tawney recorded a situation in his commonplace book to prove the point and as an illustration of "'the heart' which must be attacked." In the coal-mining community of Denaby, eight Labour members sat on the local council. Yet the houses and pubs were company owned, and the parson acknowledged "that his work would become impossible if he had a disagreement with the manager." Where was the real power? Clearly with the "despotism conferred by private property." What was needed was intervention of a magnitude great enough to produce an equitable redistribution of power: "(a) the municipalization of urban land and the regular purchase of land by the state (b) the purchase of coal-mines and railways and licensed houses (c) the creation of a really democratic system of higher education (d) heavy taxes on incomes from property." This, Tawney believed, was what the working class, as opposed to intellectuals, meant by socialism. He lamented that neither group seemed prepared to press ahead toward those reforms, and believed that the reason for their unwillingness to do so was that too many reformers remained convinced "that principles are valueless and only a fool looks more than 12 months ahead."[30]

Tawney's insistence upon democratic connection encouraged him to demand that control of the machinery of a socialist state should not be confined to "benevolent bourgeois bureaucrats." In testimony before the Poor Law commissioners, he argued that once registration was separated from relief, administration of the latter should be entrusted to workers— and not merely trade-union bureaucrats. "I think the example of putting the administration of unemployed relief not into the hands of distress committees but into the hands of workmen themselves, and of throwing the obligation of ascertaining whether a man was malingering or not on themselves, is the only principle that can succeed":[31] a radical sentiment that must have produced a grimace from both commissioners Beatrice Webb and Octavia Hill.

Tawney's democratic belief in the need for workers to share directly in deliberations and decisions affecting their own lives accounts for his enthusiastic support of the trade boards established by Parliament in 1909 to regulate wages in the chainmaking and tailoring industries. In both cases, the boards contained worker representatives, whose presence, Tawney argued, was vital to the boards' success, helping to produce decisions that were not only economically sound but morally correct. "What actually happens," he wrote of the Tailoring Board, "is that the Board crawls to an agreement along a path of which the milestones are one-sixteenth of a penny, and that its ultimate decision represents a compromise between the employer's instinct of what the trade will bear, and the desire of the workers and appointed members to establish a 'living wage.' . . . The elements of economic strength, bluff and skill in bargaining are not ruled out but merely limited by the fact that the participation of both parties . . . does something to *moralize* economic relationships, and that the ultimate decision rests with the appointed members whose duty it is to represent the *public economic conscience.*"[32]

The boards were no panacea. In both industries, although wages had been raised, they remained very low, especially for women. In some cases, higher wages had forced inefficient firms to close down, causing at least temporary unemployment. In others, speed-ups had driven workers to accomplish as much in less time for their increased hourly wage as they had formerly at lower piece rates. But despite these continuing problems, the boards had gone some way to provide large groups of exploited workers with their first opportunity to live a decent life. A minimum meant "that the workers have at last security for a wage which, though still low, is higher than a large number of them were being paid before. The result is that they are more hopeful, more alert, and more enterprising. The State has given them a little help. Therefore they are more prepared to fight their own battles and help themselves." Higher wages meant an ability for the first time to spend money on those things which too often the middle class defined as working-class luxuries. Tawney, however, argued that "expenditure on 'holidays and picnics,' 'amusements,' 'books and papers' is not a luxury: it is a necessary, if by 'necessary' one means an indispensible condition not of animal existence but of an intelligent life and energetic work."[33]

Tawney confided angrily to his commonplace book that the very need for a minimum wage "marks the extraordinary barbarism of our economic arrangements," by pronouncing "that people are not to be paid what they are worth, but what is necessary to keep them working." That, Tawney declared, was how a horse or slave was paid.[34] In a better world, perhaps minimum-wage boards would no longer be needed. In the present state of things, they were encouraging evidence of the degree to which the state could promote democracy and equality, as well as human decency. Those first two goals attest to the distance which Tawney put between his own ideals and the hierarchical authority that characterized the Toynbee ethos. Yet by insisting upon the need to free men and women so that they might fulfill the best that lay within them he demonstrated his debt both to Green and to Christian immanentism. And by perceiving a role for the privileged as bridge-builders, Tawney was restating that sense of obligation that had brought Toynbee Hall into being, that vital belief in service to an ideal that he needed if he was to justify his own life of social mission.

Tawney's demand that the state provide its citizens with opportunities for "intelligent life" and "energetic work" was a measure of his passionate conviction that the purpose of intervention was to prevent the use of men and women as slaves. The more defenseless individuals were, the greater the need for programs not simply to protect them but to encourage their eventual independence, to promote the intelligence and energy that would make them the subject and not the object of the society in which they lived. It was this conviction that led Tawney to his lifelong commitment to working-class education.

Tawney's insistence that workers deserved the best education the state could provide was fueled by his belief in individual human worth. It was grounded as well in investigations he undertook on the subject of juvenile labor while at Glasgow, work that provided him with statistical material for a book and articles in which he argued in favor of broader educational opportunities for the nation's working class. He campaigned to raise the school-leaving age from thirteen to fifteen and to institute a further program of continuing compulsory education for youths between the ages of fifteen and eighteen, with the stipulation that no one under eighteen could work more than a thirty-hour week.

> The time has come when it ought to be laid down as a principle that the years between 14 and 18 must be spent not merely on wage earning, but on preparing for a life of healthy citizenship and independence in the future. . . . An industry which uses up the strength

of its young employees and leaves them no opportunity for preparing themselves for the time when they will require a man's wage is a parasitic industry; a State which allows the rising generation to be so used up is living upon its human capital.

Tawney believed fourteen a particularly susceptible age: a time "at which the mental facilities are beginning to develop most quickly." Thus the need for education beyond that age. He did not consider voluntary programs of continuing education an adequate response to the problem. Some far-sighted employers now granted ambitious young workers time off to attend such classes. But "no employers will give time off to rivet boys or packers, or drawers-off, still less to van boys or 'labourers.' As one put it, 'you don't want a professor to work a machine,' and it never occurs to these boys themselves that they have anything to gain by continuing education."[35]

Tawney wanted to see working-class children treated with the same attention to their innate abilities and rights as were the children of the middle and upper-middle classes. He deplored the large number of pupils per classroom in board schools. Sixty had been established as the upper limit, a number Tawney believed far too great. Even so, more than one-seventh of the children in London elementary schools sat in classes of over sixty. Rather than fall back upon the "drill and discipline" so characteristic of barrack schools whose primary concern was obedience, teachers must be prepared to "adapt [their] curriculum far more closely to the needs of individual children than we have done hitherto."[36] In the end, it was a question for the community as a whole to decide: immediate expediency as opposed to long-term advantage. "It is quite possible for a town or a country by using its boys to satisfy a passion for evening newspapers and cheap cartage to court a shortage of (say) steelworkers or bricklayers or good citizens in the future. It is impossible for a nation or a city, by employing boys solely with reference to their 'immediate commercial utility' not to live on its human capital."[37]

While at Toynbee Hall, Tawney had been forced to take on faith his belief in the value of working-class men and women as precious human capital. Bridge-building in East London had not come easily to him; he left still craving the personal experience of connection that would have confirmed him in that faith. In his memoir of George Unwin, Tawney quoted a letter Unwin had written to his wife in 1901 which expressed the certainty for which Tawney was himself longing.

But belonging to them, as I do by *experience*, I have a deeper sense of the needs of the young [working-class] men with social ideals and at the same time a conviction that in their aspirations lies the future of England, if it is to have any. The future of Christianity lies with them too. They have the fresh vitality which alone can make a future and it is true in this sense that to the poor belongs the Kingdom of Heaven.[38]

Tawney wanted Toynbee Hall to connect him "by experience" to the working class, but it had not. His brief stint at Glasgow had not brought him much closer, despite his hopes, expressed to Beveridge, that "teaching economics in an industrial town" would do so. Only when we understand how central to Tawney's faith was his democratic belief in the potential of the working class, and how important it must have seemed to him to confirm that faith by experience, can we appreciate why he took with such pleasure and excitement to his teaching for the Workers' Educational Association.

The WEA was founded in 1903 in response to the belief of upper-middle-class and working-class reformers that adult working-class men and women needed and would welcome further educational opportunities beyond the secondary-school level. The association's roots lay in various nineteenth-century movements and institutions: cooperative societies, adult schools, mechanics' institutions, workingmen's colleges, and the like. Its most immediate predecessor was the university-extension program, designed at least in some measure with the expectation of serving the working class. Yet experience had proved that extension lectures in most areas attracted a largely middle-class clientele.

Out of disappointment at the inability of the university-extension scheme to respond to working-class needs, the sense arose that some additional and different organization was required to serve that purpose, a sense that became the compulsion governing the life of the WEA's founder, Albert Mansbridge. Mansbridge, the son of a Gloucester carpenter, had worked his way into the civil service by means of grammar-school scholarships and university-extension courses. A devout Anglican and cooperator, his previous work in the adult-education movement made him the friend and protégé of Charles Gore and won him the respect of such extension worthies as J. A. R. Marriott and J. Holland Rose. In July 1903, Mansbridge brought together a provisional committee of cooperators and trade unionists at Toynbee Hall to form an association whose exclusive concern was to be the provision of higher education for working-class adults. The following month the group met again at Oxford, where it received university blessing. The association's first branch was organized at Reading in 1904. By 1908, it boasted 50 branches; by 1914, 179 branches and a membership of 11,430.[39]

Much of the association's work bore a superficial resemblance to that sponsored by Toynbee Hall. Indeed, various Toynbeeites were closely associated with the WEA's early endeavors: Barnett, Bolton King, and T. E. Harvey, who served for a time as treasurer. Despite the support it received from its upper-middle-class friends, the WEA was a determinedly working-class organization and generally successful in avoiding an embrace from above that might have smothered it. Mansbridge recognized that his undertaking would not succeed without assistance from the universities. But he insisted that it be a genuinely cooperative enterprise, in which the final word lay with the workers' representatives. "It was clear," he recalled in his memoirs, "that working people had proved unresponsive, and would continue to be unresponsive, to facilities devised for them by other people. . . ." A devoted disciple of the cooperative movement, he believed that the English character would refuse to rise "to anything which it does not co-operate in creating."[40]

Not only was this to be a joint venture; it was also to be one open to all who wished to avail themselves of it. Combating the conventional wisdom of the educational establishment that higher education should be a privilege reserved for those few working-class children who had managed to climb the secondary-school ladder, the WEA declared its determination to provide a highway for all, rather than a ladder for just a few, and called its journal the *Highway* in order to make the point continually and explicitly.

These views, of course, accorded with Tawney's. The WEA, he declared, was the concrete expression of an educational movement that was a social movement as well, the statement of a "distinctive conception of the life proper to man and of the kind of society in which he can best live it." That conception was "social solidarity," the "contribution of the working class to the social conscience of our age." It meant saying farewell to that liberal-sounding shibboleth, the career open to talent: "not simply equality of opportunity," Tawney declared in a 1914 WEA pamphlet, "but universality of provision." Educationalists had to be made to understand that a great many men and women wanted to learn, not so as to improve their material position in society and to move from the working class to the middle class, "not in order that they may become something else, but because they are what they are." Once that democratic proposition was accepted, the ladder became nonsense. The purpose of education was not "to enable intellect to climb from one position to another, but to enable all to develop the faculties which, because they are the attributes of man, are not the attributes of any particular class or profession of men."[41]

Tawney's educational views, the consequence of his optimistic belief in democracy and individual human worth, contrasted with those of equally committed reformers such as Barnett, who professed to want much of what Tawney wanted, but who wanted it for quite different reasons. Tawney embraced the WEA because of its determination to lay to rest "that smiling illusion which whispers that 'culture' is something that one class—'the educated'—possess, that another—'the uneducated'—are without, and that the former, when sufficiently warmed by sympathy or alarm, can transfer to the latter in pills made up for weak digestions." Unlike Barnett, Tawney remained convinced that culture was a matter of sharing, of mutual learning, and that therefore this common possession was one to which all had an equal claim. No matter that one person spent his life as a professional and another as a laborer. "Those who have seen the inside both of lawyers' chambers and of coal mines will not suppose that of the inhabitants of these places of gloom the former are more constantly inspired by the humanities than are the latter, or that conveyancing is in itself a more liberal art than hewing."[42]

Tawney rejoiced in the degree to which the WEA seemed to him to embody his own iconoclastic attitudes. He considered the association an expression not simply of a desire for educational change "but part of the general working-class ferment, renaissance, self-consciousness—call it what you will" of the opening years of the century.[43] Tawney's eagerness to rankle an elitist bourgeoisie led him to overestimate the association's radicalism. Certainly he was a good deal further to the Left politically than was Mansbridge. He welcomed the WEA, however, not only as a way of manifesting his own democratic education philosophy but also as a means of achieving that "belonging by experience" that he had attempted unsuccessfully elsewhere. His original contact with the organization came at Barnett's suggestion—evidence of the perception with which the canon could read other men's enthusiasms. Soon Tawney was serving on its various subcommittees and, after 1905, on its executive. But it was as a teacher that he left his mark on the WEA during these years. And the WEA, in turn, left its mark on him.

The teaching he undertook as leader of small WEA-sponsored tutorial classes was the association's specific response to the disappointing nature of university-extension lectures, whose size and popularized subject matter had lent them an air of superficiality that left serious students unsatisfied. In 1907 a delegation from the Rochdale WEA appealed to the University Extension Delegacy for a tutor to conduct intensive, sustained course work over a period of two years. The delegacy, in consultation with the WEA, agreed to the scheme and to the appointment of Tawney to the tutorship. Meanwhile a similar request had come from Longton, and Tawney was eventually engaged to serve both communities.

Oxford's willingness to underwrite the tutorial classes was the result, in large part, of continuing pressure brought to bear by the association and by Tawney himself, who soon became one of its leading public apologists. In 1907, at the annual WEA conference held at the university, Walter Nield, an Oldham workingman, and Sidney Ball, the Oxford Fabian, read papers entitled "What Workpeople Want Oxford to Do" and "What Oxford Can Do for Workpeople," both of which were based on suggestions passed to them from Tawney via Barnett.[44] The result was the appointment of a committee of fourteen—seven from Oxford and seven from various working-class organizations—to draft proposals which were published the following year in a pamphlet, *Oxford and Working-Class Education*. Although Tawney was not a member of the committee, he played a large role in the drafting of the report.[45] It recommended the establishment of a committee to promote tutorials, separate from the University Extension Delegacy, a Tutorial Classes Committee, which was duly formed in November 1908, again with seven university and seven working-class representatives. The report was as important for what it said, however, as for what it did. It bore the unmistakable stamp of Tawney's educational philosophy, arguing that Oxford no longer opened itself, as had been its founders' intentions, "to practically all who desired to learn, irrespective of wealth or poverty," and that tutorial classes, supported by the university and taught by its faculties, were one means of returning Oxford to its original purposes.

These tutorials were not to be perceived as a means of declassing or reclassing men and women, an echo of Tawney's distaste for the concept of an educational ladder. "What [the working classes] desire is not that men should escape from their class, but that they should remain in it and raise its whole level."[46] Yet behind the radicalism of sentiments such as these lay the same compulsion to connect that had fired the enthusiasms and hopes of the previous generation of Toynbee Hall reformers. "The increasing complexity of industrial organisation and the growing tendency of different classes to live in different quarters of the same town . . . is making it increasingly difficult for the various sections of the community to appreciate each other's circumstances or aspirations. In modern life there is much which tends to the separation of classes, and little which brings them together." The connection tutorial classes was designed to provide, though, was not the sort that would result in the submission of students to the cultural viewpoint of a disinterested yet implicitly upper-middle-class teacher. Students were to learn how to articulate "loyalty to their order" and then to pass their newly gained knowledge to fellow workers. "Every member is a missionary of education in a continually expanding field, and spreads habits of criticism and reflection among his fellows in a way that is impossible if education is organized simply from above."[47] Despite foot-draggging by academic conservatives, by 1913 Oxford colleges were contributing a third of the Tutorial Classes Committee's annual budget of £3200; the remainder of the money came mainly from grants by local education authorities and donations from trade unions and cooperative societies. By the same year the number of Oxford classes had grown from the original two to seventeen, and other universities had begun to sponsor tutorials as well.

Enthusiasm and good will did not diminish a number of continuing administrative problems. Lack of funds constantly jeopardized the expansion, and occasionally the maintenance, of the program. Overtime made it very difficult for students to budget their hours for study. Many found the task of writing weekly essays taxing, and the drop-out rate among some groups was high. Mansbridge and Tawney continued to fear that the clientele would grow increasingly middle class. Figures for the 1913–14 Oxford tutorials, however, suggest that the student body remained primarily working class. Of the 367 men and women enrolled, the four largest occupational groups were potters (48), textile workers (37), women working at home (22), and carpenters and joiners (15). Twelve were shop assistants, and in every class, whose average size was twenty, there were usually three or four clerks or school teachers.[48]

Tutors were pleased by the extent to which students put their new knowledge and experience to work within their communities, displaying that "loyalty to their order" which the report had hoped the tutorials would encourage. F. W. Kolthammer, an Oxford BA who taught economic history to five classes, noted that several of his pupils were leading members of the local Independent Labour party: "The dream of class students becoming themselves teachers and leaders of their fellows shows clear signs of future realization."[49] That dream was further realized in the course of the following year when a group of Longton students, with Tawney's enthusiastic backing, began offering lecture courses to miners in several North Staffordshire villages. By 1913, the North Staffordshire Miners' Higher Education Movement, an official adjunct of the Tutorial Classes Committee organized by the Longton class secretary, E. S. Cartwright, was conducting twenty-one classes, fifteen of which were taught by current tutorial-class members.

Tawney took enthusiastically to tutorial teaching, both because it reflected his own personal and educational goals and because he appears to have shared none of the anti-urban and anti-industrial sentiments typical of social reformers who had attended public school and university. The north of England attracted him as it attracted few of his upper-middle-class contemporaries. Writing of Stockport, George Unwin's birthplace, Tawney celebrated its stalwart virtues. "A cotton town," Tawney acknowledged, "sometimes seems to turn an unfriendly face to the visiting southerner, who finds tall chimneys and smoky streets, even on a background of moors, drab and depressing." Yet on men and women born and raised there, a town like Stockport could "lay a spell of its own, pride in a distinctive type of community, whose rough edges have not been worn into featureless vacuity by the cosmopolitan whirlpool of a great city." Residents understood that as industrial workers they were active participants in "a stirring history still being enacted," not only aware of that present role but also linked by "moving, even heroic memories" to the events of their particular working-class past.[50] In short, they possessed a class consciousness, which Tawney, far from working to obliterate, was anxious to understand and appreciate.

Demand swelled Tawney's first classes far above the small number he had hoped for and believed most desirable: 43 at Rochdale, with a remarkably high average attendance of 39 during its three-year duration; 40 at Longton, with an average attendance of 31. The students in the first Rochdale class were predominantly working class: twelve ironworkers (eight skilled and four unskilled), ten male cotton textile workers, and a variety of other skilled laborers, in addition to a cashier, an accountant's clerk, a teacher and two journalists. The four women members were a working-class housewife, a dressmaker, a clerk and a schoolmistress. The youngest student was seventeen, the oldest fifty-seven. The first Longton class was far more middle-class in composition: only ten manual workers and fifteen elementary-school teachers.[51]

Tawney's curriculum reflected the declared purposes of the Tutorial Classes Committee: it required university-level work of its students and contained topics that would encourage working-class men and women to make academic use of their own experiences and points of view. The syllabus for a 1909 course entitled "The Economic History of the Nineteenth Century," for example, entailed sessions on the "Recent Positions of Trade Unions," with reading from A. V. Dicey and the Webbs; "Combinations of Capital," with reading from Hobson's *Evolution of Modern Capitalism;* "The Working of the 'New Poor Law,'" reading for which included selections from the reports of the commissions of 1832–34 and 1905–09, along with Beveridge's *Unemployment;* and "The Movement toward Collective Control and the Increase in Democratic Participation in Government," with reading from, among others, Graham Wallas's *Human Nature,* the Webbs' *Industrial Democracy,* Arnold Toynbee's *Industrial Revolution,* and *Fabian Essays.* Tawney's other courses were pitched at the same level: "The Early Industrial History of England"; "The Puritan Revolution"; "Nineteenth Century Reform Movements"; "Local Government"; and "Economic Theory" (which included reading from Marx's *Capital* and Alfred Marshall's *Principles of Economics.*) In addition to the reading, writing, and discussion for the classes themselves, Tawney assigned further projects: to his Longton students, for example, a vacation-time study either of economic conditions in the potteries or of the health and housing conditions of the district.[52]

Demanding courses of this sort were particularly difficult for students, who were in many cases forced to work as much as twenty hours of overtime a week. Tawney continued to write angrily every year about the pressures caused by "the systematic misuse" of overtime, "a grave scandal," he declared in his 1910 annual report, "which should be stopped by law."[53] As frustrating was the fact that most students lacked academic preparation. Tawney was attempting to serve as catalyst to a group of men and women the majority of whom had had little more than an inadequate elementary education. A student in one of Tawney's classes wrote Mansbridge in 1909 that, much as he appreciated his teacher, he found himself constantly inhibited by the intellectual demands put upon him.

> Having had practically no education I am handicapped at every point, the rules of grammar, composition, punctuation, and the sequence of historical persons and events are so absent from my knowledge as though they did not exist. . . . When I hear such names as William Pitt and Sir Walter Raleigh, I don't know until I search for their history whether they were Primates, Pirates, Peers, or Premiers. Of course until I joined the Economics class I had never found it necessary to know anything about them because my life has been spent in a sphere in which the only important thing appeared to be the devising of some scheme whereby one could escape from what seemed to be the inevitable end of one's fellow workers, viz., poverty and that old British institution, the workhouse.

One is tempted to doubt the academic disabilities of a student capable of a rhetorical flourish like "Primates, Pirates, Peers, or Premiers." But undoubtedly the reading and writing were an agony for many. Cartwright wrote to Mansbridge of "how very difficult and distasteful the mere *physical* act of writing is to a miner or a potter. . . . Sometimes one gets so overburdened that one stops and asks oneself—'To what end: will these laborious days and nights of toil bring any real and lasting fruit?'"[54]

Tawney felt the strain as well. He was faced with four not easily reconcilable tasks: to understand and appreciate his students as fellow human beings; to learn from them by designing courses that would let them speak and write from their own experience; to acknowledge, without condescension, that their own experience had in many instances afforded them almost no opportunity to express themselves; and, despite that fact, to demand of them work of university caliber. These tasks defined the sort of connection that Tawney the bridge-builder was trying to achieve. He fought the temptation to sacrifice any one of them to expediency. Despite class size, he tried hard not to lecture, thereby reducing the tutorial to the level of just another university-extension course. In this, he was as well refusing to substitute the sort of authoritarian relationship that seems so natural a concomitant of teaching for the genuine partnership between himself and his classmembers that his dedication to the principle of equality demanded. Toynbee Hall had defined education as the bestowal of a set of authoritative values. In Rochdale and Longton, education was to be the far more complicated process of mutual enlightenment. Tawney remained prepared to acknowledge his position as class leader, while struggling to avoid becoming its master—a tough assignment, as any teacher who has tried it will testify.

Though Tawney listened willingly, he believed he had every right to articulate his own brand of socialism, convinced that tutorial students must be taught the importance of first defining and then defending a political position of their own. Criticisms he wrote on student essays frequently contain the injunction to do more than set out a series of facts, to put forth, instead, a particular point of view. To one pupil writing on the set topic Tawney commented: "There is no one problem of underemployment, but half a dozen. You ought . . . to argue and discuss more. . . .you say that 'overproduction and underconsumption are the real cause of unemployment.' This may be so, but you ought to have given more space to supporting your own position with arguments." In other instances, Tawney used the comments as a chance to put his own case. An essay written in response to the question, "Does the rate of wages fix the standard of life or the standard of life fix the rate of wages?" was returned with the observation that the relationship was a double one. "It is quite true, as you say, that a man's standard depends on his income and is determined by it. . . . On the other hand the customary standard of any class does offer a barrier, because the supply of labour needed is not forthcoming. It is here that trade unions come in. The individual standard is weak. But the standard of a number of workers, when crystalized into a rule, is much stronger."[55]

How often did this sort of commentary, in class and on papers, result in the imposition of Tawney's own thoughtfully conceived, persuasively articulated point of view upon his students? Was he, in fact, doing what Toynbee Hall teachers understood it as their duty to do, what Tawney insisted the tutorial classes must not do: implanting his own ideas, rather than encouraging the ideas of his students to flourish? At one point a group of students belonging to the Socialist Democratic Federation walked out of his Longton class to protest his propagandizing on behalf of "bourgeois economics."[56] Others who professed a socialism more orthodox than Tawney's apparently managed to retain their convictions.

One student wrote him after he had moved to London that "those whom it was said you were sent to side track, etc., are still the staunchest socialists in Rochdale." Nevertheless, there is no question that Tawney was a force, both in the classes and in the communities where they were held. His presence as teacher and as personality undoubtedly pulled men and women in the direction of his own beliefs. "He has established for himself a position in the town," the secretary of the Rochdale class wrote in his report for the year 1909–10, "especially among Labour men, and his withdrawal from Rochdale would be looked upon as a calamity by a far larger circle than the members of the Class."[57]

Student response to Tawney was generally enthusiastic, in some cases to the point of adulation. One of Tawney's earliest pupils, a Rochdale general laborer, writing to Mansbridge, described his first impression as "one of surprise, first at his youth, and secondly at the sweet affable charm of his presence." Despite the fact that Tawney wore a gown—surprising, given his determination to be no more than first among equals—the student reported that "there was none of the academic manner about him, none of that air which is so inclined to freeze." T. W. Price, a Rochdale bleacher and eventual historian of the tutorials, responded to Mansbridge's request for an early report with the declaration that "we have the right man for teacher. . . . Mr. Tawney gained the entire confidence of the members in the first five minutes."[58]

Tawney once remarked of William Temple and of the effect of his WEA work upon him that "the 'we' and 'they' complex which is so marked among the more virtuous members of the privileged classes, might have clung to him as a habit, even though he knew it to be damnable in principle. It could not survive continuous co-operation with colleagues whose educational interests he shared, but whose experience of life was quite different from his own." Tawney, another virtuous member of the privileged classes, suffered from the "'we' and 'they' complex" less than most of his peers. What there was of it in him was further inhibited by the teaching he was engaged upon, the sort of teaching he undoubtedly had in mind when he wrote the following about Unwin: "The most effective teaching is done, perhaps, when teacher and pupil are too deeply absorbed in the matter at hand to be conscious of process, and 'conversation' expresses best the form of the act. . . ."[59]

Tawney maintained that whatever his influence upon his students, theirs upon him had been enormous. He insisted that he would have been unable to write *The Agrarian Problem in the Sixteenth Century* without having first tested and refined his ideas in class. "The members of the Tutorial Classes . . . with whom for the last four years it has been my privilege to be a fellow-worker," he wrote in the introduction, and "the friendly smitings of weavers, potters, miners, and engineers, have taught me much about the problems of political and economic science which cannot easily be learned from books." This is not merely another of those casual, if gracious, acknowledgements that so often fill scholars' prefaces. It reflects the intellectual position from which the book itself was conceived. "The supreme interest of economic history," Tawney declared, "lies , . . in the clue which it offers to the development of those dimly conceived presuppositions as to social expediency which influence the actions not only of statesman, but of humble individuals and classes, and influence, perhaps, most decisively those who are least conscious of any theoretical bias."[60] If the ideas and presuppositions of humble individuals were the stuff of history, the teacher's job was to encourage those individuals to articulate them, not to change them.

Any final assessment of Tawney's role in the tutorial classes he taught must rest on an understanding of the degree to which he remained a curious and respectful student of human nature. He enjoyed listening to all sorts of men and women, not simply listening but trying to hear them in terms of their own background and experience. At some point after he had begun teaching, he wrote down

a few comments by simple people on the subjects which learned people call "the social problem" and discuss in long books. I heard them in railway trains, in trams, at social and educational gatherings, and in the homes of the speakers. I write them down as far as possible in their words, but I can't reproduce the charm of their speech. [A young female millworker, speaking of an old woman whose husband was forced to enter the Poor Law hospital:] "When she told him, he said 'I'll die then,' and died 11 days later. It sounded strange to hear her tell it in the dark, while we were sitting in the mill. When a hard piece of work (course and stiff threads) came round, we used to take it in turns to do it, but the girls always skipped this old woman: she used to sit saying 'Time and Patience,' 'Time and Patience,' when we were angry at anything. . . ." [A university-extension student:] "I like the literature class very well.

> But it seems trivial to think of such things when the workers live as they do. I go to the mill at 5, and I see the little children going too in this cold weather. . . . To study Shakespeare is all right for the chapel—and 'Englands' Glory'; but when one thinks of the conditions of the workers it seems as though one has no right to spend time on such things."[61]

Tawney's biographer, Ross Terrill, has suggested with some justification that his optimistic generalizations about the nature and abilities of the working class were based too exclusively upon his experience of the elite he taught in Lancashire. He himself remarked that "Lancashire people spoil one for any more feeble stock."[62] Certainly his students *were* an elite, willing as they were to commit themselves to the rigorous demands Tawney imposed on them. Yet Tawney's optimism, though ultimately confirmed by his teaching, was grounded in a transcendent conviction that "simple people" were superior stuff; he agreed with Unwin that in their aspirations lay the future of England. Once, in a debate as to whether the middle classes should be admitted to tutorials, when a proponent argued that they should attend since God had made them as well as the working class, Tawney interjected: "Are you sure?"[63] About the working class he *was* sure. His faith in its members survived his disappointing Toynbee Hall experience. He went north, he listened to them, heard them, and was confirmed in his belief that they were people whose particular and self-defined best selves were the nation's ultimate strength.

That belief, combined with the success many of his tutorial students were achieving, fueled Tawney's determination to campaign for the admission of young working-class men and women to Oxford. He joined with a coalition—William Beveridge, William Temple, Graham Wallas, Charles Gore, and others—who were demanding a broad program of university reform based upon their sense that Oxford was not at present fulfilling its obligations to the nation. In a series of newspaper and journal articles in 1907, they demanded that the university address itself to matters of governance, admission, curriculum, examination, and cost.

The previous year, Tawney had raised most of their points in a lengthy set of articles for the *Westminster Gazette* entitled "The University and the Nation." He ridiculed a system that resulted in men being sent to Oxford "for much the same reason and with much the same result as they join any other fashionable club." He deplored the fact that colleges remained free to spend their "superfluous moneys in adorning the rounded completeness of academic culture as though unconscious of the barriers between Oxford and the nation." He wanted to see scholarships awarded not to bright, academically force-fed public-school boys but to able students who could not afford the £120 a year it took to live as an Oxford student.

Apologists for the status quo still spoke "as though humane education were for those who are to live, technical instruction for those who are to work." Oxford must see that its humaneness reached the lives of men and women most likely to profit from it, no matter what their economic circumstance. The more increasing specialization narrowed one's sights, "the more necessary does it become in a democratic state that as many men as possible should possess some knowledge of the corporate life of humanity which is expressed in literature, philosophy and history. Such knowledge it has always been the work of Oxford to impart, . . . she is still the organ through which the past experience of mankind is interpreted afresh to each generation." For this particular generation, her task was as well to function as a connector, "to bring representatives of the teachers and the taught face to face, in order that books may be confronted by fact, and that the academic and the practical mind, the scientist and the enthusiast may agree upon the principles of the cooperative effort which is the essence of higher education."[64]

These sentiments naturally led Tawney to support the suggestion, first mooted in 1912, that students from tutorial classes would profit from spending a year or more as Oxford residents. That support, however, brought him into conflict with other socialists, who feared that exposure to the co-optive contamination of an Oxford education might infect working-class men and women with a desire to deny their roots and scramble up into the middle class. In the eyes of most members of the Marxist Socialist Democratic Federation, tutorial classes were themselves little more than elitist devices designed to mask conflict by means of bogus connection. Tawney, anxious to dispel such notions, wrote to a dubious George Lansbury to reassure him that although the association was nonpolitical "in the sense of trying to aid students of all political views, . . . the backbone of the movement consists of men who are also working at the political side of the Labour and Socialist movement. Socialists predominate in all the classes I teach, and I believe that this is so everywhere, because it is they who know best what education can do for labour."[65] Tawney suspected that what these critics really objected to was the willingness of tutors to encourage serious discussion based on a variety of viewpoints. In a speech in 1912, he argued that proper university education was not "taking the views which happen to please you and labelling them 'working-class history' or 'working-class economics.'" It was, rather, "to see that all types of experience are represented in your educational institution and then to create a body of opinion which does justice to the sufferings and interest of all classes in the community." Threats to the independence of working-class minds came not only from the elitist precincts of Toynbee Hall. "No class," Tawney declared, be it a disinterested bureaucracy on the Right or a committed intelligensia on the Left, "is wise enough to do its thinking for another."[66]

Many socialists, however, feared that Oxford's intent was to do just that. In 1909, students at the workingman's Oxford foundation, Ruskin College, engaged in a bitter strike against what they charged was an unwarranted though characteristic attempt by the university to rid them of their intellectual independence. The focus of their attack was a proposal to issue certificates that would admit advanced Ruskin students to a regular Oxford course of study. The idea had originated in *Oxford and Working-Class Education*, whose authors had seen it as a means of increasing the number of working-class undergraduates. The strikers interpreted it as the university's way of denying them the right to live and learn as proletarians. "Instead of Ruskin College becoming an avenue to the emancipation of workers, it was to be converted into a gloomy archway to the reactionary university." They dismissed the notion that a university's purpose was to foster the exchange of differing ideas. "The 'impartial education' idea had its source in a very 'partial' quarter, and so long as the control of education comes from that quarter the working-class movement will be poisoned and drained."[67]

The Ruskin strikers' eventual withdrawal from Oxford and their establishment of the Central Labour College in London was a measure not just of the strength of their convictions but of the militant fears that generations of class antagonism and cultural hierarchy had produced. Writing on "Oxford and Democracy" in 1908, Ramsay MacDonald declared bluntly that "Oxford is not a university where Labour can learn anything." Oxford and Cambridge had "filched their educational birthright from the people, and for us to assist now in sending up a few workers to try and assimilate the habits of Oxford and be spoiled by its patronage is only to perpetuate the present condition of things." An anonymous correspondent, writing to attack *Oxford and Working-Class Education* in the January 1909 issue of *Highway,* argued (though less vehemently) to the same point: that the report appeared to define the goal of university education as "scientific and unbiassed" thinking—thinking such as Barnett consistently propounded, untainted by passion or by class consciousness. Such thinking when applied to the nation's problems would produce solutions drained of any real effectiveness and therefore favoring the status quo. The chief defect of an Oxford education, the writer concluded, was that "no provision is made for the emotional side of the student: the dreary cultivation of intellect is not to be relieved by one scrap of feeling."[68]

Tawney agreed that disinterestedness by itself accomplished nothing. He and those Oxford reformers who thought as he did wanted workingmen at the university in part because of their optimistic belief that they could rouse it from its disinterested, passionless existence. If, as one of their number, the classicist A. E. Zimmern, wrote, they could summon up "the power to withstand the isolating and disintegrating effects of the intellectual life," they could "help to give [the middle-class university student] some of the inspiration and sympathy which . . . students find it hard to retain." MacDonald could not agree. "You cannot recreate Oxford by an infusion of workingmen," he wrote Mansbridge after the latter had nervously reproached him for his "Oxford and Democracy" essay. "Oxford is a settled social organism. The pilgrims you sent to it have not that character. Therefore, Oxford will assimilate them, not they Oxford."[69]

Tawney's certainty about the possibilities and virtues of connection overcame his egalitarian suspicions about the degree of Oxford's commitment to democracy. He responded sharply to a memorandum from Mansbridge urging that the WEA oppose the limitation of specially provided university admissions to tutorial students: "The question is not whether facilities shall be 'confined' to Tutorial Class students but whether Tutorial Class students shall have any facilities at all. It is not yet necessary to beg the universities not to make too much provision for students from Tutorial Classes." Mansbridge was also anxious to throttle criticism coming from the Left to the effect that the transfer of students from the tutorials to the university was further evidence that the classes existed solely to facilitate the passage of co-opted proletarians up the ladder and into the bourgeoisie. "This particular objection," Tawney rejoined, "seems to rest, in fact, on the conventional idea that universities are 'finishing schools,' an idea which I hope Tutorial Classes and the W.E.A. will do something to destroy." Tutorials were not part of one national ladder, whose top rung was Oxford and Cambridge. They were the beginning of a new kind of educational system designed to provide English men and women with alternative routes to the same goal: a humane education. That fact should not, however, preclude an opportunity for resident university work. "It is no criticism of the classes to affirm what is obviously true, that a year's leisure for study enables a student to make greater progress than he can if he is working hard all day and studying at night": circumstances, Tawney remarked, that were not the fault of the classes but of the present economic system.[70]

The matter was the subject of protracted debate among tutorial students themselves. Their particular concern remained the ladder. They feared, as MacDonald and others did, that Oxford would carry its working-class students into the middle class. The scheme would have merit only if class members went away with the intention of returning to take up positions as class teachers themselves. A report of the Longton class deliberations states flatly that "in case such employment could not be found at once, the class were of the opinion that students should be prepared 'to go back to the bench' or resume their previous occupations until teaching work could be found." When H. H. Turner, the Oxford astronomer and tutorial enthusiast, went to Longton himself to question the class about Oxford residency, he encountered a generally hostile response. Resentment centered upon the notion that only two or three from each class would be chosen. "Workpeople have as much right in Oxford as anyone," a student told Turner, "but not in ones and twos. . . . Tell the committee straight we absolutely refuse their offer, thanking them for nothing."[71]

Two years later, student opposition to the scheme had diminished to the point that the Longton class nominated seven candidates for admission. Oxford selected three: Arthur Emery, a potter's thrower; John Elkin, a miner; and Maud Griffiths, an elementary school teacher. Emery was financed by a grant from Balliol, the Stroke-on-Trent Educational Authority, and by private donations; Griffiths by a scholarship from St. Hilda's. Support for Elkin, who was forty-one and had a family to maintain, never materialized. Emery was prevented by the university's language requirements from pursuing an Honours degree in history and was compelled instead to settle for a diploma in economics and political science, which he received "with distinction." He competed for the Chancellor's Prize with an essay on John Bunyan, which, though it was adjudged a "striking" piece of work, lost out to a competitor possessed of "a far better knowledge of English Literature as a background." Griffiths, according to the vice principal of St. Hilda's, "learned that some forms of intellectual work were harder than one would have imagined for some types of mind." Hers, the vice principal opined, contained "little literary or philosophical capacity," yet "a real power of mastering a subject which she takes in hand." Emery returned to teaching in the North Staffordshire Miners' Movement; Griffiths, though she applied there as well, failed to obtain a post, the number of classes having been sharply curtailed following the outbreak of war. Instead she took a position on the staff of Bournville, the garden community founded by the philanthropic Cadbury family outside Birmingham.[72]

Connection eluded the tutorial scheme as it had eluded Toynbee Hall. Though Tawney himself made friends among the Lancashire working class and though, as the hall had enjoined bridge-builders to do, he did his best to learn from those friends by means of individual connection as much as they learned from him, his students were impatient for the time when they would no longer need a middle-class teacher, confident that they could learn as well—better, perhaps—from one of their own. They were comfortable with Tawney because he had come to them on their terms and on their territory. He found virtue in the towns where they lived and the culture the towns had created. Their experience as workers in those towns convinced them that despite Tawney, connection, no matter how defined, in fact meant hierarchy and domination—at best the sort of benign authoritarianism of a Toynbee Hall conversazione, more often the officious snooping of a cos lady visitor. Class had imparted a pattern of assumptions both to workingmen and -women and to the social reformers determined to connect with them. Working-class experience taught that economic fact made disinterestedness a myth. Reformers continued to operate as if connection need not imply equality, whether economic, political, or social. The result was the masking of class position with the language of authority and the rejection of such language by those who thought they understood it for what it really was.

This language encouraged reformers to continue talking of community in hierarchical terms. Tawney was the exception. He defined community as he defined democratic government—"a government in which all types of experience are represented, and from which all classes receive intelligent consideration."[73] His imagination was fired by trade boards, as Beveridge's had been by labour exchanges. Their contrasting enthusiasms are instructive. Both men began with a common goal, derived in great measure from their Balliol tutelage: the endowment of community with a moral objective. Both agreed that to relieve working people of the hardships of economic uncertainty would assist in the realization of that goal. To achieve it, Beveridge favored state machinery manned by bureaucratic connectors, whose disinterested sense of the needs of management and labor set them apart as the essential catalytic element in a harmoniously functioning community. Tawney's community, on the other hand, was one in which all were equally essential, all connectors cooperating democratically to moralize society by endowing it with what he called "economic conscience."

Tawney's work to establish an equalitarian educational system was a lifelong manifesto of his early conviction that regardless of class all men and women were worth listening to, that genuine equality of opportunity was as vital to the national community as was equality of treatment. Such a notion has not fared particularly well in twentieth-century England. Insistence upon equality has run counter to the continuingly powerful traditions of hierarchy and authority, in which there is no place for the sort of democratically inspired connection Tawney championed. The result has been an elitist educational system bound to preserve the "we and they complex" he so deplored and a bureaucracy staffed in the main by those who have managed to climb to the top of the ladder he despised.

Tawney's failure is negative evidence of Beveridge's triumph. It is Beveridge's point of view that has far more often prevailed: the belief that social morality depends ultimately on the efforts of disinterested reformers, whose education and consequent position have fitted them specially to undertake for others the "intelligent consideration" that produces a community of best selves. This attitude indubitably encouraged the pattern of twentieth-century governmental behavior Keith Middlemas has analyzed in *Politics and Industrial Society*.[74] The capitalist triangle he has discovered in the insistence of progressively minded industrialists, trade-union bureaucrats, and civil servants that they are best suited to make decisions on behalf of the country is no more than Harold Perkin's "fourth class," reorganized to suit twentieth-century needs. It is based and sustained on assumptions that were part of the Toynbee Hall ethos, that class antagonisms must be discouraged—and that the best way to do so is by surrendering leadership into the hands of a supposedly classless, disinterested elite.

When Beveridge began work on the famous report that lay the foundations for the post-1945 welfare state, he did so convinced, in the words of his mentor, Beatrice Webb, "that he and his class have to do the job. . . . He agrees that there must be a revolution in the economic structure of society: but it must be guided by persons with training and knowledge—i.e., by himself and those he chooses as his colleagues."[75] He also believed, however, that those with training and knowledge would, like himself, be most aware of the need to plan with a transcendent moral goal in mind. Like John Bunyan, Beveridge was out to slay evil giants, and in his report he gave them specific, capitalized names: Ignorance, Squalor, Idleness, Want, and Disease. The Beveridge Report, testament to the philosophical assumptions its author had adopted in his youth from his experiences at Balliol and at Toynbee Hall, was testament as well to the enduring influence of the ethos those experiences produced.

NOTES

CHAPTER 1.

1. G. M. Young, *Victorian England: Portrait of an Age* (London, 1953), p. 71.
2. David Newsome, *Godliness and Good Learning* (London, 1961), p. 60.
3. Young, *Victorian England*, p. 70.
4. Harold Perkin, *The Origins of Modern English Society* (London, 1969), p. 252; Noel Annan, "An Intellectual Aristocracy," in J. H. Plumb, ed., *Studies in Social History* (London, 1956), pp. 241–87.
5. David Roberts, *Paternalism in Early Victorian England* (London, 1979).
6. Beatrice Webb, *My Apprenticeship* (London, 1971), pp. 192–93.
7. Margaret Simey, *Charitable Effort in Liverpool* (Liverpool, 1951), p. 106.
8. Baldwin Leighton, *Letters and Other Writings of the Late Edward Denison* (London, 1872), pp. 37, 29.
9. "Technical Education," *ibid.*, pp. 59, 21.
10. Elinor S. Ouvry, ed., *Extracts From Octavia Hill's "Letters to Fellow Workers," 1864 to 1911* (London, 1933), p. 3.
11. *Ibid.*, pp. 15–16.
12. *Ibid.*, p. 20.
13. R. K. Webb, "John Hamilton Thom: Intellect and Conscience in Liverpool," in P. T. Phillips, ed., *The View from the Pulpit: Victorian Ministers and Society* (Toronto, 1978), p. 237.
14. Although Mearns is listed as the author on the title page of *The Bitter Cry of Outcast London*, the writer was W. C. Preston, another Congregational minister and former newspaper editor to whom Mearns turned over his field notes. See P. d'A. Jones, *The Christian Socialist Revival, 1877–1914* (London, 1968), pp. 413–18.
15. Gareth Stedman Jones, *Outcast London* (Oxford, 1971), p. 26.
16. Sheldon Rothblatt, *The Revolution of the Dons* (London, 1968).
17. *Ibid.*, p. 246.

18. Matthew Arnold, *Mixed Essays, Irish and Others* (London, 1894), p. 246.

19. Matthew Arnold, *Culture and Anarchy* (New York, 1895), pp. 67–69, 85, xi.

20. *Ibid.*, p. 38.

21. Melvin Richter, *The Politics of Conscience: T. H. Green and His Age* (Cambridge, Mass., 1964), pp. 46, 49.

22. Arnold Toynbee, introduction to T. H. Green, *The Witness of God and Faith: Two Lay Sermons* (London, 1884), pp. iii–iv.

23. *Ibid.*, p. 32; R. L. Nettleship, *Memoir of T. H. Green* (London, 1906), p. 149.

24. Green, *Witness of God*, pp. 16, 41.

25. T. H. Green, *Lectures on the Principles of Political Obligation* (London, 1937), p. 209.

26. T. H. Green, *Liberal Legislation and Freedom of Contract* (Oxford and London, 1881), pp. 11–13.

27. Green, *Political Obligation*, p. 209.

28. *Ibid.*, p. 220.

29. Richter, *Politics of Conscience*, p. 345.

30. Nettleship, *Green*, p. 170.

31. T. H. Green, "Lecture on the Work to be Done by the New Oxford High School for Boys," in R. L. Nettleship, ed., *The Works of T. H. Green* (London, 1885–88), 3:475–76.

32. Richter, *Politics of Conscience*, p. 95.

33. Green, *Political Obligation*, p. 130.

34. A. L. Illingworth, *Life and Work of J. R. Illingworth* (London, 1917), p. 316; Michael Sadler, "Learning from Those who Differ from Us," quoted in Peter Gordon and John White, *Philosophers as Educational Reformers: The Influence of Idealism on British Educational Thought and Practice* (London, 1979), p. 99.

35. Stephen Paget, *Henry Scott Holland* (London, 1921), p. 47.

36. Letter to Maitland Hobday, 2 October 1875. G. Toynbee, ed., *Reminiscences and Letters of Joseph and Arnold Toynbee* (London, 1910), pp. 123–24.

37. Alfred Milner, introduction to Arnold Toynbee, *Lectures on the Industrial Revolution* (London, 1919), p. 39; Arnold Toynbee, "'Progress and Poverty': A Criticism of Mr. Henry George," 1883, quoted in Beatrice Webb, *My Apprenticeship*, p. 195.

38. See Arnold Toynbee, "Wages and Natural Law," *Lectures on the Industrial Revolution* (London, 1884), pp. 155–77.

39. Arnold Toynbee, "The Ideal Relation of Church and State," *ibid.*, pp. 232–35.

40. Arnold Toynbee, "Are Radicals Socialists?", *ibid.*, p. 216.

41. *Ibid.*, p. 238.

42. Arnold Toynbee, "The Education of Co-operators," *ibid.*, p. 228.

43. Arnold Toynbee, "'Progress and Poverty': A criticism of Mr. Henry George," quoted in Beatrice Webb, *My Apprenticeship*, p. 195; "Industry and Democracy," *Industrial Revolution* (1884), p. 179.

44. Alfred Milner, introduction to Arnold Toynbee, *Industrial Revolution* (1919), p. 21.

45. Albert Mansbridge, *University Tutorial Classes: A Study in the Development of Higher Education Among Working Men and Women* (London, 1913), p. 10.

46. Henry Jones and J. H. Muirhead, *The Life and Philosophy of Edward Caird* (London, 1921), p. 4.

47. Edward Caird, *The Moral Aspect of the Economical Problem* (London, 1888), p. 14.

48. *Ibid.*, p. 3; speech in support of the University Settlement Association, 1892, in Jones and Muirhead, *Caird*, pp. 115–16.

49. Edward Caird, *Lay Sermons and Addresses* (Glasgow, 1907), p. 5.

50. Sidney Ball, *The Moral Aspects of Socialism*, Fabian Society tract no. 72 (London, 1896), p. 9.

51. Mrs. Humphry Ward, *Robert Elsmere* (Lincoln, Nebraska), 1967, p. 158.

52. *Ibid.*, p. 356.

53. *Ibid.*, p. 499.

54. Paget, *Holland*, pp. 31–33. See also Richter, *Politics of Conscience*, pp. 31–32.

55. Janet P. Trevelyan, *Life of Mrs. Humphry Ward* (London, 1923), p. 59.

CHAPTER 2.

1. Henrietta O. Barnett, *Canon Barnett, His Life, Work and Friends* (London, 1919), 1:5.

2. *Ibid.*, 1:15.

3. *Ibid.*, 1:11.

4. *Ibid.*, 1:13.

5. *Idem.*

6. Samuel A. Barnett, Journal. Barnett Papers, (hereafter BP), Greater London Council, F/BAR/577.

7. James Fraser, *Charge* (Manchester, 1872), pp. 76–77, quoted in K. S. Inglis, *Churches and the Working Classes in Victorian England* (London, 1963), p. 25.

8. Barnett, *Barnett*, 1:22–23.

9. *Ibid.*, 1:29.

10. *Ibid.*, 1:32.

11. To Mary Harris, 27 November 1870. BP.

12. Barnett, *Barnett*, 1:37.

13. *Ibid.*, 1:67.

14. *Ibid.*, 1:68.

15. *Ibid.*, 1:69.

16. *Ibid.*, 2:305.

17. Jerry White, *Rothschild Buildings: Life in an East End Tenement Block, 1887–1920* (London, 1980), pp. 4–5.

18. Arthur Winnington-Ingram, *Work in Great Cities: Six Lectures on Pastoral Theology* (London, 1895), p. 129.

19. See Jeffrey Cox, *The English Churches in a Secular Society* (New York and Oxford, 1982).

20. Circular dated 7 March 1873. BP, F/BAR/466.

21. Hugh McLeod, *Class and Religion in the Late Victorian City* (London, 1974), pp. 112–13, 105.

22. 7 February 1879. Lambeth MSS, 1465/25.

23. To Mary Harris. Emily S. Maurice, ed., *Octavia Hill, Early Ideals* (London, 1928), p. 105; Beatrice Webb, *My Apprenticeship*, p. 223.

24. 18 June 1879. Lambeth MSS, 1465/28.

25. Barnett, *Barnett*, 1:194.

26. Walter Besant, "On University Settlements," in W. Reason, ed., *University and Social Settlements* (London, 1898), pp. 12–13.

27. Barnett, *Barnett*, 1:306.

28. Inglis, *Churches and the Working Classes*, pp. 68, 91.

29. Samuel A. Barnett, "University Settlements," in Samuel A. Barnett and Henrietta O. Barnett, *Practicable Socialism*, 2d ed. (London, 1894), pp. 168ff.

30. Barnett, *Barnett*, 1:311.

31. *Ibid.*, 1:313.

32. T. H. Darton to Henrietta Barnett, 23 November 1917. *Ibid.*, 1:316.

33. *Ibid.*, 1:37.

34. Beatrice Webb, *My Apprenticeship*, pp. 219–20.

35. Barnett, *Barnett*, 1:264, 319.

36. Beatrice Webb, *My Apprenticeship*, pp. 223, 220. 6 August 1880. Hill Papers, Library of Political and Social Science (hereafter LPSS), Misc. 512.

37. Barnett, *Barnett*, 1:279.

38. General Information Bulletin, 1887. Toynbee Hall Papers (hereafter THP), Greater London Council, A/TOY/5.

39. Samuel A. Barnett, "Preachers and People," *The Service of God* (London, 1897), p. 124; Barnett, *Barnett*, 1:320.

40. José Harris, *William Beveridge* (Oxford, 1977), p. 45.

41. Samuel A. Barnett, "Sensationalism in Social Reform," in Barnett and Barnett, *Practicable Socialism*, p. 233.

42. Samuel A. Barnett, *Class Relations in East London* (London, 1889), p. 2.

43. Samuel A. Barnett, "'Settlement' or 'Missions,'" in Samuel A. Barnett and Henrietta O. Barnett, *Towards Social Reform* (London, 1909), pp. 279–80.

44. Samuel A. Barnett, *A Sermon Preached on Advent Sunday, November 27, 1887* (London, 1887), pp. 10–11.

45. Samuel A. Barnett, introduction to Toynbee Hall *Annual Report* (London, 1892), pp. 13–14.

46. Toynbee Hall *Annual Report* (London, 1884), p. 13.

47. P. Lyttleton Gell, *The Municipal Responsibilities of the "Well-to-Do"* (n.d., n.p.). THP, A/TOY/5.

48. Stedman Jones, *Outcast London*, p. 286.

49. Nettleship, *Green*, p. 14.

50. To Francis G. Barnett, 22 May 1886. BP.

51. Samuel A. Barnett, "A Scheme for the Unemployed," *Nineteenth Century* (November 1888): 754–55.

52. Samuel A. Barnett, "The Church and Labour Dispute," in Barnett and Barnett, *Practicable Socialism*, p. 203.

53. Samuel A. Barnett, "Class Divisions," *Commonwealth* (November 1903): 347.

54. 13 April 1883. Barnett, *Barnett*, 1:165–66.

55. Samuel A. Barnett, "Class Divisions," *Commonwealth* (November 1903): 347.
56. *Ibid.*, pp. 348–49.
57. Beatrice Webb, *My Apprenticeship*, p. 222.
58. Barnett, *Barnett*, 2:47.
59. To Francis G. Barnett, 9 May 1885; 26 June 1886; n.d. [1893]. BP.
60. E. K. Abel, "Canon Barnett and the First Thirty Years of Toynbee Hall" (Univ. of London, Ph.D. diss., 1969), p. 134.
61. Toynbee Hall *Annual Report* (London, 1892), p. 14.
62. J. A. Spender, "Barnett of Toynbee Hall," *Westminster Gazette* (19 June 1913):1–2.
63. Barnett, *Barnett*, 1:216.
64. H. F. Wilson, "Toynbee Hall," *Cambridge Review* (18 February 1885): 214.
65. To Francis G. Barnett, 23 October 1886. BP.
66. Barnett, *Barnett*, 1:315.
67. *Ibid.*, 2:51, 41, 42.
68. *Toynbee Record* (October 1889): 8; *ibid.* (December 1889): 26.
69. Barnett, *Barnett*, 2:42.
70. Quoted by Benjamin Jowett in his memoir of Toynbee, in Arnold Toynbee, *Industrial Revolution*, p. xxi.
71. Leonard Woolf, *Growing* (London, 1961), pp. 24–25.
72. A. P. Laurie, *Pictures and Politics: A Book of Reminiscences* (London, 1934), pp. 73–74; Stephen H. Hobhouse, *Forty Years and an Epilogue: An Autobiography* (London, 1951), p. 133.
73. Samuel A. Barnett, "University Settlements," in Reason, ed., *University and Social Settlements*, p. 19.
74. Barnett, *Barnett*, 1:293–94.
75. J. F. C. Harrison, *A History of the Working Men's College, 1854–1954* (London, 1954), pp. 21, 33. See Beatrice Webb, *My Apprenticeship*, p. 222.
76. Charles Booth Papers, LPSS, Notebook B, p. 227.
77. Toynbee Hall untitled brochure (25 October 1884). THP, A/TOY/5.
78. Barnett, *Barnett*, 1:322.
79. *Ibid.*, 2:83.
80. Samuel A. Barnett, "Hospitalities," in J. M. Knapp, ed., *The Universities and the Social Problem* (London, 1895), p. 64.
81. To Francis G. Barnett, 5 April 1890. BP.
82. *Toynbee Record* (October 1893): 2–3.
83. *Ibid.* (March 1889): 81.
84. Toynbee Hall, *Annual Report* (London, 1892), p. 29; *ibid.* (London, 1885), p. 30.
85. Samuel A. Barnett, introduction to Toynbee Hall *Annual Report* (London, 1890), p. 10.
86. Samuel A. Barnett, "Philanthropists and Others' Needs," *Service of God*, p. 79; to Francis G. Barnett, 3 July 1886. BP.
87. Henrietta O. Barnett, "'At Home' to the Poor," in Barnett and Barnett, *Practicable Socialism*, p. 159.

88. Toynbee Hall *Annual Report* (London, 1885), p. 36.
89. Toynbee Hall *Annual Report* (London, 1890), pp. 16, 17.
90. Samuel A. Barnett, "Short Hours and Leisure." BP, F/BAR/524.
91. To Francis G. Barnett, 1 April 1899. BP.
92. Toynbee Hall *Annual Report* (London, 1889), p. 22; *Toynbee Record* (November 1898): 23; *ibid.* (December 1907): 35.
93. Charles Booth Papers. LPSS, Notebook B, p. 227.
94. Toynbee Hall *Annual Report* (London, 1885), pp. 33, 34; Barnett, *Barnett*, 1:373; Nevinson, *Changes and Chances*, p. 131; *Toynbee Record* (December 1902): 31.
95. To Francis G. Barnett, 29 October 1887; 12 April 1890; n.d. [1894]. BP.
96. Toynbee Hall *Annual Report* (London, 1885), p. 22.
97. Henrietta O. Barnett, *The Making of the Home* (London, 1885), p. 161.
98. H. E. Meller, *Leisure and the Changing City* (London, 1976), pp. 243, 154.

CHAPTER 3.

1. "The Rev. Canon S. A. Barnett: Interview and Sketch," *Christian Commonwealth* (23 November 1893): 123–24.
2. Samuel A. Barnett, "Foreign Politics and Home Progress." BP, F/BAR/528.
3. Samuel A. Barnett, "Social Reformers, Past and Present," in Barnett and Barnett, *Social Reform*, p. 25.
4. Samuel A. Barnett and Henrietta O. Barnett, Journal. BP, F/BAR/546, fols. 36, 18, 37.
5. *Ibid.*, fols. 181, 185, 172.
6. Samuel A. Barnett, "A Retrospective of Toynbee Hall," in Barnett and Barnett, *Social Reform*, p. 263; Ernest Aves, interview. Charles Booth Papers, LPSS, Notebook B, p. 227.
7. *Toynbee Record* (November 1900): 18.
8. Barnett, "A Retrospective," in Barnett and Barnett, *Social Reform*, p. 263.
9. Samuel A. Barnett, "School Boards and Liberals." BP, F/BAR/546.
10. Toynbee Hall *Annual Report* (London, 1888), p. 9.
11. Samuel A. Barnett, *Pastoral Address and Report of* [*St. Jude's*] *Parish Work* (London, 1890), p. 24.
12. Toynbee Hall *Annual Report* (London, 1889), p. 22.
13. To Francis G. Barnett, 3 December 1887; 30 August 1899; 15 April 1893. BP.
14. To Francis G. Barnett, n.d. [1892]; 1 March 1890. BP.
15. Samuel A. Barnett, "Wages and Work." BP, F/BAR/525.
16. Samuel A. Barnett, *Haste and Faith* (London, 1886), p. 5; *Toynbee Record* (November 1892): 15; *Pastoral Address and Report*, pp. 8–9.
17. Barnett, *Barnett*, 2:231.
18. George Lansbury, *My Life* (London, 1928), p. 12.
19. Samuel A. Barnett, *Sermon . . . Preached before the University of Oxford on June 15, 1884* (n.d., n.p.), p. 6.
20. Barnett, *Barnett*, 1:30.

21. Samuel A. Barnett, "Practicable Socialism," in Barnett and Barnett, *Practicable Socialism*, pp. 242–43.
22. Samuel A. Barnett, "A Twenty Years' Retrospect," *ibid.*, p. 6.
23. Samuel A. Barnett, "Distress in East London," *Nineteenth Century* (November 1886), p. 678; to Francis G. Barnett, n.d. [1889]. BP.
24. Henrietta O. Barnett, "What Has the Charity Organisation Society to Do with Reform?", in Barnett and Barnett, *Practicable Socialism*, p. 211; Samuel A. Barnett, "University Settlements," *ibid.*, p. 165; *Toynbee Record* (March 1891): 59.
25. Beveridge Papers (hereafter Bev P) LPSS B. XIV, 8.d.; Samuel A. Barnett, "A Scheme for the Unemployed," *Nineteenth Century* (November 1888): 759.
26. C. S. Loch, diary entries for 30 October and 1 October 1888, pp. 164, 150. Goldsmith's Library, Univ. of London; to Francis G. Barnett, 1888. BP.
27. *Draft of the Toynbee Hall "Unemployed" Committee* (London, 1892), pp. 3–4; *Toynbee Record* (January 1893): 40–41.
28. Samuel A. Barnett, "Charity Reform," *Service of God*, p. 339.
29. Samuel A. Barnett, "Practicable Socialism," in Barnett and Barnett, *Practicable Socialism*, p. 242; "The Sick and the Old." BP, F/BAR/517/1.
30. Samuel A. Barnett, "Charity Reform," *Service of God*, p. 337.
31. *Ibid.*, p. 336.
32. *Westminster Gazette* (20 September 1895): 1–2.
33. Barnett, *Barnett*, 2:267.
34. Arnold J. Toynbee, "Are Radicals Socialists?", *Industrial Revolution* (1884), p. 230; Samuel A. Barnett, "The Unemployed." BP, F/BAR/517/1.
35. Samuel A. Barnett and Henrietta O. Barnett, introduction to *Practicable Socialism*, p. v.
36. *The Oxford House in Bethnal Green* (London, 1940), p. 12; Barnett, *Barnett*, 2:29.
37. K. S. Inglis, *Churches and the Working Classes*, pp. 158–61.
38. Arthur Sherwell, "Settlements and the Labour Movement," in Reason, ed., *Universities and Social Settlements*, p. 132; Sir Walter Besant, "On University Settlements," *ibid.*, pp. 4, 40; Sir John Gorst, introduction to Knapp, ed., *Universities and the Social Problem*, pp. 3–4; Maud Corbett, "Mayfield House," *ibid.*, pp. 116–17.
39. J. Scott Lidgett, "Settlements and the Administration of the Poor Law," in Reason, ed., *University and Social Settlements*, pp. 67–68.
40. Percy Alden, "The University Settlement in Relation to Local Administration," in Knapp, ed., *Universities and the Social Problem*, p. 74.
41. Percy Alden, "Settlements in Relation to Local Administration," in Reason, ed., *University and Social Settlements*, p. 43.
42. Samuel A. Barnett, "University Settlements," *ibid.*, p. 19.
43. J. G. Lockhart, *Cosmo Gordon Lang* (London, 1949), p. 50; C. R. Ashbee, *The Building of Thelema* (London, 1910), pp. 181, 175–76.
44. Nevinson, *Changes and Chances*, pp. 90–91.
45. Samuel A. Barnett, "Social Reform," *Independent Review* (August 1903): 38.
46. Samuel A. Barnett, "University Settlements," in Reason, ed., *University and Social Settlements*, p. 15.

47. Barnett, *Barnett*, 2:23.

CHAPTER 4.

1. Samuel Hynes, *The Edwardian Turn of Mind* (Princeton, 1968), p. 63.
2. C. F. G. Masterman, "Realities at Home," in C. F. G. Masterman, ed., *The Heart of the Empire* (New York, 1973), p. 8.
3. P. W. Wilson, "The Distribution of Industry," *ibid.*, pp. 233–34.
4. Masterman, "Realities," *ibid.*, p. 30.
5. F. W. Laurence, "The Housing Problem," *ibid.*, p. 105.
6. Masterman, "Realities," *ibid.*, pp. 30, 35, 92, 4, 34.
7. G. R. Searle, *The Quest for National Efficiency* (Berkeley and Los Angeles, 1971), pp. 150–51.
8. Alfred Marshall, "Memorandum and Evidence to the Royal Commission on the Aged Poor," *Official Papers*, ed. J. M. Keynes (London, 1926), p. 245.
9. *Ibid.*, p. 365.
10. Alfred Marshall, *The Principles of Economics* (London, 1890), 1:4.
11. J. A. Hobson, *The Problem of the Unemployed* (London, 1906), p. 102.
12. J. A. Hobson, *The Industrial System* (London, 1910), p. 230.
13. L. T. Hobhouse, *Democracy and Reaction* (London, 1904), p. 78.
14. J. A. Hobson and M. Ginsberg, *L. T. Hobhouse: His Life and Work* (London, 1931), p. 184.
15. L. T. Hobhouse, *The Labour Movement* (London, 1898), p. 90.
16. L. T. Hobhouse, *The Elements of Social Justice* (London, 1921), pp. 88–89; *Liberalism* (London, 1911), p. 202.
17. Hobhouse, *Liberalism*, pp. 158–59, 182–83.
18. *Ibid.*, p. 40.
19. Sidney Webb and Beatrice Webb, *The Prevention of Destitution* (London, 1911), p. 98.
20. Sidney Webb and Beatrice Webb, *Problems of Modern Industry* (London, 1902), p. 250.
21. Beatrice Webb, *Our Partnership* (London, 1948), p. 340.
22. Webb and Webb, *Prevention of Destitution*, pp. 166–67, 182, 204.
23. J. A. Hobson, *The Crisis of Liberalism: New Issues of Democracy* (London, 1909), p. 85.
24. Webb, *Our Partnership*, p. 133.
25. *Ibid.*, pp. 120, 300.
26. Paget, *Holland*, p. 170.
27. *Ibid.*, pp. 242–43.
28. *Commonwealth* (February 1906); 22.
29. H. S. Holland, "Property and Personality," in Charles Gore, ed. *Property: Its Duties and Rights* (London, 1913), p. 175; Arthur Winnington-Ingram, *The Weakness of West End Christianity* (London, 1910), p. 11.

198

30. Charles Booth Papers, LPSS, Notebook B, p. 227; Peter d'A. Jones, *The Christian Socialist Revival* (Princeton, 1968), p. 164.

31. G. L. Prestige, *Life of Charles Gore* (London, 1935), p. 274.

32. Conrad Noel, *An Autobiography* (London, 1945), p. 71.

33. *Church Socialist* (January 1912): 3.

34. Report of the Annual Conference of the Church Socialist League (n.p. May 1912), bound into *Church Socialist* (May 1912).

35. P. E. T. Widdrington, "Some Church Societies and their Views," *Church Socialist* (November 1912): 5.

36. Stewart Headlam, *Christian Socialism* (London, 1892), p. 2.

37. Conrad Noel, *Socialism in Church History* (London, 1910), p. 8.

38. Charles L. Marson, *Charity Organisation and Jesus Christ* (London, 1897), pp. 40–41.

39. Maurice Reckitt, "Charles L. Marson," *Christ and the People* (London, 1968), p. 96.

40. N. Dearmer, *The Life of Percy Dearmer* (London, 1940), p. 71.

41. R. Kenyon, "The Case Against the District Visitor," *Commonwealth* (January 1909): 4. Italics added.

42. Stewart Headlam, *The Socialist's Church* (London, 1907), p. 24.

43. Percy Dearmer, "The Social Work of the Undivided Church," in Andrew Reid, ed., *The New Party* (London, 1897), p. 287; Headlam, *Socialist's Church*, pp. 48–49.

44. *Ibid.*, p. 53.

45. William Temple, "The Church and the Labour Party," *Economic Review* (April 1908): 201, 190.

46. Noel, *Autobiography*, p. 69; Charles L. Marson, *Church Socialist* (May 1914): 85.

47. The fact that a number of Christian Socialists were attracted to Guild Socialism further supports the argument that they could appreciate the positive contributions of intermediate institutions. See Peter d'A. Jones, *Christian Socialist Revival*, p. 117; J. N. Figgis, *Churches in the Modern State* (London, 1913).

48. Headlam, *Socialist's Church*, p. 20; Percy Dearmer, *Socialism and Christianity* (London, 1907), pp. 11–12.

49. Noel Annan, "The Curious Strength of Positivism in English Political Thought," *L. T. Hobhouse Memorial Lecture* (London, 1959), p. 18.

50. Philip Abrams, *The Origins of British Sociology: 1834–1914* (Chicago, 1968), pp. 3, 23.

51. Frederic Harrison, "Sociology," *The Sociological Review* (April 1910):101

52. T. S. Simey and M. B. Simey, *Charles Booth, Social Scientist* (Oxford, 1960), p. 42.

53. T. Lummis, "Charles Booth, Moralist or Social Scientist?," *Economic History Review* (Feb. 1971): 100.

54. E. J. Urwick, *A Philosophy of Social Progress* (London, 1912), pp. vi, 246–47.

55. L. T. Hobhouse, editorial, in *Sociological Review* (January 1908): 5, 6.

56. Abrams, *Origins of British Sociology*, p. 95.

57. *Ibid.*, pp. 107, 62, 65.
58. E. J. Urwick, *Social Progress*, p. 111.
59. Martin J. Wiener, *Between Two Worlds: The Political Thought of Graham Wallas* (Oxford, 1971), p. 66.
60. Graham Wallas, "Darwinism," in May Wallas, ed., *Men and Ideas* (London, 1940), p. 94.
61. Graham Wallas, *The Great Society* (London, 1914), p. 138.
62. Graham Wallas, "Property under Socialism," in G. B. Shaw, ed., *Fabian Essays* (London, 1920), p. 132.
63. Abrams, *Origins of British Sociology*, pp. 110–13.
64. *Ibid.*, p. 106; Reba N. Soffer, "Why Do Disciplines Fail? The Strange Case of British Sociology," *English Historical Review* (Oct. 1982): 782. See also Stefan Collini, "Sociology and Idealism in Britain, 1880–1920," *European Journal of Sociology*, 19 (1978): 3–50. which attempts to trace links between idealism and sociology, and, by the same author, *Liberalism and Sociology: L. T. Hobhouse and Political Argument in England, 1880–1914* (Cambridge, U.K., 1978).

CHAPTER 5.

1. To Francis G. Barnett, 5 October 1901. BP.
2. [Samuel A. Barnett], "Pax Pandemonica," *Saturday Review* (7 June 1902): 723–24.
3. Samuel A. Barnett, *Religion and Politics* (London, 1911), p. 66.
4. To Francis G. Barnett, 20 January 1906. BP. But see below, p. 119.
5. Samuel A. Barnett, "Poor Law Reform," in Barnett and Barnett, *Practicable Socialism*, new ed. (London, 1915), pp. 172–73.
6. *Ibid.*, p. 175.
7. Samuel A. Barnett, "School Boards and Liberals." BP, F/BAR/546.
8. Samuel A. Barnett, *Religion and Politics*, pp. 13–14.
9. Samuel A. Barnett, "The Poor Law Report," in Barnett and Barnett, *Practicable Socialism* (1915), pp. 186–87.
10. Samuel A. Barnett, introduction to *New Poor Law or No Poor Law* (London, 1909), pp. ix–x.
11. Samuel A. Barnett, *Religion and Politics*, p. 39.
12. Samuel A. Barnett, "The Unemployables," *Social Reform*, p. 65; introduction to *New Poor Law*, p. xi.
13. To Francis G. Barnett, 19 October 1902. BP; Samuel A. Barnett, "Social Reformers, Past and Present," *Social Reform*, p. 21.
14. To Francis G. Barnett, 8 October 1899. BP.
15. *Toynbee Record* (October 1904): 8–9.
16. To Francis G. Barnett, n.d. [1890]. BP.
17. To G. C. Moore Smith, 22 January 1903; Barnett, *Barnett*, 2:54, 53.
18. Samuel A. Barnett, "Charity Up-to-Date," in Barnett and Barnett, *Practicable Socialism* (1915), p. 234.
19. Samuel A. Barnett, "Social Reform," *Independent Review* (August 1903): 37.

20. Barnett, *Barnett*, 2:313–14; "Town Planning," in Barnett and Barnett, *Practicable Socialism* (1915), p. 267.
21. Barnett, *Barnett*, 2:324.
22. Henrietta O. Barnett, in James Hand, *Science in Public Affairs* (London, 1906), pp. 65–66.
23. Samuel A. Barnett, "Labour & Culture," *Tribune* (18 January 1906): 2.
24. Barnett, *Social Reform*, p. 12.
25. E. J. Urwick, "The Settlement Ideal" (I, II), *Charity Organization Review* (Mar. 1902): 121, 126; (Dec. 1902): 330, 336.
26. To Francis G. Barnett, 24 and 28 November 1900. BP.
27. To Francis G. Barnett, 14 November 1903. BP; E. J. Urwick, "The Settlement Ideal," *Charity Organization Review* (March 1902): 119.
28. To Francis G. Barnett, 5 October 1901; 12 October 1901; 18 January 1902. BP.
29 *Toynbee Record* (May 1902): 116–17.
30. Toynbee Hall *Annual Report* (London, 1905), p. 13.
31. To Annette J. Beveridge, 8 September 1903. LPSS, IIa77.
32. *Toynbee Record* (December 1913): 43.
33. Lansbury, *My Life*, p. 130.
34. J. A. Salter, *Memoirs of a Public Servant* (London, 1961), p. 46; *Toynbee Record* (October 1905); 2; *ibid.* (November 1905): 18; *ibid.* (March 1909): 117; *ibid.* (June 1910): 138.
35. Committee on Unemployed, Minute Book. BevP, III.
36. *Toynbee Record* (October 1903): 8–10; *ibid.* (December 1903): 35.
37. William H. Beveridge, "Report of Canvass as to Sunday Trading." BevP, III 2; Harris, *Beveridge*, pp. 58–59.
38. J. J. Mallon, introduction to J. A. R. Pimlott, *Toynbee Hall* (London, 1935).
39. Salter, *Memoirs*, p. 46.
40. *Toynbee Record* (January 1911), p. 53.
41. To Francis G. Barnett, 28 November 1905. BP.
42. To Mrs. Francis G. Barnett, 2 November 1906. BP. Barnett had accepted a canonry at Bristol in 1893, which he resigned upon his appointment to Westminster.
43. *Toynbee Record* (October 1909): 4.
44. To Alfred Milner, 25 May 1913. THP, A/TOY/6/1.
45. Memorandum, undated. THP, A/TOY/6/6.
46. Werner Picht, *Toynbee Hall and The Settlement Movement* (London, 1914), pp. 93, 97–98.

CHAPTER 6.

1. Undated memorandum on school life; William Beveridge to Annette S. Beveridge, February, 1907; Annette S. Beveridge to William Beveridge, undated. BevP, Ia36; IIa21.
2. To Annette S. Beveridge, 27 January 1901. BevP, IIa48.
3. William Beveridge, "The George Eliot Aspect of the Absolute." BevP, IXbl.

4. To Jeannette Beveridge, 16 March 1898; 6 July 1898. BevP, IIa76.

5. To Annette S. Beveridge, 13 February 1898. BevP, IIa44.

6. William Beveridge, *Power and Influence* (London, 1955), p. 9.

7. Harris, *Beveridge*, pp. 41–42.

8. To Jeannette Beveridge, 3 March 1902. BevP, IIa.

9. To Annette S. Beveridge, 16 January 1900. BevP, IIa.

10. Annette S. Beveridge to William Beveridge, 20 October 1900; William Beveridge to Annette S. Beveridge, 23 October 1900. BevP, IIa18; IIa47.

11. To Annette S. Beveridge, 24 February 1902. BevP, IIa.

12. To Annette S. Beveridge, 19 January 1902; 25 January 1903. BevP, IIa49; IIa50.

13. Annette S. Beveridge to William Beveridge, 28 January 1903; William Beveridge to Henry Beveridge, 3 February 1903; Henry Beveridge to William Beveridge, 24 April 1903. BevP, IIa19; IIa37; IIa3.

14. To Henry Beveridge, 24 April 1903; to Annette S. Beveridge, 11 May 1903. BevP, IIa50.

15. To Francis G. Barnett, 3 May 1903. BP.

16. Samuel A. Barnett to William Beveridge, 13 May 1903; William Beveridge to Henry Beveridge, 28 April 1903; William Beveridge to Annette S. Beveridge, 11 May 1903. BevP, IIb2; IIa37; IIa50.

17. To William Beveridge, 21 May 1903; 19 March 1904. BevP, IIb2; IIb3.

18. William Beveridge, Diary entry for 5 March 1905. BevP, Ic2.

19. To Annette S. Beveridge, 3 December 1905; 22 September 1903. BevP, IIa51; IIa50. *Toynbee Record* (July-September 1905): 167.

20. To Annette S. Beveridge, 15 November 1903; 20 April 1904; to Richard Denman, 3 October 1904. BevP, IIa50; IIa51; IIb4.

21. To Richard Denman, 3 October 1904. BevP, IIb4.

22. To Annette S. Beveridge, 25 and 27 October 1905. BevP, IIa51.

23. Bentley B. Gilbert, *The Evolution of National Insurance in Great Britain* (London, 1966), p. 242.

24. *Ibid.*, pp. 262–64.

25. Harris, *Beveridge*, pp. 189–94.

26. William Beveridge, *Labour Exchanges and Unemployment Insurance: Report of the Proceedings of the Board of Trade under the Labour Exchanges Act, 1909, and under Part II of the National Insurance Act, 1911 to July 1914* (London, 1915), p. 43.

27. William Beveridge, "Settlements and Social Reform," *Oxford and Cambridge Review* (Michaelmas 1907): 114–15.

28. To Annette S. Beveridge, 1 October 1905. BevP, IIa51.

29. To Annette S. Beveridge, 20 April 1904; 28 November 1904. BevP, IIa51.

30. William Beveridge, untitled essay on the application of the thought of Plato and Aristotle to the present (1905). BevP, IXb.

31. William Beveridge, "The Unemployed Workmen Act in 1906–7," *Sociological Review* (January 1908): 5.

32. See above, p. 13.

33. *Morning Post* (27 February 1906): 6; *ibid.* (2 November 1906): 4.

34. *Ibid.* (9 February 1906): 6.

35. William Beveridge, "The Economics of Socialism"; to Annette S. Beveridge, 31 January 1906. BevP, IXb4; IIa52.
36. William Beveridge, "The Problem of the Unemployed," *Sociological Papers,* (London, 1907), 3:327. Italics added.
37. William Beveridge, "Unemployment in London," *Toynbee Record* (March 1905): 101–02.
38. William Beveridge, "The Economics of Socialism." BevP, IXb4.
39. To Annette S. Beveridge, 3 December 1906; 12 March 1908; n.d. [February, 1910]. BevP, IIa52; IIa54; IIa56.
40. William Beveridge, untitled essay on the application of the thought of Plato and Aristotle to the present. BevP, IXb.
41. To Annette S. Beveridge, 25 January 1913. BevP, IIa59.
42. William Beveridge, *Unemployment: A Problem of Industry* (London, 1912), p. 194.
43. To Annette S. Beveridge, 31 December 1912. BevP, IIa58.
44. Harris, *Beveridge,* p. 106.
45. *Morning Post* (5 June 1906):2.
46. William Beveridge, "The George Eliot Aspect of the Absolute." BevP, IXbl.

CHAPTER 7.

1. Ross Terrill, *R. H. Tawney and His Times* (Cambridge, Mass., 1973), pp. 23–24.
2. R. H. Tawney, *Commonplace Book,* ed. J. M. Winter and D. M. Joslin (Cambridge, U.K. 1972), pp. 78–79. Tawney kept this record from April 1912 until December 1914.
3. R. H. Tawney, ed., *Studies in Economic History: The Collected Papers of George Unwin* (London, 1927), pp. xiv, xviii, xxix.
4. Terrill, *Tawney,* p. 178.
5. Tawney, ed., *Studies in Economic History,* pp. xxvi–xxvii.
6. Toynbee Hall *Annual Report* (London, 1904), pp. 23–24. Italics added.
7. To William Beveridge, 7 November 1903; 15 December 1903. BevP, IIa106.
8. Cyril Jackson, "The Children's Country Holiday Fund and the Settlements," in Knapp, ed., *Universities and the Social Problem,* pp. 96, 90.
9. To E. J. Palmer, 17 September 1906. Lambeth Palace Library, LAM 3010/64.
10. BevP, IXb3; Beveridge, *Power and Influence,* p. 31.
11. *Ibid.,* p. 26.
12. To William Beveridge, 20 September 1905. BevP, IIa106.
13. To William Beveridge, 29 April 1907. BevP, IIa106.
14. Tawney, *Commonplace Book.* pp. 8–10.
15. R. H. Tawney, "The New Leviathan." Tawney Papers (hereafter TP), LPSS, T/10/10.
16. *Idem.*
17. See above, p. 14.
18. Tawney, *Commonplace Book,* p. 23.
19. *Ibid.,* pp. 13, 67.
20. *Ibid.,* p. 34.

21. *Ibid.*, p. 9.
22. *Ibid.*, pp. 27–28.
23. *Ibid.*, p. 40.
24. R. H. Tawney, *Poverty as an Industrial Problem* (London, 1914), pp. 15–16.
25. Tawney, *Commonplace Book*, pp. 50–51.
26. *Ibid.*, p. 22.
27. *Ibid.*, pp. 16–17, 43.
28. Terrill *Tawney*, p. 151.
29. Tawney, *Commonplace Book*, pp. 51, 46.
30. *Ibid.*, pp. 52–53, 56.
31. Royal Commission on the Poor Law and Relief of Distress. Minutes of Evidence, Parliamentary Papers, Cd. 5068, 49 (1910): 344, 346.
32. R. H. Tawney, *The Establishment of Minimum Rates in the Tailoring Industry* (London, 1915), p. 35. Italics added.
33. *Ibid.*, pp. 134–35, 130.
34. Tawney, *Commonplace Book*, p. 48.
35. R. H. Tawney, "Blind Alley Occupations," *Women's Industrial News* (October 1910): 9; R. H. Tawney and N. Adler, *Boy and Girl Labour* ([London], 1909), pp. 12, 10.
36. R. H. Tawney, *Education and Social Progress* (Manchester, 1912), p. 5.
37. R. H. Tawney, "The Economics of Boy Labour," in J. H. Whitehouse, ed., *Problems of Boy Life* (London, 1912), p. 51.
38. Tawney, ed., *Studies in Economic History*, p. xxv.
39. For details of the early years of the Workers' Educational Association see Albert Mansbridge, *An Adventure in Working-Class Education* (London, 1920); his *The Trodden Way* (London, 1940); T. W. Price, *The Story of the Workers' Educational Association from 1903 to 1924* (London, 1924); Mary Stocks, *The Workers' Educational Association: The First Fifty Years* (London, 1953).
40. Albert Mansbridge, *Trodden Way*, pp. 54–55, 58.
41. R. H. Tawney, "An Experiment in Democratic Education" [1914], repr. in Rita Hinden, ed., *The Radical Tradition* (London, 1964), pp. 72–74.
42. *Ibid.*, pp. 76–77, 71–72.
43. R. H. Tawney, undated MS, fragment of a speech. TP, T/18/6.
44. See Tawney's note appended to a letter from Ball to Barnett, asking for suggestions, 21 March 1907. Tawney Correspondence, Temple House, London (hereafter TH).
45. Albert Mansbridge to Tawney, 6 April 1908. Early Tutorial Classes Correspondence, TH.
46. *Oxford and Working-Class Education* (Oxford, 1908), p. 50.
47. *Ibid.*, pp. 48–49, 50.
48. Oxford University Extension Delegacy [OUED], Tutorial Classes Committee, *Report for the Year 1913–1914* (Oxford, 1914), pp. 3–4.
49. OUED, Tutorial Classes Committee, *Report for the Year 1909–1910* (Oxford, 1910), p. 15.
50. Tawney, ed., *Studies in Economic History*, p. xi.

51. Tutorial Classes Committee Papers, Rewley House, Oxford (hereafter RH). Early Tutorial Classes Correspondence, TH.

52. Early Tutorial Classes Correspondence, TH; OUED, Tutorial Classes Committee, *Report for 1909–1910*, p. 11; T9, T10, TP.

53. OUED, Tutorial Classes Committee, *Report for 1909–1910*, pp. 8–9.

54. C. B. Caldecott to Albert Mansbridge, 26 December 1909; E. S. Cartwright to Albert Mansbridge, 9 October 1909. Tutorial Classes Correspondence, RH.

55. Essay file, Tutorial Classes Papers, RH.

56. E. S. Carpenter to Albert Mansbridge, 23 February 1907. Tutorial Classes Committee Correspondence, RH.

57. J. Warburton to R. H. Tawney, 31 October 1913. Tawney correspondence, TH; OUED, Tutorial Classes Committee, *Report for 1909–1910*, p. 2.

58. J. Henigan to Albert Mansbridge, 2 February 1908; T. W. Price to Albert Mansbridge, 2 February 1908. Early Tutorial Classes Correspondence, TH.

59. F. A. Iremonger, *William Temple* (London, 1948), p. 88; Tawney, ed., *Studies in Economic History*, p. xlix.

60. R. H. Tawney, *The Agrarian Problem in the Sixteenth Century* (London, 1913), pp. ix, vii.

61. Undated notes in Tawney's hand. Early Tutorial Classes Correspondence, TH.

62. Tutorial Classes Committee Minute Book, 29 January 1910, RH.

63. Conversation reported in Ross Terrill, *Tawney*, p. 44.

64. [R. H. Tawney], "The University and the Nation," *Westminster Gazette*, 15, 16, 17, 23, 24 February; 2, 3, 10 March, 1906.

65. To George Lansbury, 9 December 1910. Lansbury Papers, LPSS, 4, fols. 134–37.

66. Tawney, *Education and Social Progress*, p. 10.

67. The 'Plebs' League, *The Burning Question of Education* (Oxford 1909), p. 14; *'Plebs' Magazine* (May 1909): 63.

68. J. R. Macdonald, "Oxford and Democracy," *Labour Leader* (27 November 1906): 757; W.E.B., "The Oxford Report" [i.e., *Oxford and Working-Class Education*], *Highway* (January 1909): 56–57.

69. A. E. Zimmern, "What is the Use of the University to the Working Man," *Highway* (November, 1908): 27; J. R. MacDonald to Albert Mansbridge, 4 December 1908. Tutorial Classes Correspondence, RH.

70. To Albert Mansbridge, n.d. [March–April 1914]. Early Tutorial Classes Correspondence, TH.

71. "Report on University Scholarships held by Tutorial Students," November 1916, p. 4. Longton Papers, RH; Report of Professor H. H. Turner, January 1911. Tutorial Classes Committee Correspondence, RH.

72. "Report on University Scholarships held by Tutorial Students," pp. 6–12. Longton Papers, RH.

73. Tawney, *Education and Social Progress*, p. 8.

74. Keith Middlemas, *Politics and Industrial Society* (London, 1979).

75. Beatrice Webb, diary entry for 11 August 1940, quoted in Paul Addison, *The Road to 1945* (London, 1975), p. 118.

INDEX